SHAKESPEARE AND SOCIAL DIALOGUE
Dramatic Language and Elizabethan Letters

Shakespeare and Social Dialogue opens up a new approach to Shakespeare's language and the rhetoric of Elizabethan letters. Moving beyond claims about the language of individual Shakespearean characters, Magnusson develops a rhetoric of social exchange to analyze dialogue, conversation, sonnets, and particularly letters of the period, which are normally read as historical documents. The verbal negotiation of social and power relations such as service or friendship is explored in texts as diverse as Sidney family letters and Shakespeare's sonnets, merchant correspondence and *Timon of Athens*, Burghley's state letters and *Henry IV Part 1*.

The book draws on ideas from discourse analysis and linguistic pragmatics, especially "politeness theory," relating these to key ideas in epistolary handbooks of the period, including those by Erasmus and Angel Day. Chapters on *Henry VIII*, *King Lear*, *Much Ado About Nothing*, and *Othello* demonstrate that Shakespeare's dialogic art is deeply rooted in the everyday language of Elizabethan culture. Magnusson creates a way of reading both literary texts and historical documents which bridges the gap between the methods of new historicism and linguistic criticism.

LYNNE MAGNUSSON is an Associate Professor of English at the University of Waterloo, where she teaches Shakespeare, discourse analysis, and early modern literature in English. In addition to publishing articles, she has co-edited *The Elizabethan Theatre XI: The Theatre of the 1580s*, *XII: The Language of the Theatre*, *XIII: Actors and Acting*, and *XIV: Women and the Elizabethan Theatre*.

SHAKESPEARE AND SOCIAL DIALOGUE

Dramatic Language and Elizabethan Letters

LYNNE MAGNUSSON

PUBLISHED BY THE PRESS SYNDICATE OF THE UNIVERSITY OF CAMBRIDGE
The Pitt Building, Trumpington Street, Cambridge, CB2 IRP, United Kingdom

CAMBRIDGE UNIVERSITY PRESS
The Edinburgh Building, Cambridge CB2 2RU, United Kingdom   http://www.cup.cam.ac.uk
40 West 20th Street, New York, NY 10011–4211, USA   http://www.cup.org
10 Stamford Road, Oakleigh, Melbourne 3166, Australia

© Lynne Magnusson 1999

This book is in copyright. Subject to statutory exception and to the provisions of relevant collective licensing agreements, no reproduction of any part may take place without the written permission of Cambridge University Press.

First published 1999

Printed in the United Kingdom at the University Press, Cambridge

Typeset in Baskerville 11/12.5 pt [VN]

A catalogue record for this book is available from the British Library

Library of Congress cataloguing in publication data
Magnusson, Lynne,
Shakespeare and social dialogue: dramatic language
and Elizabethan letters/Lynne Magnusson.
p. cm.
Includes bibliographical references and index.
ISBN 0 521 64191 8 (hardback)
1. Shakespeare, William, 1564–1616 – Political and social views.   2. Literature and society – England – History – 16th century.   3. English language – Early modern, 1500–1700 – Style.   4. England – Social life and customs – 16th century.   5. Shakespeare, William, 1564–1616 – language.   6. English letters – History and criticism.   7. Social history in literature.   8. Discourse analysis, Literary.   9. Dialogue in literature.   10. Drama – Technique.   I. Title.
PR3024.M34   1999
822.3'3–dc21   98–35821   CIP

ISBN 0 521 64191 8 hardback

*To my mother, Gudlaug Magnusson,
and to the memory of my father,
Agnar Rae Magnusson*

Contents

Acknowledgments ix

Introduction 1

PART I. THE RHETORIC OF POLITENESS

1 Politeness and dramatic character in *Henry VIII* 17

2 "Power to hurt": language and service in Sidney household letters and Shakespeare's sonnets 35

PART II. ELOQUENT RELATIONS IN LETTERS

3 Scripting social relations in Erasmus and Day 61

4 Reading courtly and administrative letters 91

5 Linguistic stratification, merchant discourse, and social change 114

PART III. A PROSAICS OF CONVERSATION

6 The pragmatics of repair in *King Lear* and *Much Ado About Nothing* 141

7 "Voice potential": language and symbolic capital in *Othello* 163

Notes 183
Bibliography 208
Index 217

Acknowledgments

In a book that treats the social shaping of early modern texts, it is a special pleasure to acknowledge the persons and communities that have helped to make this text. The book has taken shape, above all, as a rejoinder within the diverse and fractured conversation in Shakespearean and early modern studies between language critics and historicist scholars. In my text and notes I mention specific positions taken by many of the participants in this social dialogue, but here I wish to acknowledge how much I value the diversity and range of scholarship in this field, how much it has stimulated and taught me.

My more personal debts begin with that to my long-term mentor, Sheldon Zitner: he has provided me with an exemplary and enduring model for intellectual inquiry and original scholarship. I am deeply grateful for the intellectual generosity of Margreta de Grazia, Keir Elam, Bruce Smith, and Frank Whigham, each of whom read and commented on an early version of the plan for this book. I benefited a great deal from their gentle criticisms, acute suggestions, and encouragement. Early in the writing stages, I also benefited from stimulating conversations with David Goodwin about language and social relations. Throughout the later years of picking up and putting down this project while other work took priority, I have been sustained and encouraged in important ways by my colleague and fellow Shakespearean, Ted McGee. I am grateful to Sarah Stanton at Cambridge University Press for her expert editorial guidance and to the anonymous Press readers for detailed and thoughtful commentaries.

My own experience in completing this long-term project has been my best test of one idea explored within the book: that being heard enables speaking – that linguistic production is shaped in part by its reception. The hearing, contesting, correcting, qualifying, and agreeing of the many audiences to whom I have presented portions of the developing book affected its content and spurred its completion. I am grateful for the generous hearing I have had for papers presented to the Association of Canadian College and University Teachers of English, the Canadian Society for Renaissance Studies, the International Shakespeare Conference, and the Shakespeare Association of America. I especially wish to thank Irena Makaryk, Elizabeth Hanson, and Patricia Rae for inviting me to speak on my research at the University of Ottawa and at Queen's University and for their continuing encouragement. Within the distinctive and learned scene of the Canadian scholarly community, Christina Luckyj, Helen Ostovich, Camille Slights, Marta Straznicky, Judith Weil, Karen Weisman, Paul Werstine, and Paul Yachnin have also been generous with their knowledge and their responses. Furthermore, the book has benefited from the rich and lively exchanges it has been my pleasure to share with the University of Waterloo graduate students in my seminars on "Pragmatics, Dialogism, and Social Practice."

An earlier version of chapter 1 appeared in *Shakespeare Quarterly* (1992), a version of chapter 2 in *ELH* (1998), and a portion of chapter 7 in *Shakespeare Survey* 50 (1997). I am grateful for permission to use this material.

The research for this book has been very generously supported by a grant from the Social Sciences and Humanities Research Council of Canada. My debt of gratitude to SSHRC does not end with the material support from this grant: from the early days when the Council made my graduate education thinkable to more recent times when I have had the pleasure of working directly with its committees, SSHRC has stood out as a friend to learning and a model for institutional integrity.

Together with my parents, to whom this book is dedicated, my greatest debt is to Paul Stevens. There is no sentence in this book with which I have not troubled him for a response. At every stage he has found the answer best suited to the occasion. I can wish for no better context for thinking and writing than our enduring conversation.

Introduction

This book focuses on verbal interaction in the language of Shakespeare's plays and Elizabethan letter-writing. I argue that to make further advances in understanding Shakespeare's verbal achievement, it is necessary to turn attention away for a time from his private craftsmanship in words and to develop a better understanding of social invention in language – and of the richly complex rhetoric of social exchange in early modern England. We need to take a closer look at how language is organized as interaction, how dialogue and other verbal exchanges can be shaped by the social scene or context as much as the individual speakers, how "the word in living conversation" – in Bakhtin's intriguing formulation – "is directly, blatantly, oriented toward a future answer-word."[1] We need to know more about what everyday speech genres Shakespeare had to draw upon; how language demarcated class, social position, and relative power in Elizabethan England; how friendship, subjection, authority, intimacy, alienation, enmity and the like were constructed and inflected in words; how the language scripts for early modern relationships might have constituted and reproduced patterns of social organization on the one hand or of individual psychology on the other; how relational scripts for friendship or service might have changed over time and changed, with them, the repertoire of available personal relationships. The Elizabethans enacted their personal relationships with a rhetorical complexity and eloquence that Shakespeare assimilated, a historically situated eloquence that has been largely neglected in the formalist study of Shakespeare's stylistic artistry. To learn to read the socially situated verbal interaction of his time is to make a good start at understanding the fascinating social life of the languages that Shakespeare appropriated and embedded in dramatic writings. I employ two principal means to this end: a methodological use of modern-day discourse analysis (including linguistic pragmatics) and a comparative study of the theory and practice of Elizabethan letter-writing.

As one key strategy, this book makes a selective use of recent interdisciplinary developments in discourse analysis, an approach to language which places its accent on dialogic interaction and on the situated use of language in its varied contexts and which chooses conversational discourse and other types of socially situated verbal exchange as its object of study in preference to decontextualized sentences from written texts.[2] Given the primacy of dialogue representing conversation in Shakespeare's plays and the social orientation to language use evident in his time, discourse analysis is better suited to the goal of making the eloquence and the politics of these early modern exchanges visible than are formalist or affective stylistics, deconstruction, semiotics, Chomskyan grammar, or the other available methods. The appropriateness of the emergent discipline of discourse analysis to this study has been enhanced in the late 1980s and early 1990s by an increased awareness of its points of intersection with politically inflected social theory.[3] In this book, I bring some tools for practical criticism from discourse analysis together with theoretical perspectives on discourse as a social phenomenon, drawing especially on the work of M. M. Bakhtin and Pierre Bourdieu. A politeness model developed out of speech-act theory by cultural anthropologists Penelope Brown and Stephen C. Levinson is the practical tool I have found most useful to make visible how verbal exchanges figure the complex and variable power dynamics of historically specific social relationships.[4] Linguists have long since identified one isolated feature of verbal exchange in early modern English that can serve as an index to social relationships. It is generally accepted that the selection of "thou" or "you" (T/V), the pronouns of address, can register relations of power and solidarity, although the other contextual factors governing selection seem to be so complicated that no one can be said to have entirely cracked this code.[5] What is so exciting about the Brown and Levinson politeness model is its capacity to demonstrate how verbal exchange inscribes the complexities of social relations at many different levels of message construction, making it a matter of much more general interest and significance to the interpretation of Shakespeare's discourse than the alternation of two pronouns, however mysterious, could ever be. Drawing on other resources from discourse analysis, in this book I also make some recent theories about how conversation works the starting point for arguing that such Shakespeare plays as *Much Ado About Nothing* and *Othello* exemplify a sophisticated rhetoric based not so much upon literary artifice as upon the potentialities of conversation.

As a second strategy, I set Shakespeare's language in relation to the theory and practice of Elizabethan letter-writing. The most widely available epistolary handbooks, including handbooks Shakespeare made use of, are the main rhetorical texts which conceptualize interpersonal exchange in language. These texts have not been adequately studied from this point of view. The significance of Erasmus's treatise "On the Writing of Letters" (*De conscribendis epistolis*), for instance, goes far beyond the immediate goal of teaching letter-writing.[6] For Erasmus, the dialogic forms of address developed in the epistolary scripts for various occasions are not just forms in words: they are forms of life, the material substance of relationships. For him, the language of the letter is always primarily determined by the situated event taken together with the relative positioning of the addressor and the addressee, which is imagined as almost infinitely various, depending on the relative ages, temperaments, moods, wealth, education, and a multitude of other factors. For Angel Day in *The English Secretary*, the language of the letter is also a function of relative positioning but primarily determined by the social superiority or inferiority of the addressee. The world he represents, like the Elizabethan court, is a world of vertical relations, in which one is almost always negotiating one's position within a graduated hierarchy, and all the while reproducing the forms of symbolic domination and subordination that reinforce the hierarchy. Epistolary handbooks by William Fulwood and John Browne address social groups distinct from the gentlemen or aspiring gentlemen reading Erasmus and Day: addressing merchants, burgesses, and citizens, they offer insights into the social stratification of Shakespeare's universe of discourse, the languages of its diverse classes and occupational groups.[7] Elizabethan epistolary rhetoric presents its own version of "discourse analysis," and this study aims to build a practical criticism of interaction around their points of intersection.

We cannot hear the Elizabethans speak, but, for early modern England, letters – what Erasmus called "mutual conversation between absent friends"[8] – give us access to the written language of social exchange. While we must always remember the degree to which any historical understanding is mediated through various linguistic and cultural frames of reception, letters exchanged in Shakespeare's day nonetheless give the clearest idea of how relative social positioning affected language and style in ways that have seldom been discussed. Few studies of Shakespeare's language have tried to read the dialogue within the historical context of verbal exchange in early modern England: "historicizing" Shakespeare's language is usually confined to glossing word meanings or, in the more specialized work of linguists, mapping grammatical shifts. Nonetheless, this study does not read Elizabethan letters merely as background for Shakespeare's plays, as contexts for "the text." My point is not to show that Shakespeare's artistry builds up complex structures out of more primitive verbal forms such as letters but to show that Shakespeare's prized artistry partakes of the sophisticated social creativity also on display in the Elizabethan language of letter-writing. In this book, I am also making a beginning at the serious rhetorical study of early modern administrative letters, treating them as texts in their own right, an agenda suggested by new historicist assertions about the rhetoricity of historical documents but generally left undeveloped.

This book about the rhetoric of social interaction in Shakespeare's works and in Elizabethan letters began as a study of dialogue in Shakespeare's plays. Despite the commonplace observation that dialogue is a basic element of drama, it struck me that Shakespeare studies had neglected the interactive features of Shakespeare's language.[9] Instead, approaches to Shakespeare's language have been restricted by two tendencies: to focus on the speech rather than the exchange as the unit of dramatic discourse; and to regard the speech as issuing from within the character rather than from interactions among characters. But even as I worked to develop a new approach to thinking through how Shakespeare's dialogue is organized as interaction, how words answer preceding words and anticipate "answer-words," and how addressor and addressee are shaped as subjects within these exchanges, the problem began to change shape. I soon came to see that a study of dialogue could turn out to be as decontextualized as a study of individual dramatic speeches, for what shapes answer-words is never wholly given in the immediate speech situation, in the dynamics of the interpersonal exchange. To think about two individuals exchanging speeches – however one might construct them as listening and responding, or emphasize the coordination of their efforts, or consider the specific context of the speech event – can still be to hold on to ideologically loaded assumptions about how the inner world of the character or the private craftsmanship of the author shapes utterances.[10] It can be to look at dialogue essentially as monologue, to shift the accent back from social interaction to individual expression. The challenge, it became apparent, was to take a broader view of social discourse: to learn to look closely at collective invention in language – at how and to what extent speech and other verbal activities shape and are shaped by social organization and by social relations.

To meet this challenge is also to speak to an impasse that developed within Renaissance and Shakespeare studies with regards to close verbal analysis as the new historicism or cultural poetics took hold in the 1980s – for it drained much of the energy and interest out of language-oriented studies. The traditional equipment available for analyzing Shakespeare's language and style – the new critical and formalist models – met with serious criticisms. New historicism together with other poststructuralist theories challenged the orientation of close readings to traditional conceptions of literary texts as autonomous and unified wholes, separated from other texts of the culture; of authors as largely independent originators of the verbal intricacies in texts; and by extension of dramatic characters as individuated by stylistic demarcators. A gap was developing between the newer theories underlying current critical practices and the long-standing taxonomies for close verbal analysis. With the widespread repudiation of formalism and the new criticism and with the questioning of traditional categories that formerly directed close readings (text, author, and character), we were left to a large extent without adequate ways of engaging the complex language of Shakespeare's plays or of other Renaissance texts. Despite the frequent invocation of "discourse," recent work in Shakespeare studies has tended to avoid language-oriented close reading, moving instead outward from the text to look at its relations to other cultural formations.

When Stephen Greenblatt opposed his "poetics of culture" to readings attentive "to formal and linguistic design," he observed that "textual analyses . . . convey almost nothing of the social dimension of literature's power."[11] Yet in constructing this opposition, Greenblatt was not entirely condemning verbal analysis, or even formalism, *per se*: he was, instead, criticizing the usual privileging by formalist critics of individual artistry over collective invention as the principal agent in literary production – that is, the ideology informing even apparently descriptive practices. It is not surprising that the titles of such important books of the 1970s and early 1980s as *Shakespeare's Grammatical Style, Shakespeare's Dramatic Language, Shakespeare's Styles, The Making of Shakespeare's Dramatic Poetry, Shakespeare's Universe of Discourse,* and *Shakespeare's Metrical Art*[12] tend to confirm Greenblatt's point: that however different the approaches, the shared orientation was at that time to the agency of the individual author. What is surprising is, on the one hand, how few stylistic studies of Shakespeare's work since the emergence of the new historicism have taken up the challenge to relate linguistic texture to social, cultural, and ideological practices and, on the other hand, how few historicist studies have found ways to reengage linguistic detail or texture in any sustained way that accords with their theoretical principles and political enterprise.

Among stylistic studies, Juhani Rudanko's stance in his recent book on *Pragmatic Approaches to Shakespeare* exemplifies a prevailing tendency to bracket off language study from social and historicist concerns. The book takes the view that "man is an essence and not a construct of 'special discourses' or of 'social context.'"[13] Yet Rudanko's conceptual orientation, with its dissociation of the linguistic from the social, is strangely at odds with the analytical tools he has selected from linguistic pragmatics, for the explicit concern of pragmatics is with how language works in social contexts. If the analytical techniques of the new criticism and of formalism presumed an orientation to the writer as private craftsman, one would certainly expect the tools from pragmatics that Rudanko is innovative in introducing to orient the analyst towards the social context of a writer's discourse. A similar tension between conceptual orientation and analytical tools is increasingly encountered in close readings of Shakespeare, but the tension is usually between newer outlooks and older tools – between the transformed scene of political and contextual criticism and the largely unchanged practices of close reading. The collection of essays, *Shakespeare Reread: The Texts in New Contexts*, stands apart, with Russ McDonald's lucid articulation of the fortunes of close reading in an age of politically inflected cultural criticism, and yet the tension between historicist criticism and close reading is strongly marked in opening essays by such masterful analysts as Helen Vendler and Stephen Booth, essays which nonetheless stay very much within the confines of recognizable formalist practice.[14] Despite the battle lines drawn when early new historicist critics set up language-oriented analysis as a defining Other, the impulse towards a synthesis has also found expression among cultural theorists. According to Louis A. Montrose in "Professing the Renaissance: The Poetics and Politics of Culture," for example, cultural studies does not oppose "the linguistic and the social" but instead "emphasizes their reciprocity and mutual constitution": "On the one hand, the social is understood to be discursively constructed; and on the other, language use is understood to be always and necessarily dialogical, to be socially and materially determined and constrained." While this formulation places issues of language at the center of Montrose's project, there is nonetheless no further treatment of language in the essay beyond the comment that "The propositions and operations of deconstructive reading" (often argued to be ahistorical) "may be employed as powerful tools of ideological analysis."[15] As with Rudanko's stance, a gap opens up, here one between the conceptual orientation to language as a social phenomenon and the analytical tools: the demonstration of how deconstructive readings manifest social determination or constraint in language use is missing. In more general terms, the frequent references within historicist criticism to discourse and to discursive practices have seemed at times to gesture towards a sophistication of linguistic concept that is not always carried over into practical analysis.

It is time to negotiate some common ground between close reading and cultural poetics and, in particular, to propose taxonomies for verbal analysis that can address the place of collective invention in the production of Shakespeare's complex texts. A first step is to acknowledge that the separation described above between linguistically oriented criticism and historicist criticism may not be entirely, or even primarily, a matter of ideological difference. It may be instead a matter of uncoordinated resources among disciplines, of mismatches between concepts and analytical tools that are not particular to Shakespeare studies, and even of timing differences in how related ideas develop in different fields. If Greenblatt was right to claim that close textual analyses in the 1980s conveyed "almost nothing of the social dimension of literature's power,"[16] it was not because the linguistic and the social are inherent opposites. Language is a complicated – an inexhaustible – subject. Efforts to explain or contain it have always met with competing claims and been subject to endless revision, and yet the pace of that revisionism is at times slowed by the level of complexity demanded by investigation of language and at times diffused by the fragmented dispersal of the investigation across many disciplines. This study does not propose to synthesize interdisciplinary work bringing together the linguistic and the social but instead to identify some productive points of intersection that can take the practical criticism of Shakespeare's language in a new direction. As an important example, it will identify some points of contact between the empiricist research into politeness undertaken by Brown and Levinson on a social-science model and the theoretical insights into linguistic exchange developed by thinkers such as Mikhail Bakhtin and Pierre Bourdieu to develop a practical analysis of how social relationships are constructed both in dramatic dialogue and in epistolary exchanges.

Underlying my project is an effort to think about verbal discourse as a social phenomenon. "Social discourse" has gathered so many different resonances – some complementary and others contradictory – in deconstruction, cultural studies, post-colonial studies, and linguistic discourse analysis that it becomes important to situate one's use of the term and offer some preliminary identification of key issues. The new historicist ideas about social discourse draw most heavily upon the work of Foucault, but Foucault's "discourse," while enormously productive for sociohistorical reading, is not primarily a linguistic concept. In this study I am primarily concerned with language use – with the actual words exchanged among speakers and writers. For this reason, some of the basic distinctions made by Bakhtin provide a more immediately relevant point of departure. Furthermore, theorizing discourse as a social phenomenon, Bakhtin's work anticipated by about thirty years the first steps in discourse analysis and anticipated by about forty-five years the recognition among its practitioners of a need to interrogate theoretical presuppositions that were limiting the interpretive power of its descriptions.

For Bakhtin, to argue that verbal discourse is a social phenomenon was to oppose a "stylistics of 'private craftsmanship'" prevailing when he wrote "Discourse in the Novel" and long afterwards.[17] It was also to interrupt the Saussurian binary opposition between *langue* and *parole*, between a unified language system and individual language use. Verbal production cannot be accounted for by imagining the "speaking individual" drawing for his or her utterance on a "unitary language system."[18] To understand discourse as a social phenomenon is to imagine a multi-languaged world – a plenitude of colliding and overlapping discourses – discourses associated with the huge range of human enterprises specific to any time and place, discourses of groups, discourses of classes, of professions, of generations, and the like. Language is stratified, plural, heteroglossic. Discourses are specific to their historical, institutional, relational – and other – contexts, but they are also migratory, hybridizing, shape-shifting, continuously changing.

Discourse, so conceived, is neither the product of individual invention nor a mere derivative from a general system of language. Instead, the word, as Bakhtin puts it, is always oriented towards encounters with other jostling discourses. Discourse is *social* in that it is *dialogic*. In Bakhtin's writings, "dialogic" takes on a number of different meanings.

It does not usually refer primarily to verbal exchange, to one person speaking to another person in consecutive turns – what in "Discourse in the Novel" he calls "intra-language" or external dialogue. For Bakhtin, all language use is caught up in the "internal dialogism of the word" – a concept he explains in terms of two ways that the "word" is oriented toward "alien words."[19] First, he develops what is the foundation of "intertextuality": the idea that discourse is oriented toward the "already uttered," that the word "is shaped in dialogic interaction with an alien word that is already in the object."[20] That is, no subject matter, no topic for discourse, presents a blank sheet for the individual's marking or invention. Invention is collective in that competing and jostling discourses are already in place for every topic, and discourse has always to situate itself in relation to this ongoing conversation or dialogue. Our discourse, as Bakhtin puts it, is made up largely of quotations: words are somebody else's words – discourse is invariably quotation and hence appropriation – and such an encounter of the word with others' words is an integral part of what makes discourse social.[21] Furthermore, the speaking subject is formed partly out of this unceasing play of dialogue, for the language helping to shape subjectivity always "lies on the borderline between oneself and the other."[22]

It is Bakhtin's account of how the word is oriented not merely to alien words in the object but also to the alien word of the listener which first drew my attention. I quoted part of it earlier: "The word in living conversation is directly, blatantly, oriented toward a future answer-word: it provokes an answer, anticipates it and structures itself in the answer's direction."[23] In this formulation, anticipation of an answer-word is conceived as a fundamental feature of social discourse production. A dialogic utterance is not, surprisingly, structured to answer a preceding utterance; instead, it is structured to answer its own future answer. This idea of social discourse as anticipatory is borne out and developed in the theorizing of some later writers: Pierre Bourdieu, for example, emphasizes how the anticipated conditions of reception shape discourse production, constraining the speech of dominated speakers and enabling the speech of dominant speakers;[24] politeness theory, as another example, emphasizes how the mitigating strategies of politeness anticipate potentially threatening effects of speech acts, repairing damage – so to speak – before it occurs.[25] My study focuses a good deal of attention on forms of "external dialogue," and, despite Bakhtin's disclaimer of attention to external dialogue, this concept of anticipation is an extremely fruitful one for the analysis of verbal exchanges.

I have reviewed two senses in which Bakhtin construes social discourse as words oriented to the words of others. For Bakhtin, social language is also a matter of repetitive forms. In producing discourse, we are not always merely quoting, or replicating and appropriating, the words of other individual speakers; in doing so, we draw on collective repertoires, what Bakhtin calls social speech genres, routinized verbal behaviors appropriate to particular situations and relations.[26] As forecast by Erasmus, speech genres can be conceived as fragmentary scripts, the stuff out of which life's diverse activities, roles, and relationships are improvised. In placing emphasis on repetitive form, an understanding of language as a social phenomenon places significance on the maintenance work done by discourse – on its construction of the quotidian and on its reproductive role. Through the part language plays in the elaboration of repetitive social practices, discourse can be said to contribute to the construction and reproduction of subject positions and personal identities, relationships, and systems of knowledge and belief.[27] The idea that language is instrumental in creating and maintaining the social order has a long history. For much of that long history, the idea had a eulogistic cast, as in Cicero's celebration (much "quoted" in Shakespeare's time) of how oratory and civil conversation first brought people together in communities and subsequently sustained the bonds that keep people working together. More recently accounts tend to have a dyslogistic cast: Althusser's work, for example, brought home how language supports and sustains social formations perpetuating oppression. For political criticism, social discourse, together with other recurring material practices, produces and reproduces social relations – with social relations being conceived primarily as power relations, relations of domination and subjection. Ideology works out its gentle violence in language use. These ideas are commonplace today, and yet it is far from common to hear particular accounts of how ideology, or social relations, are figured in the grain of particular discourses – and this provision of practical tools for such analysis is one of my aims in seeking common ground between cultural criticism and close reading.

For all Bakhtin's insistence on quotation and repetition, he nonetheless is less concerned to emphasize the conservative and reproductive dimension of discourse than to accent the potential for creativity and invention. Is it possible, he asks, to talk about social or collective invention in language? Or, to talk about creativity in language, does one need to fall back upon the idea of the private craftsman, the individual author? Bakhtin finds social invention and creativity arising partly where recited words and repeated forms are accented anew within changing material contexts, so that it is possible to talk about discursive innovations that are social and anonymous in terms of the non-repeatability of situated utterances.[28] His perspective invites one to take a microscopic perspective on how language relates to social change: discourses encountering change in alien contexts can recombine or be otherwise transformed, and they in turn can reaccent or reorient the shifted context of situation. This idea that ordinary language scripts, encountering new situations, exhibit a kind of prosaic creativity is important to an understanding of how social invention and Shakespeare's invention intersect, since Shakespeare's creativity with language has itself been often aligned with processes of recontextualization.[29] Indeed, most of these general social discourse themes relating language use to social differentiation, intersubjectivity, the behavioral genres constituting forms of relationship, the social maintenance work of civility, the reproduction of the quotidian, the corresponding reproduction of symbolic forms of domination, and, finally, to social creativity and change get taken up and developed in specific relation both to Shakespeare's writing and to Elizabethan letter-writing at some point in this study.

Part I of *Shakespeare and Social Dialogue* develops a rhetoric of social interaction by adapting Brown and Levinson's politeness model to an analysis of the verbal forms of early modern civility. In chapter 1, I demonstrate how much of the complicated eloquence of characters like Katherine and Wolsey in *Henry VIII* arises not as a matter of their individual expression but instead out of the contexts of their interactions – both out of the immediate relations of their dialogue and out of their long-term, habituated social speech positions. By way of the politeness model, the chapter proposes some new ways to understand character construction in language. Given the traditional belle-lettristic convention of the practical criticism of literary language, readers may initially resist the use of Brown and Levinson's social-scientific vocabulary as having the feel of "alien words," for in chapter 1 I begin by using the model as a hermeneutic tool in a fairly straightforward and faithful way. I am not, finally, proposing that theirs is a fully adequate language for a sociological stylistics of Shakespeare's writing, but I do not think we will arrive at an adequate language without exploring the utility of discoveries in other disciplines.

In chapter 2, I begin to historicize and adapt the model, showing how the insights it generates complement those from epistolary rhetoric to help us characterize with precision the involved language of such hierarchical early modern relationships as that between servant and master. In "Power to hurt," I juxtapose the complicated epistolary language in which Edmund Molyneux negotiates the problematic verbal action of answering-back Sir Philip Sidney, his master's son, with the language in which Shakespeare's speaker in sonnet 58 answers back his aristocratic friend. My argument is that the verbal intricacy in each case arises out of a historically specific social relation and situation. In answer to claims often made that Shakespeare, through his private craftsmanship in language, invents a new language of inwardness or individuated subjectivity in the sonnets, I propose that the effect of subjectivity exhibited in this sonnet is, at least in part, a social invention.

Part II turns to the epistolary tradition for early modern accounts of social discourse and for practical instruction in the verbal production of Elizabethan social relations. In chapter 3, I suggest that Erasmus's teaching about letter-writing presents social relations as not merely expressed in language but actually constructed through language. If a relation like "friendship" is for Erasmus a self-conscious discursive production, then his pedagogy can aim not merely at teaching his students how to negotiate the existing social world but at teaching them to change it for the better. Whereas Erasmus's letter manual offers readers the equipment to alter the imperfections of existing social relations, Angel Day's *English Secretary* promotes social reproduction, while at the same time making room for individual mobility. In this chapter I therefore treat Day's book as a practical guide to the language of typical social relations, an Elizabethan's map of lived relations. It is just such a map that Shakespeare, the Stratford native, must have required when he began to ventriloquize, in writings for the London stage, the voices of gentlemen speaking to earls and of kings speaking to knights.

Chapter 4 moves from the theory to the actual practice of Elizabethan letter-writing. What is surprising and neglected about Elizabethan letter-writing is the rhetorical complexity and the eloquence with which writers negotiate even the practical tasks of administration undertaken in letters preserved as state papers. As a route towards eventually illuminating the social conditions of early modern discourse which fostered Shakespeare's stylistic accomplishment, and as a topic of interest in its own right, I propose in chapter 4 some new reading practices intended to open up the particular eloquence of the Elizabethan business letter and to show how its verbal intricacies are caught up in the linguistic display of hierarchical relationships.

Although we have much more information about the discursive and social practices of the uppermost echelon of Elizabethan society than about other groups, the epistolary handbooks I consider in chapter 5 open up ways to understand the social stratification of Shakespeare's verbal world. Not only the patterns of emulation but also the failures of competence on display in William Fulwood's *The Enimie of Idlenesse* offer insight into the comic collisions among social groups in *Love's Labour's Lost* and *A Midsummer Night's Dream*. Chapter 5 also opens up issues of discourse and social change by considering how a friendship style commonly exchanged among gentry in local communities migrates into merchant circles, undergoing transformations and, in turn, reaccenting the life forms of its new contexts. Specifically, I trace the transmutations of a relational script I call "pleasuring friends" from *The English Secretary* through *The Marchants Avizo*, John Browne's business letter-manual for merchant apprentices, coming finally to Shakespeare's recontextualizations of the script in *The Merchant of Venice* and *Timon of Athens*.

In part III, with the help of recent discoveries in pragmatics and conversational analysis about the workings of face-to-face social interaction, I try to show how deep was Shakespeare's understanding, or at least his plays' knowledge-in-practice, of the much-neglected complexity and interest of day-to-day conversation – how he both makes it his theme and develops his dialogue in full cognizance of how face-to-face interaction in talk occurs. In chapter 6, I show how *King Lear* and *Much Ado About Nothing*, with very different accents, foreground the housework of language, its rituals of maintenance and repair. In *King Lear*, this emerges in the intersubjective construction of identity, which is caught up with the characters' unceasing need for acknowledgment that is played out in the microcosms of conversational repair work. In *Much Ado About Nothing*, mistake-making and repair are represented as the mainstays of social life both in the macrocosm of the play's action and in the microcosms of its conversations.

In *Othello*, a speaker's words are weighed not so much for their linguistic virtuosity as for their power to move credit or belief in particular social contexts. Chapter 7 employs Pierre Bourdieu's economic model for linguistic exchange to explore how utterances in *Othello* receive their values in particular contexts and how, in turn, the conditions of reception affect discourse production for characters like Othello and Desdemona. Bourdieu's market analogy for social exchange opens up a new perspective on Iago's rhetorical performance in the play. Not only is Iago the supreme rhetorician of conversation, he is the rhetorician of social context, adept in manipulating voice power – his own and other characters' – by manipulating the context of utterance. Furthermore, chapter 7 adapts Bourdieu's perceptions to offer a new perspective on how social discourse shapes dramatic character, a perspective that complements and extends the perspective on character and dialogue developed using politeness theory in chapter 1.

Shakespeare and Social Dialogue offers an exploratory rather than an exhaustive treatment of its subject, a treatment which, I hope, will contribute to opening up further research on Shakespeare's language and early modern social discourse.

PART I

The rhetoric of politeness

CHAPTER I

Politeness and dramatic character in Henry VIII

In *Henry VIII*, when the class-conscious Duke of Buckingham, conversing with the Duke of Norfolk and the Lord Abergavenny, becomes increasingly heated in his criticisms of the upstart Cardinal Wolsey, Norfolk offers this advice:

> I advise you
> (And take it from a heart that wishes towards you
> Honor and plenteous safety) that you read
> The cardinal's malice and his potency
> Together; to consider further, that
> What his high hatred would effect wants not
> A minister in his power.   (1.1.102–08)[1]

In the construction of Norfolk's speech, two features of the language may be said to serve reparative functions, undoing deficiencies of the utterance-in-the-making. One such feature is restatement: the final *that* clause restates the preceding *that* clause, compensating with redundancy for the "high communication loss" associated with oral delivery in a theatre setting.[2] The second instance of repair work, which occurs in the parenthesis, is motivated not by a desire for clarification but for social maintenance. A recent account of the social logic of civil conversation, developed by anthropologists Penelope Brown and Stephen Levinson, can help to characterize the work of social maintenance accomplished here.[3] Brown and Levinson argue that the most commonplace speech acts negotiated in everyday conversation – advising, promising, inviting, requesting, ordering, criticizing, even complimenting – carry an element of risk, for they threaten potential damage to the persona of either hearer or speaker (or to those of both). *Politeness*, in the special sense that Brown and Levinson define it, consists of the complex remedial strategies that serve to minimize the risks to "face," or self-

17

esteem, of conversational participants.[4] Coming between Norfolk's specification of his speech act as advice and the advice he offers, the parenthetical reassurance redresses the trespass constituted by advice-giving. While advice is not as openly intrusive as criticism, to advise a social equal is clearly to trespass on the other's sense of self, for it implies that the person advised would not take a sound course of action without the intervention of the advisor. Brown and Levinson's model of politeness does not merely account for the occurrence of social-maintenance practices where speech actions create risk. Rather, as they argue, the specific configuration of the social relation between speakers, including relative power and social distance, directs the particular verbal strategy employed to accomplish the repair work of politeness. In other words, the rhetorical strategy Norfolk employs is not an expression of his individual personality but is instead determined by the immediate social context of his utterance, or his social positioning.

One can, of course, assert that Norfolk's rhetorical strategy is determined by Shakespeare's verbal artistry. But Shakespeare's artistry is itself affected by this social poetic of maintenance and repair, the social rhetoric of politeness. Brown and Levinson's politeness model can permit us to examine complex features of normal social discourse, usually neglected in the study of Shakespeare's style, which are embedded in all of his plays just as they are embedded in such other written texts of his culture as letters, even though their main showplace is face-to-face conversation. While these politeness strategies commonly operate apart from the controlling artistry of speakers and writers, they can also be deliberately manipulated. In Shakespeare's plays they can be placed in the foreground of our attention, and so treated as theme. This occurs in particular when Shakespeare represents breakdowns in the effective practice of verbal maintenance, as at the beginning of *King Lear* or *The Winter's Tale*. Indeed, in everyday conversation it is also in such circumstances of breakdown that these social strategies become visible; in more normal circumstances the strategies are generally exchanged among people without attention being turned to them. In *Henry VIII*, while politeness strategies contribute significantly to the discourse of the characters, I shall not argue that they are foregrounded as theme. Instead I shall illustrate how Brown and Levinson's model is predictive of the social language of characters in the play, and I shall demonstrate in very specific ways how gender and class are caught up in the social positioning that affects speech patterns. I shall also argue that an analysis of politeness forms, specifically in the speeches of Katherine and

Wolsey, can help to articulate a new understanding of the social construction in language of dramatic character.

In the introduction I suggested that our current resources for analyzing social discourse are uncoordinated – that we do not have at our command the practical procedures for testing in close reading the richly suggestive observations of discourse theoreticians like Bakhtin and Vološinov. In this chapter, I am less concerned to provide an overall interpretation of *Henry VIII* or even a comprehensive overview of its language techniques than to show how Brown and Levinson's politeness model can provide Shakespeare scholars with a practical inventory of distinctions that will permit analysis of characters' concrete utterances as products of social intercourse. The politeness model can open up a way to analyze and test, for example, Vološinov's claims that an utterance is "the product of the reciprocal relationship between speaker and listener, addresser and addressee" and that the "immediate social situation and the broader social milieu wholly determine . . . the structure of an utterance."[5] To do so is to take a first step toward closing the gap between cultural poetics and close verbal analysis. I turn now to a summary of the politeness model before testing its application on *Henry VIII*.

POLITENESS THEORY

As I noted above, Brown and Levinson make the striking claim that most of the commonplace actions that people negotiate in words carry a considerable element of risk: these include not only speech acts usually considered threatening or damaging, such as insults, criticisms, admissions of guilt, commands, curses, or dares, but also speech acts generally regarded as positive, such as offers, compliments, thanksgiving, and invitations. One piece of compelling evidence that such verbal negotiations are fraught with risk is the existence in all known languages of a complex and extensive repertory of verbal strategies apparently directed towards minimizing damage and managing risk. In the early 1970s, as speech acts theorists worked to classify the kinds of illocutionary acts performed in speaking and to understand the relation between the speech acts performed and their linguistic realizations, they began to call attention to the apparent overabundance of ways of, for example, making a request or issuing a "directive."[6] "Come with me" seems to deliver a simple, clear, and serviceable message. Why then do we say instead "Would you like to come with me, dear?" or "Let's go together" or "You wouldn't like to come with me, would you?" or "Your mother can manage on her own for a few minutes"? According to Brown and Levinson, "the abundance of syntactic and lexical apparatus in a grammar seems undermotivated by either systemic or cognitive distinctions and psychological processing factors"; they argue that the motivation is "social, and includes . . . face-risk minimization."[7] In defining what is at risk in conversation, they adapt Erving Goffman's concept of "face," or publicly projected self-image.[8] They propose that the overabundance of linguistic apparatus for speech acts begins to make sense if participants in speech exchanges are conceived as having a reciprocal or mutual interest in maintaining face. Furthermore, they distinguish positive and negative face: positive face is the "positive consistent self-image or 'personality' (crucially including the desire that this self-image be appreciated and approved of) claimed by interactants"; negative face is "the basic claim to territories, personal preserves, rights to non-distraction – i.e. to freedom of action and freedom from imposition." Some acts (these include both verbal and non-verbal acts associated with social interaction) intrinsically threaten either a participant's "want to be approved" or "want to be unimpeded." Brown and Levinson call these "face-threatening acts."[9] The role of politeness strategies is to minimize these threats to face.

It has usually been assumed that, where social motives enter conversation, all logic is abandoned. Indeed, J. L. Styan's first principle for understanding dramatic dialogue – "Dramatic Dialogue is More than Conversation" – assumed, without making any serious study of conversation, that conversation itself is virtually devoid of logical or systematic progression, built up instead of irrelevant clutter.[10] H. Paul Grice's influential article, "Logic and Conversation" (1975), which established how indirect messages in conversation are logically organized and decoded by interactants, did much to make such dismissive treatment of conversational organization untenable.[11] Brown and Levinson go still further, for they refuse to treat the social dimension of conversation as haphazard. They argue that a logic informs the deployment of "politeness" strategies, a logic whereby the face-saving strategy adopted in any instance correlates to the assessed seriousness or weight of the face-threatening act. Three factors added together make up this weighting: Distance – the social distance between speaker and hearer; Power – the relative power of speaker and hearer; and Ranking – the culture-specific ranking of impositions.[12] If potential face threats are very slight, speakers perform acts without redressive action ("on-record"); if threats to face are very great, speakers tend to avoid them or perform them only indirectly ("off-record"). Between these extremes, Brown and Levinson position their two main politeness "super-strategies" – "positive" strategies for lesser face threats and "negative" strategies for greater ones. The positive strategies address the hearer's wish for approval, and the negative his or her wish for noninterference.[13]

What is perhaps most impressive about Brown and Levinson's account is also what resists summary: their enormously detailed and suggestive classification of specific politeness strategies and their linguistic realizations, and their abundant examples drawn from modern English, Tamil, and Tzeltal languages. Brown and Levinson do not call their richly delineated inventory of strategies for performing face-threatening acts with minimized risk a "rhetoric," but if we recognize that they have indeed gone a long way toward developing a rhetoric of social interaction, the potential applications and importance of their work become clearer.

POSITIVE POLITENESS

This rhetoric of social interaction can help us toward an analysis of how the characters use directives in *Henry VIII*, permitting us not only to describe and categorize the politeness strategies deployed to manage risk but also to predict which politeness super-strategies would normally occur based on distance between speakers, their relative power, and the speech action involved.[14] With lower-risk threats one expects positive politeness: it works upon an interactant's desire for approval, especially through strategies for claiming common ground between speaker and hearer and through strategies for conveying that the speaker and hearer are cooperators. With higher-risk threats one expects negative politeness, redressive action addressed to the interactant's desire to be unimpeded. While positive politeness asserts or suggests identification between participants, negative politeness puts distance between participants through strategies conveying the speaker's effort to avoid assumptions about the hearer's condition or volition, to avoid coercion, to communicate the wish not to impinge, or to impersonalize the threat. Positive politeness is basically a rhetoric of identification.[15] Negative politeness is basically a rhetoric of dissociation.

Let us return to the advice Norfolk offers Buckingham, to see whether the specific reparative strategies correspond to these patterns. It is useful to recall the context of the advice-giving. After Norfolk describes the extravagant display of the Field of the Cloth of Gold, the conversation turns to an account of the ruinous expense incurred for lavish wardrobe and other travel costs by the nobility whose attendance was required by Cardinal Wolsey. All three of the speakers voice their intense resentment of the cardinal. Their antipathy toward Wolsey is repeatedly accounted for as class resentment, resentment that "A beggar's book / Outworths a noble's blood" (1.1.122–23). Norfolk's advice-giving to Buckingham is interrupted by the passage of the cardinal and his train across the stage, with such disdainful looks exchanged between Wolsey and Buckingham as confirm for the audience the legitimacy of Norfolk's warnings. Observing Buckingham's anger at Wolsey's disdain, Norfolk reiterates his warnings, so that his advice-giving is itself a main action of the scene and one that anticipates the climax of Buckingham's arrest. I have marked the repair features in Norfolk's speeches with symbols that I will link to their specific functions; as the Brown and Levinson model predicts, positive politeness predominates.

> ... Like it[a] your grace,[b]
> The state takes notice of the private difference
> Betwixt you and the cardinal. I advise you
> (And take it from a heart that wishes towards you
> Honor and plenteous safety)[c] that you read
> The cardinal's malice and his potency
> Together; to consider further, that
> What his high hatred would effect wants not
> A minister in his power. You know his nature,[d]
> That he's revengeful; and I know[e] his sword
> Hath a sharp edge ...   (1.1.100–10)

> Stay, my lord,[b]
> And let your reason with your choler question[f]
> What 'tis you go about. To climb steep hills
> Requires slow pace at first.[g] Anger is like
> A full hot horse, who being allowed his way,
> Self-mettle tires him.[g] Not a man in England
> Can advise me like you.[h] Be to yourself
> As you would to your friend.[h]   (1.1.129–36)

The parenthetical assurance of good will we have already noted (*c*) expresses most blatantly the orientation of Norfolk's speeches toward positive politeness: it attends directly to the advisee's need for approval.

Norfolk reinforces the claim to common ground with Buckingham, first by attributing knowledge to the advisee – specifically, knowledge of Wolsey's nature (*d*) – and second by acknowledging shared and approved values – specifically, the belief that reason can and should guide action (*f*). Norfolk's speeches also illustrate Brown and Levinson's other main category of positive politeness: the implication that the speaker and the hearer are cooperators. In alluding to Buckingham's own sound advice-giving (*h*), Norfolk claims reciprocity by recontextualizing the one-way speech action of advice-giving to place it within a larger speech continuum between them of reciprocal counsel. The pronominal shift in the "you know-I know" formulation (*e*) also assumes reciprocity between them. These positive politeness strategies, while greatly multiplied in the risky context of advice-giving, nonetheless also extend an "in-group" language already established in the conversation. Perhaps its most explicit previous assertion is Norfolk's announcement of his shared class membership with Buckingham: "As I belong to worship and affect / In honor honesty" (39–40). Furthermore, an in-group rhetoric of identification recurs predictably in the regularly occurring scenes of gossiping gentlemen or peers which are peculiar to this play.[16]

While it is clear that positive-politeness strategies predominate in Norfolk's usage above, strategies that Brown and Levinson classify as negative politeness do occur, including distancing devices and respect forms. In developing his comparison of anger to a horse (*g*), Norfolk employs generalizing sententiae to amplify the content of his advice-giving. He thus distances and impersonalizes his criticism of Buckingham's gathering anger against Wolsey, using the general precepts to dissociate himself from the role of fault-finder and his hearer from the role of fault-maker. Finally, the opening "Like it your grace" (*a* and *b*) exemplifies highly conventional forms of the respect behavior I will discuss in the next section, behavior which minimizes the risk of imposing by implying that the power or status of the hearer exempts him or her from such risk.[17]

Where does this analysis of Norfolk's advice-giving take us? The analysis accounts for a surprisingly large number of stylistic features in Norfolk's speeches. If this kind of analysis, oriented toward social situation (social situation conceived not as static social organization but as dynamic interaction) explains much, then it should lead us to call into question other standard ways of accounting for the same stylistic features. For example, it should lead us to question the assumption that "The style is the man" – that is, that stylistic phenomena correlate to individual personalities in Shakespeare's plays. The modification Bakhtin proposes – "Style is at least two persons" – may be more adequate to the preceding analysis, for Norfolk's language constantly anticipates and attends to Buckingham's face wants and so – to use again Bakhtin's locution – is oriented toward a "future answer-word."[18] What we get is not Norfolk's individualistic style but the style of a person giving advice (Ranking of the imposition) to a high-ranking social equal (Power) with whom he has more than a passing acquaintance (Distance). Such a style is predictably marked by positive politeness.

NEGATIVE POLITENESS

King Henry VIII yields many examples of negative politeness because so many of its speech situations involve address to King Henry, whose power relative to all other persons in the play is very great. Imperatives, with their assumption of the right to impose on others, are an obvious prerogative of power. Henry claims as another defining prerogative of his power the right to non-imposition. This is made explicit when the approach of the dukes of Norfolk and Suffolk to Henry's presence draws this rebuke: "Who's there, I say? How dare you thrust yourselves / Into my private meditations? / Who am I? ha?" (2.2.63–65). Clearly, speaking to the powerful gives rise to a dilemma, for speech interaction cannot be sustained without the need arising on both sides for directives and other face-threatening acts – that is, the need to impose. Indeed, a large power difference multiplies the number of potential face-threatening acts, so making their performance still less avoidable; for power brings into the realm of risk such acts as small involuntary body movements or the very fact of entering into speech, even to answer questions. Speakers addressing directives to the powerful must negotiate glaring clashes. These extreme situations are interesting not only in themselves but also for the light they shed on the contradictions always inherent in performing face-threatening acts. Negative politeness displays these inherent contradictions more directly in its strategic rhetorical products than does positive politeness. This is so because positive politeness is "free-ranging" compensation, defusing risk by the general practices of expressing interest in and approval of the other, while "negative politeness is specific and focused ... minimizing the particular imposition that the [face-threatening act] unavoidably effects."[19] Hence negative politeness often puts on display the simultaneous effort to do and to undo the imposition.

Performing directives involves making assumptions about the hearer's willingness and ability to comply; furthermore, directives are coercive. Hence negative politeness works to repair or undo assumptions about the hearer's wants and to undo coercion. We can see that these motives inform the most conventional politeness formula displayed in the play, one that explicitly retracts any assumption about the hearer's willingness:

> KATHERINE [to Henry]
> ... *Please you*, sir,
> The king your father was reputed for
> A prince most prudent ...
> (2.4.42–44; emphasis added)
>
> WOLSEY [to Katherine]
> *May it please you*, noble madam, to withdraw
> Into your private chamber ...
> (3.1.27–28; emphasis added)

At one point in the play, when Henry's anger is stirred by the Council's affront to Archbishop Cranmer, he asserts his power by denying the efficacy of this repair strategy:

> SURREY   May it please your grace –
> KING   No, sir, it does not please me.   (5.3.134)

We get a further variation in Katherine's trial scene when she makes her request for Spanish counsel. She undoes the coercive force of her directive by using a post-posed "If not" clause to make fully explicit Henry's option not to act:

> ... Wherefore I humbly
> Beseech you, sir, to spare me till I may
> Be by my friends in Spain advised, whose counsel
> I will implore. *If not*, i'th' name of God,
> *Your pleasure be fulfilled!*   (2.4.51–55; emphasis added)

Whereas positive politeness associates the speaker with the hearer, the negative politeness of deference behavior – either the raising of the other or the lowering of oneself – dissociates the speaker from the hearer. By making explicit the magnitude of a power difference obtaining, a speaker can signal the hearer's immunity from imposition. Respectful titles of address and humbling self-representations like Wolsey's "me (poor undeserver)" (3.2.175) work this way. Verb choices such as "beseech" can also mark the power difference between speaker and hearer. Directives in English, in Shakespeare's time as in ours, are so lexicalized as to provide gradations of illocutionary force. Hence when Lear wavers in determining the level of his speech force ("The King would speak with Cornwall. The dear father / Would with his daughter speak, commands, tends service" [2.4.96–97]), these alterations bespeak his altered power. In *Henry VIII* we find a range of negatively polite verb forms that register directives of weak force:

> MESSENGER [to Katherine]
> I humbly do *entreat* your highness' pardon.
> (4.2.104; emphasis added)
>
> KATHERINE [to Capuchius]
> Sir, I most humbly *pray* you to deliver
> This to my lord the king.
> (4.2.129–30; emphasis added)

When Katherine sues Henry in 1.2 to remove unfair taxations imposed on the people by Wolsey, a bold speech action interrupting Wolsey's own agenda of undoing Buckingham, her style illustrates some more complicated but characteristic practices of negative politeness:

> KATHERINE
> Thank your majesty.[a]
> That you would[b] love yourself, and in that love
> Not unconsidered[c] leave your honor nor
> The dignity of your office, is the point
> Of my petition.[d]
> KING   Lady mine, proceed.
> KATHERINE
> I am solicited, not by a few,
> And those of true condition,[e] that your subjects
> Are in great grievance . . .
> . . . yet the king our master,[f]
> Whose honor heaven shield from soil! – even he escapes not
> Language unmannerly[c]; yea such which breaks
> The sides of loyalty[g] and almost[h] appears
> In loud rebellion.   (4.2.13–29)
>
> KATHERINE
> I am much too venturous
> In tempting of your patience, but am bold'ned
> Under your promised pardon.[i]   (4.2.54–56)

Katherine begins here by thanking Henry for his courteous offer that she arise, "take place by us," and assume "half our power." Whatever response Katherine might render through her bodily demeanor to Henry's invitation,[20] her words work to repair the risk of her suit by asserting a power difference between them. Thanking him as "your majesty" (*a*), she positions him above her. Transparent indirection is a characteristic strategy of negative politeness. The indirection of posing a criticism as an injunction to self-love (*d*) is reinforced at the level of the syntax by the double negatives (*c*) and by the conditional force of the "would" (*b*). Similarly, with the qualifying "almost" (*h*), we get an obvious undercutting of the force of the complaint. As already noted, negative politeness works by dissociation. At *e*, Katherine dissociates herself as speaker from the direct reporting of the subjects' grievances; at *f*, by addressing Henry in the third person, Katherine dissociates Henry as hearer from the criticism. Furthermore, what Brown and Levinson call "point-of-view distancing"[21] comes into play to redirect the harm-giving from Henry's subjects to the depersonalized "sides of loyalty" (*g*). And finally, we get at *i* one of the most easily recognizable strategies of negative politeness: perform the face-threatening act and apologize for the face-threatening act, or – as another Renaissance heroine is urged in a very different context – "Be bold. Be not too bold."

SPEECH POSITION AND CHARACTER

I have been considering these discursive practices as effects, caused not by the control and decision-making of the individual speaker but by the motive of politeness and the socially defined site of the subject. Now let us consider the possibility of regarding the discursive forms themselves as causes, as partial determiners of personality, including inner experience in real persons and the illusion of its effect in the artificial persons of drama. For even if we take as our starting point Vološinov's principle that the "organizing center of any utterance . . . is not within but outside – in the social milieu surrounding the individual being," a cumulative effect of such utterances will be to shape subjectivity in the speakers. Indeed, by his account (which I consider helpful but too extreme), "the personality of the speaker" is "wholly a product of social interrelations."[22] By this logic the external forms of politeness may help to organize the psychology of real persons[23] and its illusion in the presentation of dramatic characters. If we examine the disjunctive speech behavior of Katherine in the scene where the Cardinals Wolsey and Campeius visit her in her private chamber, and consider how her words at the end of the scene relate to her character, we may get a glimpse at how politeness can pattern personality.

Katherine's words are apologetic and self-deprecating:

> Do what ye will, my lords; and pray forgive me;
> If I have used myself unmannerly,
> You know I am a woman, lacking wit
> To make a seemly answer to such persons.
> Pray do my service to his majesty,
> He has my heart yet, and shall have my prayers
> While I shall have my life. Come, reverend fathers,
> Bestow your counsels on me. She now begs
> That little thought, when she set footing here,
> She should have bought her dignities so dear. (3.1.175–84)

This speech stands in apparent sharp contrast with the bold defiance of her behavior toward Cardinal Wolsey earlier in the play. Further, to a modern audience these words, with their demeaning account of womanhood, their self-humiliation, their apology – and spoken by a character who to this point in the play we have been able to admire for her strength – may seem an embarrassment. There are a number of things we can do about this source of embarrassment. As a first alternative we can blame the words on Fletcher, who has never seemed so much our contemporary as Shakespeare.[24] Second, we can cut these words in performance, even if it is not our current practice to cut such bad words in our written texts of the Bard. Third – and this comes easiest to a generation of readers trained in reconciling apparent contradictions to produce texts and characters that are autonomous and coherent wholes – we can understand Katherine's words here as sarcasms, so that they register her continuing strength of character, defiance, and rhetorical self-possesion. Of course, if our reading of Katherine's words and their relation to her character were not conditioned by assumptions about Shakespeare's own exemplary rhetorical control, we might be less inclined to read ironic reversal. It may therefore be useful to recall that the speech is drawn from Holinshed's *Chronicles*, where it appears as follows: "And my lords, I am a poore woman, lacking wit, to answer to anie such noble persons of wisedome as you be, in so weightie a matter, therefore I praie you be good to me poore woman, destitute of freends here in a forren region, and your counsell also I will be glad to heare."[25] It is a fourth alternative that I want to take seriously: that is, to recognize in the discontinuity between

Katherine's boldness and her self-deferential apologizing the expected discourse of "the socially defined site from which it is uttered," to use here Pierre Bourdieu's words.[26] Katherine's disjunctive language, juxtaposing bold speech and apology, is entirely consistent with the Janus-faced negative politeness that a hierarchically arranged culture makes it her part to use in most of the speech positions she habitually occupies. Her "character" then is, at least in part, an effect of negative politeness.

Just as unsettling, I think, to some present-day feminist readers of the play as Katherine's self-humiliating deprecation of her sex is the meek discourse of religious humility, patience, and obedience she adopts as she awaits her death. To this point, I have tended to write about the language of *Henry VIII almost* as if it provided direct transcriptions of real social scenes. Much of the language is, in fact, taken over from Holinshed's *Chronicles* and from Foxe's *Acts and Monuments*, works that claim to record direct quotations of their speakers, making my blurring of the real and the poetic perhaps less problematic than would be the case for *Hamlet* or *King Lear*. Still, it is obvious that the shifted context of the borrowed speeches alters their significance, that there can be no direct transcriptions of real social scenes into Shakespeare's plays, and that we are looking at at least slightly different "textual" Katherines in *Henry VIII*, in Holinshed's *Chronicles*, and indeed in a letter purportedly written by the historical Katherine to which I will refer later. Such differences will obtain no matter what the intention or "private craftsmanship" the dramatist strives to effect. Nonetheless, in *Henry VIII* we are made privy to at least one of Shakespeare's purported intentions. We are told in the Epilogue that we have been shown a "merciful construction of good women" (10). In other words, alterations have been made to the historical representations aimed at giving us a favorable view of Queen Katherine and of Queen Anne.

In Anne's case it would seem that the main linguistic means to construct her goodness is to keep her silent.[27] Presumably a construction of her goodness could not be sustained by assertive language such as the historical Anne is reputed to have used.[28] The jokes in *Henry VIII*, 2.3, one of only two scenes where Anne Bullen does speak, salaciously concern whether or not Anne's "back will bear a duchess" (99) or a queen. In this play the "good" woman learns to "bear" – on her back a king's weight, and in her labor a future queen. In other words, the play does in a very objectionable way show how Anne shifts her position to fit her new role, but it does not show the historical Anne's shift from the speech position of a "blushing handmaid" (72) to the speech position of a queen.

While the situation with Katherine is more complicated, it seems to me that Shakespeare's "merciful construction" of her religious piety also performs the ideological work of patriarchy by idealizing nonassertive speech. The dramatist invents a symbolic Patience to be her handmaiden, and he delivers as her new voice a religious discourse of humility, meekness, passivity. Her heavenly coronation – with garlands she says she feels "not worthy yet to wear" (4.2.92) – comes to her not through her own exertions but after she has wished Patience to "set [her] lower" (76). Therefore, while Katherine's "goodness," unlike Anne's, is constructed in language, it is significant that the particular discourse Shakespeare permits her is a discourse of religious piety. In one very interesting way this verbal situation does accurately reflect the situation in Shakespeare's culture, where a main discursive space open to women was indeed religious discourse. Renaissance Englishwomen were permitted access as readers and as writers to this discourse when many other kinds of discourse were kept closed to them, and it is to a large measure true that Renaissance women would have been "silent but for the Word."[29] We can choose, if we wish, to represent this discursive situation as wholly negative and repressive for women, a putting of them – like Katherine in *Henry VIII* – into their quiet places. But this is not the whole truth. Religious discourse at the time was not just a safe and quiet space permitted by the allowance of others to women. The fact that women managed copious performances within this discursive space shows that it was also a space of opportunity for them – a space in which at least some of them found it comfortable to speak and write.[30] Furthermore – and here is where I would suggest that the play's idealizing construction of Katherine as a "good" woman mutes and misrepresents the female discourse of religious piety – it could be a very bold speech. While it would be wrong to represent the discourse of religious piety as univocal, we can nonetheless say that in sixteenth-century England such discourse was very often marked by the speech actions of exhortation and admonition. Religion, in other words, gave women access to the imperative – that is, to the speech action of the powerful. I imagine that this access (though perhaps on an unconscious level) was at times as attractive as was (on a conscious level) the promised access to heaven. And for a woman like the historical Katherine, religious discourse, with its characteristic disjunctions between boldness and humility, was entirely continuous with the Janus-faced speech modes of her secular behavior, molded, as I have argued, on negative-politeness strategies. At any rate, in a letter of religious counsel which the historical Katherine purportedly sent in 1535 to Dr. John Fisher, who was to be beheaded for refusing to take the Oath of Supremacy, we can discern not the insipid speech of the play's passive "good" woman but the by-now familiar alternating accents of apology and boldness which mark this strong woman's language elsewhere:

My revered father,
Since you have ever been wont in dubious cases to give good counsel to others, you will necessarily know all the better what is needed for yourself, being called to combat for the love of Christ and the truth of the Catholic faith. If you will bear up under these few and short pains of your torments which are prepared for you, you will receive, as you well know, the eternal reward . . . But perhaps I have spoken [of her own longing to die] as a foolish woman. Therefore, since it appears that God has thus ordained, go you, my father, first with joy and fortitude, and by your prayers plead with Jesus Christ for me, that I may speedily and intrepidly follow you through the same wearisome and difficult journey; and, meanwhile, that I may be able to share in your holy labours, your torments, punishments and struggles . . . As to the rest, I think it would be an extravagant thing in me to exhort you to desire above all other things that immortal reward . . . you being of such noble birth, gifted with such excellent knowledge of divine things, and (what I ought to mention first) brought up from youth in a religion so holy, and in the profession of the most glorious father St. Francis . . .[31]

SPEECH POSITION AND CLASS TRAJECTORY

We have now looked at one kind of relation that can obtain between standard practices of politeness and character. Our look at Katherine has suggested that the politeness practices to which a person is habituated by virtue of the speech positions he or she most frequently occupies will help to structure that person's makeup. However, a look at Cardinal Wolsey's practice with directives must introduce some new elements into the discussion. The first has to do with Wolsey's reputation as a self-made man, and a man who made himself partly through his mastery of eloquence. It is easier to imagine the speech production of sixteenth-century women being largely determined by social discourses working apart from their control than it is to imagine this of Wolsey. In Shakespeare's representation of Wolsey, we expect to find the "private craftsmanship" in language more pronounced. If a rhetoric of social interaction plays a part in the "honey of his language" (3.2.22), we might expect it to be a rhetoric he has mastered, that he has made his tool and works to his advantage. In the light of such expectations, it is interesting to find that Shakespeare emphasizes politeness phenomena in Wolsey's speech and that a deviation from standard forms of politeness particularizes his speech behavior.

Queen Katherine characterizes Wolsey's speech, equating his "cunning" in language and his deployment of "negative politeness":

> My lord, my lord,
> I am a simple woman, much too weak
> T'oppose your cunning. Y'are meek and humble-mouthed;
> You sign your place and calling, in full seeming,
> With meekness and humility; but your heart
> Is crammed with arrogancy, spleen, and pride.
> You have, by fortune and his highness' favors,
> Gone slightly o'er low steps, and now are mounted
> Where pow'rs are your retainers, and your words
> (Domestics to you) serve your will as't please
> Yourself pronounce their office.   (2.4.103–13)

What Katherine says is complicated, but the gist of it is a rebuke aimed against the hypocrisy of Wolsey's reverential verbal manner. She exposes his negative politeness as a posture at odds not only with his high inward self-estimation but also with the enormous power his words wield. It is easy enough to see how Wolsey's humble words jar with his place and power. The conventional forms of negative politeness are often on his lips, as in the instance which draws Katherine's rebuke – his "I do beseech / You, gracious madam, to unthink your speaking . . ." (101–02). But the interest of Wolsey's language does not reside merely in this contradiction between its forms and his power. Instead, contradictions are on display within the idiosyncratic constructions of his speech acts. Consider, for example, how the main orientation of his speech toward "humble-mouthed" negative politeness is twisted askew when he asks Henry to clear him of malice in bringing the divorce suit against Queen Katherine:

> Most gracious sir,
> In humblest manner I require your highness
> That it shall please you[a] to declare in hearing
> Of all these ears (for where I am robbed and bound,
> There must[b] I be unloosed, although not there
> At once and fully satisfied)[c] whether ever I
> Did broach this business to your highness, or
> Laid any scruple in your way . . .   (2.4.141–48)

Here we get a strongly marked disjunction between the unctuous and the imperious: the noncoercive "If it please you" or "May it please you" is strangely altered to the commanding "it shall please you" (*a*), the attenuated "would" of negative politeness replaced by the uncompromising "must" (*b*), and the parenthetical turn away from the direct progress of the utterance occupied with the prerogatives of the self rather than the face requirements of the other (*c*). Shakespeare may have caught a hint of this accent in Holinshed and then exaggerated both the deferential and the arrogant tones: "With that quoth Wolseie the cardinall: Sir, I most humblie require your highnesse, to declare before all this audience, whether I haue beene the cheefe and first moouer of this matter vnto your maiestie or no, for I am greatlie suspected heerein."[32] The speech quoted is no isolated example.[33] The curious hybrid of deference and self-aggrandizement is Wolsey's oral signature in the play.

What are we to make of Shakespeare's accent on Wolsey's distorted courtesy? It does not appear to celebrate the self-made man, nor to emphasize how Wolsey fashions with the craft of eloquence his own image. Indeed, Shakespeare brings out in Wolsey's language not the evidence of Wolsey's mastery but that of his subjection – the anomaly of Wolsey's socially situated speech position, the mark of the butcher's son pronouncing to kings and queens. That is not to say that Wolsey is unable to use the distinctiveness of his speech behavior to charm and to manipulate. But by giving Wolsey a speech that exposes his anomalous social situation, Shakespeare emphasizes the way in which the forms and resources people have available for manipulation are those speech forms that they habitually live within.

It may be only fanciful to hear in the complaints of the aristocrats against Wolsey's "witchcraft / Over the king in's tongue" (3.2.18–19) –

> Which of the peers
> Have uncontemned gone by him, or at least
> Strangely neglected? When did he regard
> The stamp of nobleness in any person
> Out of himself? (9–13)

– a parallel to the complaint of Robert Greene, who signed himself "M.A. and Gent.," against "an vpstart Crow, beautified with our feathers, that with his *Tygers heart wrapt in a Players hide*, supposes he is as well able to bumbast out a blanke verse as the best of you: and being an absolute *Iohannes fac totum*, is in his owne conceit the onely Shake-scene in a countrie."[34] Even if we can derive some small part of Wolsey's style in *Henry VIII* from the cardinal's social place and origin, we will never manage to derive Shakespeare's linguistic productions from provincial-glover's-son-turned-player, however much Shakespeare may himself have felt the constraints of his social position upon his writing, as he seems to express in sonnet 76:[35]

> Why write I still all one, ever the same,
> And keep invention in a noted weed,
> That every word doth almost tell my name,
> *Showing their birth and where they did proceed?*
> (5–8; emphasis added)

Shakespeare is nonetheless a writer acutely sensitive to the social situation of people's language. For that reason alone we must have at our command a working inventory of the tropes of social interaction before we can give a richly articulated account of his language and style. The analysis in this chapter of the various styles for doing directives in one play should at least suggest how the Brown and Levinson model of politeness can help us toward such an inventory.

I have been arguing that the conversational logic of politeness helps to determine linguistic interaction among the play's characters. If the ordinary (and yet eloquent) forms of social politeness direct characters' speeches to such a large extent, then we must question the usual assumptions that stylistic features express either a character's individual "personality" or Shakespeare's personal style. It would nonetheless be premature to conclude that style is simply reflective of the immediate contingencies of particular social interactions. It is still possible to conceptualize a connection between style and character, if we reach towards a dialogics of the speaking subject and a pragmatic reading of dramatic character. Subsequent chapters will explore this possibility further, but we have seen in this chapter how character "effects" can be shaped by the speech patterns of the speakers' relative social positions, both as given in the present moment of the verbal interaction and as gathering up the cumulative trajectory of accustomed speech positions.

CHAPTER 2

"Power to hurt": language and service in Sidney household letters and Shakespeare's sonnets

"Power to hurt": my starting point is a phrase shared by Edmund Molyneux and William Shakespeare. In an eloquent and rhetorically complicated letter to Sir Philip Sidney, answering a rebuke from him, his father's secretary, Edmund Molyneux writes of having "neither Will nor Power to hurt in this Case if I wolde."

Letter 1
Edmund Molyneux, *Esq*; *to Sir* Philip Sidney.

SIR,
I have receaved your Lettres, and doe acknowledge the same as a speciall Note of your lovinge Favour, that it wold please you to write vnto me; and what may lye in me in any Sorte to doe, you shall not need to requier me: But you have (yf it may soe lyke you) full Power and good Warrant to commaund me. Sir, yt semethe by your said Lettres, that you have beene enformed, that I either have already, or in some Sorte pretend hereafter, to be an Adversarie to Mr. *Grivell* in his Sute heere; and that I make not that good Accounte of the Validitie and Goodnes of his Patent, as in Reasone and cowrtewse frindlie Dealinge, I should doe, somwhat, as you gather, to his Disadvantage, beinge a Matter, as you saye, of noe Bennefite to my selfe; which, yf I showld soe forgett my selfe (yf it were only in Respect that you esteeme Mr. *Gryvell* as your deere and entier Frend) I showld justlie condemne my selfe of vnadvised and twoe great inconsiderat Dealinge. And therfore I pray you, and soe effectuallye desyre him to hold a better Opinion of me, till you have further Proofe howe I doe deale, and have dealt, in the Cawse from the Beginynge. *And as I have neither Will nor Power to hurt* in this Case if I wolde, havinge onlie to walke in the Pathe I am directed: So yf I had either, beinge otherwise directed by you, I wold not. And therfore beseche you, what soever Cowrse be held in the Matter, lay noe further Fawlt in me, then I justlie deserve: For assure your selfe, you and yours have, and ever shall have, that vndowbted Interest in me, as I will obey your Commaundement, as farre as in Dewtie and Credit I may, which I crave yt maye lyke you to accept. And evenso I take my Leave. From *Salloppe*, the xxviijth of *Aprill*, 1581.

Yours ever in all to be comaunded
as your obedient Servant,
E. Molyneux.[1]

In sonnet 94, Shakespeare's speaker comments on those "that haue power to hurt and will do none." The connection which this chapter aims to articulate between Molyneux's language in correspondence with Sidney and Shakespeare's language in some sonnets to the Young Man (for example, sonnets 57, 85, 88, 89, and 94, but especially sonnet 58) is not, however, of direct borrowing. What I consider is how the shared phrase arises within a particular social relation and situation – both instances involve the relation between a subordinate and a superior he is engaged to serve, and in both cases the subordinate is negotiating problematic speech actions involving the correction or the rebuke of the superior. Speech or written answer is problematic in this situation since, as the puritan divine William Perkins put it, "in case of rebuke or controlment" by the master, it is the part of the servant to "answer not again."[2] In this chapter I will make use of the politeness model which I introduced in chapter 1 to analyze the speech interactions and social shaping of dramatic characters in Shakespeare's *King Henry VIII*. Here I will draw on the distinctions offered by the politeness model to define the constraints that Molyneux's particular social speech position imposes and, more significantly, the verbal repertoire that is available to a speaker so situated. I aim to show the complexity and interest of Molyneux's rhetoric, or rather less *his* rhetoric than the rhetoric of his particular social situation.[3] It is my thesis that the same social moment to some extent informs the rhetoric of Shakespeare's speaker in the sonnets I have mentioned, and that Shakespeare's language in these sonnets derives something of its peculiar power from it.[4]

In the well-known terms of Catherine Belsey's claim that "[s]ubjectivity is discursively produced and is constrained by the range of subject positions defined by the discourses in which the concrete individual participates,"[5] I am arguing that the same subject position constrains Molyneux's and the poet-speaker's discourse and subjectivity. While there can be no doubt that the kind of thinking about discourse, social relations, and subject positions exemplified by scholars like Belsey has transformed Renaissance criticism, nonetheless one important element of the project has still been given only superficial treatment – that is, there has been no detailed account of how words match up with social relations, how words delineate subject positions. We have no adequate stylistics of the early modern subject. Mikhail Bakhtin's work takes us one step towards it by making us aware that a stylistics of the subject can not be a stylistics of the individual voice if "[s]tyle is at least two persons":[6] it must be a stylistics of interaction. Pierre Bourdieu's insights help to qualify and develop the interactionist view, by emphasizing how beyond two speaking persons we must see that "the whole social structure is present in each interaction . . . what happens between two persons – between an employer and an employee or . . . in the post-colonial situation, between two members of the formerly colonized nation . . . derives its particular form from the objective relation . . . between the groups who speak those languages."[7] To study the stylistic repertoire of the "speaking subject," his or her linguistic "habitus," is to analyze the languages of the interaction situations in which he or she is typically or habitually a verbal participant, that is, the scripts available for giving voice to historically specific social relationships.

In this chapter I focus on Molyneux's letter, related Sidney family correspondence, and sonnet 58 primarily to show with what complexity, eloquence, and precision historically specific social relations of power are figured in the language. That social rank – or more precisely relative social status – was strongly marked in both medieval and early modern verbal exchange through the courteous use of titles, forms of address, salutations and farewells, and pronouns of address expressing deference, condescension, and solidarity is well understood.[8] Less well understood but clearly exhibited in Elizabethan vernacular letter-writing and epistolary handbooks such as Angel Day's *The English Secretary* is the extent to which power relations in civil exchanges come to extend more deeply into the grain of the language – into the discourse that enacts the heart of the business rather than the flourishes that accompany it. In the early modern period, increasingly more subtle and complex verbal tools serve the important social functions of civility, which include the mutual acknowledgment and display of the relative power of interlocutors, the management and repair of aggression, and the maintenance of the hierarchical social arrangement. Although it is commonplace to claim that discourse inscribes power relations, the detailed demonstration of this phenomenon in specific instances of discourse has proved elusive for at least two important reasons we must take into consideration in sketching out the interaction repertoires shared by Edmund Molyneux and Shakespeare's speaker. First, and most obvious, power relations cannot be articulated through the single lens of social rank: even in a society so highly stratified as sixteenth-century England, age, gender, family and household position, occupation, affective bond, sexual interest, financial and other material circumstances – even the most temporary exigencies – can all color and modify the power relation. The power on display in the verbal repair work of social exchanges takes account, to adopt Pierre Bourdieu's term, of the various forms of culturally specific "symbolic capital" that interlocutors have accumulated.⁹ Bourdieu asserts, then, that civility, or politeness as it will be broadly understood in this chapter to encompass interpersonal repair and maintenance in language use, "contains a politics, a practical, immediate recognition of social classifications and hierarchies, between the sexes, the generations, the classes, etc."¹⁰ Nonetheless, while Bourdieu is correct to link social power to a spectrum of social classifications and to locate the language that registers power in the forms of politeness, we must consider the second reason for the elusiveness of discourse as a register of power in order to understand why the politics of politeness is not quite as transparent as he suggests. What must qualify his claim that politeness yields an "immediate" recognition of hierarchy is the speech act or verbal event under negotiation. Politeness, as Brown and Levinson demonstrate, is strategic and context specific: the work it does to prevent, mitigate, and repair damage to immediate relations and to the overall social fabric intensifies at points of stress or threat.¹¹ Hence, it varies not only with relative power but also with the risk level of particular speech events, and for this reason we will not find a static match between the stylistic forms of civility and the relative power of participants. To read the power politics on display in the discourse of service enacted in early modern letters and sonnets, then, we must be particularly attentive to the complex determiners of the power relations and to the speech events under negotiation.

In making the link between Molyneux's letter and sonnet 58, I will also speculate about how social interaction styles might relate to emotions and inner mental experience. A Shakespeare sonnet like 58 has more usually been read and valued as the verbal expression of an inward state than as the verbal negotiation of an outward social relation. Yet social-discourse theorists like V. N. Vološinov have proposed a close connection between "inner" and "outer" speech, encouraging questions about the possibly social and discursive genesis of structures of feeling.¹² Did the complex and often self-contradictory speech actions of men positioned like Molyneux or Shakespeare's speaker go hand in hand with distinctive forms of feeling? Does complex social speech affect the inner shape of the subject's mental experience and the sense of self?¹³ Indeed, much has been written on Shakespeare's invention in the sonnets of new forms of feeling, even of a new and individuated subjectivity. But poetic invention, or genius, can by no means account fully for the "subjectivity effects" Joel Fineman finds in Shakespeare's sonnet language.[14] This chapter will suggest how significant is the role that the hierarchical social discourse of early modern England played in inventing the subjectivity of the sonnets.

THE INSTITUTION OF SERVICE AND ITS AMBIGUITIES

What do we know of the sets of relationships in which Molyneux's self-defense against Sidney's accusation of blame arises? Speech acts, like the social relations they articulate and create, are produced from and producing of power relations and grow out of material conditions. As soon as we turn to a detailed account of Molyneux's situation, it becomes apparent that we cannot understand the subject position of the servant in the Elizabethan household in terms of the simple opposition between social inferior and social superior. In the 1570s and early 1580s, Edmund Molyneux served as secretary to Philip Sidney's father, Sir Henry Sidney, who held – in Queen Elizabeth's own words – "two of the best Offices in the kingdom":[15] Lord President of the Marches of Wales and, until his second recall in 1578, Lord Deputy of Ireland. Usually resident with Sir Henry in Wales or Ireland, Molyneux also served at times as his agent in London, pursuing suits and negotiating other business matters at court not only for Sir Henry, but also – as we shall see in the letters to be analyzed later – for his sons Philip and Robert and for his wife Lady Mary (Dudley) Sidney. Important to our understanding of the power relations obtaining between the Sidney family members and the servant Molyneux is his employer's representation of him in a 1576 letter of recommendation in what may seem to us today to be almost contradictory terms: both as "a Gentlemen [*sic*] of woorshipfull Parentage" and as "my Servaunt."[16] In the same letter, Sir Henry is recommending equally his servant Molyneux and his own son Robert as joint incumbents for the lucrative office of Supervisor of Attorneys in Wales which he is urging Sir Francis Walsingham to create. He also mentions how "longe agoe it was commended to the Lords, by my Lettres, to have passed in the Name of *Fowke Grivell*, and *Molyneux*," but now he names his son Robert because Greville, Philip's close friend and the frequent beneficiary of Sir Henry's patronage, "is spedd so well alreadye" with "the Reversions of twoe of the best Offices" in Wales.[17]

As this ambiguous network of power relations suggests, the institution of service constitutes one of the most basic differences between early modern English society and our own. Servants were not drawn from any single social class or status group: a very large proportion of the population was employed as servants at some stage in their lives, including those deriving from high-ranking families, most often for a transitional period during youth or early adulthood. The term "servant" applied to a broad range of roles, encompassing both the personal servingman and the wage-earning agricultural laborer. What servants had in common was that "they worked for one master, and were maintained by that master."[18] In upper-gentry and aristocratic households, most of the servants were male, even those employed in preparing food, serving at table, and cleaning house.[19] In *A Health to the Gentlemanly Profession of Serving-Men* (1598), I. M. makes a distinction that may help to account for the apparent contradiction between Edmund Molyneux as "a Gentlemen of woorshipfull Parentage" and a "Servaunt." The distinction is between "Servingmen" and other categories of servants, or between those in daily attendance upon their masters, partakers in their employments and pastimes, and those employed in "holding the Plough" and "whipping the Carthorse."[20] "Amongst what sort of people," he asks, "should then this Servingman be sought for?" and responds with a logic that accounts for the high birth of many servingmen: "Even the Dukes sonne preferred Page to the Prince, the Earles seconde sonne attendant upon the Duke, the Knights seconde sonne the Earles Servant, the Esquires sonne to weare the Knightes lyverie, and the Gentlemans sonne the Esquiers Servingman: Yea, I know at this day, Gentlemen younger brothers, that weares their elder brothers Blew coate and Badge . . ."[21] In his lament for the decay of the servingman's profession, I. M. contends that this social organization provided for "the preservation of ancient Houses, and, the mayntenance of the Commons in their calling."[22] That is, the institution of well-born servingmen supported the system of primogeniture by providing suitable roles for younger brothers and permitting them a "credite and esteeme alwayes equall with their birth and callyng."[23] In this highly idealized account of the servingman's lost contentment, I. M. thinks of the servingman as a member of the master's family, partaking with wife and child in the network of familial affective bonds:

the one did commaunde, the other was to obey: the due obedience to which commaunde was had in so reverent regarde, and the Servant so fearefull to offende his Maister, no servile, but as it were a filial feare, as the Maister was almost as carefull in his commaunde, as the Servant diligent in his duetie. For in these dayes what greater love could almost be found, then betwixt the Maister and the Servant: it was in maner equall with the Husbandes to the Wyfe, and the Childes to the Parent.[24]

The equivalences set out in I. M.'s pairings make the power relations within the household seem not only benign but also transparent. What remains unexamined here and in similar prescriptive treatments, however, is a whole complicated network of relationships within which the day-to-day business of living is negotiated: the relations, for example, of servant to master's wife and of servant to master's child, relations that figure prominently in the Sidney family correspondence surrounding Molyneux's letter of self-defense. Empirical studies like Alice T. Friedman's examination of the disfunctional upper-gentry household of Sir Francis Willoughby at Wollaton Hall have begun to show how the material circumstances of the Elizabethan household could make these servant–family power relations extremely competitive and ambiguous. With high-born children often living, from an early age, apart from their parents and with the wife's sphere of activity often constricted both to a narrow range of affairs and a limited public presence, gentlemen servants could capitalize on their proximity to the master: "their day-to-day familiarity with their master's business affairs and their constant attendance on him placed them in a good position to gain his confidence and even to replace his own wife or children as his principal allies."[25]

Thus we can see that "servant" is both a highly variable and a relational term, and it becomes less surprising that Sir Henry Sidney's "servant" comes of "woorshipfull Parentage," or that the office to which Sidney recommends Molyneux after his "good many Yeres Service"[26] is an office in which he hopes his son Robert can share both patent and financial rewards. Indeed, in what William Fulwood, instructing on modes of address suited to social rank, calls a person's "permanent dignities,"[27] Henry Sidney does not far outrank Molyneux. Molyneux styled himself "Esquire": he was the third son of Sir Edmund Molyneux, who had been a justice of the common pleas and was created a knight of the Bath on the occasion of Edward VI's coronation.[28] Henry Sidney was knighted with William Cecil on 11 October 1550, but he bore no higher title of nobility. Of course, in what Fulwood calls "mutable dignitie," to be added to the superscription of a letter after the addressee's "permanent dignities," Henry Sidney – as deputy of Ireland and president of Wales – clearly outranks his secretary Molyneux. Nonetheless, within the complex politics of Elizabethan address, in which Henry Sidney greets both his brother-in-law Leicester and his son-in-law the Earl of Pembroke as "my good lord,"[29] and in which Philip Sidney is instructed by Queen Elizabeth to answer the Earl of Oxford's insult with deferential language, remembering "the difference in degree between earls and gentlemen,"[30] the Sidneys are not situated in terms of any absolute ranking far above Molyneux's own station.

However complex the status differential between Henry Sidney and Edmund Molyneux begins to appear, still other factors must enter into an account of the power relation between the son Philip and the father's secretary. It is important to recognize that Philip Sidney's authority, his power to command and be heard, derives in large part from or through his mother: as a schoolboy, his father enjoined him to "Remember, my Sonne, the noble Blood yow are descended of, by your Mothers Side; and thinke that only, by vertuous Lyf and good Action, yow may be an Ornament to that illustre Famylie."[31] The family took pride in the mother's family connections, despite the shadow of her father's execution for bringing Jane Grey to the throne: the heralds' bills for funeral expenses in 1586 styled her in noble fashion "the right honorable the Lady Sidney daughter of the high and mighty John late Duke of Northumberland."[32] Although without title himself when he rebuked Molyneux in 1581, Philip Sidney's very considerable "symbolic capital," his power as registered in his speech acts and as recognized and acknowledged in the answering speech acts from others, drew not only upon the importance of his father's offices and the evidence of his own abilities but primarily upon his mother's network of relatives: as a Dudley he was heir apparent to his mother's brothers, to the two great Earls of Leicester and of Warwick. At the same time, the mother's rank does not necessarily guarantee her the symbolic or the verbal power that her son gains through it. On the one hand, Mary Sidney's rank, her education, her early ties to Queen Elizabeth and Queen Elizabeth's continuing desire for her attendance at court, and her husband's frequent need for access to her court ties may all contribute to the potential power of her speech acts, to the expectation she could have that her words would be listened to and obeyed. On the other hand, her gender, the permanent disfiguration she suffered from nursing Queen Elizabeth through the smallpox in 1562, her resultant preference to avoid the court, her frequent ill health, and her apparently slight involvement with her sons all could be expected to diminish her linguistic capital and to complicate her negotiation even of household power relations.[33] As is now becoming clear, the power relations we shall find figured in the language of the Molyneux–Sidney family correspondence reflect an extremely complex set of variables, including differences in rank, office, gender, abilities, family connections, and future prospects but nonetheless registering, above all, a subordinate positioning of the servingman.

SOCIAL RELATION AS STYLISTIC DETERMINANT

My general point about how significant social relation can be as a stylistic determinant is best illustrated by writings that exhibit a range of relations. With specific regard to relations involving service, the Molyneux–Sidney family correspondence supplies a fascinating group in which the rhetorical and stylistic contrasts across the different relations are very strongly marked. To avoid over-simplification in interpreting Molyneux's positioned language of subordination, I will situate his letter not in relation to the correspondence of master and servant but in relation to the correspondence of master's child and servant and of master's wife and servant. I quote below three letters from the Sidney sons to Molyneux, each issuing instructions on how Molyneux is to behave in the furtherance of a suit on behalf of the writer or his friend. The first of these is the letter Molyneux answers back: Philip Sidney's letter accusing Molyneux of obstructing Fulke Greville's efforts to obtain the income he expected to receive from one of the offices (the Clerk of the Signet) he had obtained in the Council of the Marches of Wales.[34]

Letter 2
Sir Philip Sidney *to* Edmund Molyneux, *Esq*;

I pray yow, for my Sake, yow will not make yowr self an Instrument to crosse my Cosin *Fowkes* [*Grevill*] Tytle in any Part, or Construction of his Letters Patentes. It will turne to other Boddies Good, and to hurte him willingly weare a foolish Discourteisy. I pray yow, as yow make Accownt of me, lett me be sure yow will deale heerein according to my Request, and so I leave yow to God. At *Bainards* Castell, this 10th of *Aprill*, 1581.

Your louing Frend,
Philip Sidney.[35]

Letter 3
Sir Philip Sydney *to* Edm. Molyneux, *Esq*;

Mollineaux,

I pray thee write to me diligently. I woold yow came down your self. Solicitt my Lord Treasurer, and Mr. Vice Chamberlain for my beeing of the Cownceill. I woold fain bring in my Cosin *Conningesby* if it wear possible: Yow shall do me much Pleasur to labour it. Farewell, even very well, for so I wish you. From *Hereford*, this 23d of *Juli*, 1582.

Your loving Frend,
Philip Sidney.[36]

Letter 4
Robert Sidney (*after Earl of* Leicester) *to* Edm. Molyneux.

Good Mr. Mullinax,
I pray yow sett doune in Writing the Reasons why her Maiestie showlde erect the Office I sue for. Yow must doe it in good Terms, for it is to be shewed to her Maiestie. I pray yow lett me heare quickly from yow, for the Queene will be spoken to, very shortly about it. Farewell. Court, this *Sonday*, 1582.

Yours assuredly,
Robert Sidney.[37]

In the letters of the Sidney brothers, how the language constructs the power difference between the master's sons and servant is unambiguous: they speak with the master's voice, an unequivocal language of command. Any contest for power between the servant and the son that may underlie Philip Sidney's explosive accusation is not acknowledged in the stylistic inscription here of the power relation. The forms of civility unambiguously assert social difference and, insofar as they summon a response, demand asymmetrical markers of difference. Relevant here is Angel Day's explanation, in his letter-writing manual *The English Secretary*, that a noble personage writing to his inferior should not "with ouer large entreatie be charged, but rather with fewer speeches, and lesse circumstances to demaunde what hee purposeth."[38]

In striking contrast is Mary Sidney's style for issuing directions to Molyneux. In letters 5 and 6, Mary Sidney instructs Molyneux on how he should convince the Lord Chamberlain to make an extra room available at Hampton Court for Sir Henry, on the occasion of his recall in 1578 from his post in Ireland.

Letter 5
Lady Mary Sydney *to* Edmund Mollineux, *Esq*;

Molenox,
I thoght good to put you in Remembrance to moue my Lord Chamberlein, in my Lords Name, to haue some uther Roome then my Chamber, for my Lord to haue his Resort unto, as he was woont to haue; or ells my Lord wilbe greatly trubled, when he shall haue enny Maters of Dispache: My Lodginge, you see, beinge very lytle, and my sealfe continewaly syke, and not able to be mouche out of my Bed. For the Night Tyme, on Roofe, with Gods Grace, shall serue vs; for the Day Tyme the Quen will louke to haue my Chamber always in a Redines, for her Maiesties Cominge thether; and thoghe my Lorde him sealfe cann be no Impediment thearto by his owen Presens, yet his Lordshipe trustinge to no Playce ells to be provyded for him, wilbe, as I sayd before, trubled for Want of a conuenient Playce, for the Dispache of souche People as

shall haue Occasion to come to him. Therefore I pray you, in my Lords owen Name, moue my Lord of *Susex* for a Room forthat Porpose, and I will haue hit hanged, and Lyned for him, with Stoof from hens. I wish you not to be vnmyndfull hear of: And so for this Tyme I leue you to the Almyghty. From *Chiswike* this xi of *October*, 1578.

*Your uery assured, louing
Mistris and Frend,*
M. Sydney.[39]

Letter 6
Lady Mary Sydney *to* Edmund Mollineux, *Esq*;

You have vsed the Matter very well; but we must do more yet for the good dear Lord then let him thus be dealt withall. *Hampton Courght* I never yet knue so full, as ther wer not spare Rooms in hit, what hit hath ben thryse better fylled then at this Presenn hit is. But some would be sory, perhaps, my Lord should haue so suer Footinge in the Courght. Well, all may be as well when the good God will. The whylst, I pray let us do what we may for our Lords Eas and Quyet. Whear vnto I think, yf you go to my Lord *Howard*, and in my Lords Name also moue his Lordshipe, to shew his Brother, my Lord, as they cawle eache other, to shew him a Cast of his Offis, and that hit shall not be knone, and aleadge your former Cawsis, I think he will fynd out some Place to serve that Purpose; and also, yf you go to Mr. *Bowyer*, the Gentelman Vsher, and tell him, his Mouther requyreth him, which is my sealf, to healpe my Lord with some on Room, but only for the Dispache of the Multitude of *Irish* and *Welsh* People, that follow him; and that you will giue your Wourd in my Lords Behalf and myne, hit shall not be accounted as a Lodginge, nor knone of. I beleue he will make what Shyft he cann; you must assure him hit is but for the Day Tyme for his Besines, as indead hit is for my Brothers Answer of my Stay hear for five or six Dayes; he knowes I have ventured farr allredy, with so long Absens, and am ill thought on for hit, so as that may not be. But when the woorst is knowne, old Lord *Hary* and his old *Moll*, will do as well as the cann in partinge lyck good Frends, the small Porsion alotted our longe Servis in Courght; which, as lytle as hit is, seams somethynge to mooche. And this beinge all I cann say to the Matter. Farewell, Mr. *Ned*. In Hast this *Mondaye*, 1578.

Your assured lovinge Mistris and Frend,
M. Sydney.

Yf all this will not serve prove Mr. *Huggins*, for I know my Lord would not for no Good be destitude in this Time for some convenient Playce for his Folowers and Frends to resort to him, which in this Case I am in, is not posyble to be in my Chamber, tell after Sun set; when the dear good Lord, shalbe as best becoms him, Lord of his owen.[40]

Where Sir Philip or Robert Sidney address Molyneux, the letters are terse; the sentences, mostly imperative in mood, are short and staccato;

the commands are direct. Mary Sidney's directions to Molyneux are leisurely in their unfolding; long sentences take up reasons for requests made; some direct imperatives are issued, but on the whole the task is proposed as a shared enterprise. The sons' mode is off-hand command; the mother's elaborated and sensitive request. Like Mary Sidney's letters, Molyneux's answer to Sidney's rebuke is very fully elaborated, both in length and sentence structure. Nonetheless, the rhetorical complication works in opposite ways: Mary Sidney's letters work out strategies for *associating* writer and reader while Molyneux's letter *dissociates* reader and writer, taking care to establish and preserve the differences between them. The stylistic contrasts across this rich matrix of family relations strongly suggest how radically social positioning affects style and how Molyneux's complicated language is less particular to his individual person than it is to his social place.

The Brown and Levinson model, which hypothesizes that speakers match politeness strategies to levels of speech-act risk arising in particular social contexts, can help to analyze and situate the social rhetoric of these letters more fully. As I have previously described it, the model delineates four distinct politeness levels, ranging from unmitigated directness to silent restraint. It proposes three factors as the determinants of overall speech-act risk and corresponding politeness level – the relative *power* of speaker to hearer, the social *distance* between speaker and hearer, and the estimated *ranking*, or risk level, associated in a specific culture with a particular face-threatening speech act.[41] The model can predict where a speaker might judge risk level so low as to issue a command without any politeness modifications (as Philip Sidney might to Molyneux); it can also predict where the speaker might estimate risk so high as to dictate making only an "off record" (or indirect) request or avoiding a potentially offending speech act altogether (as where Perkins advises the rebuked servant to "answer not again"). But what we find on display in the letters of Mary Sidney and Edmund Molyneux are the more elaborate politeness levels. When Mary Sidney directs Edmund Molyneux, her language anticipates the repertoires Brown and Levinson call "positive politeness," the rhetoric of association whereby the speaker minimizes speech-act risk by strategies that include claiming common ground with the hearer, conveying that speaker and hearer are cooperators, and fulfilling some want of the hearer. When Edmund Molyneux answers Philip Sidney's rebuke, his language anticipates the repertoires of "negative politeness," the rhetoric of dissociation whereby the speaker avoids assumptions about the hearer's wants, avoids the appearance of coercing the hearer, and may make explicit assertions about his or her wish not to impinge on the hearer.

MARY SIDNEY'S SITUATED ELOQUENCE

Before coming to the resemblances between Molyneux's language of servitude and that of Shakespeare's speaker, it is necessary to examine Lady Mary Sidney's socially situated eloquence in order to ascertain the specific accents of her positive politeness and to reflect on how material conditions help to create it. My characterization of her letters as eloquent is not merely whimsical. Although Lady Sidney is not known to have "authored" any of the "original" writings we separate out as "literature," she nonetheless received public recognition for her excellence in writing and in speaking in a eulogy printed in 1587 as part of Holinshed's *Chronicles*. Both Mary Ellen Lamb and Margaret Hannay have drawn attention to the bizarre and yet mundane circumstance that created the opportunity for the performance of eloquence that gained her most credit – that is, her death:

> During the whole course of her sicknesse, and speciallie a little before it pleased almightie God to call her hense to his mercie, she used such godlie speeches, earnest and effectual persuasions to all those about hir, and unto such others as came of freendlie courtesie to visit hir, to exhort them to repentance and amendement of life, and dehort them from all sin and lewdnesse, as wounded the consciences, and inwardlie pearsed the hearts of manie that hear hir. And though before they knew hir to exceed most of hir sex in singularitie of vertue and qualitie; as good speech, apt and readie conceipt, excellencie of wit, and notable eloquent deliverie (for none could match hir, and few or none come neere hir either in the good conceipt and frame of orderlie writing, indicting, and speedie dispatching, or facilitie of gallant, sweet, delectable, and courtlie speaking; at least that in this time I my selfe have knowen, heard, or read of) yet in this last action and ending of hir life . . . she . . . farre surpassed hir selfe . . .[42]

Beyond the public recognition, fortuitously, we are privy here as well to the judgment of her letters' recipient upon Lady Mary's way with words, since the Holinshed biographer who notes the "orderlie writing" in which few could match her is Edmund Molyneux himself.

In letters 5 and 6 above, Lady Sidney directs Molyneux to take whatever action is necessary to acquire a suitable chamber at Hampton Court for her husband upon his recall from his administrative post in

Ireland. What is striking about her instructions is, first, her lengthy provision of detailed reasons for the directions she is giving. Without a room for his business use, "my Lord wilbe greatly trubled, when he shall haue enny Maters of Dispache: My Lodginge, you see, beinge very lytle, and my sealfe continewaly syke, and not able to be mouche out of my Bed." These are the "circumstances" which Angel Day claims a superior's demand need not develop. Second, Lady Sidney represents Molyneux's assigned task as a joint venture. This cooperative approach is evident in her use of the first person plural pronoun ("*we* must do more yet for the good dear Lord . . . I pray let *us* do what *we* may for *our* Lords Eas and Quyet" [emphasis added]); and in her division of the labor for "my Lords" benefit into his part and her own ("Therefore I pray you, in my Lords owen Name, moue my Lord of *Susex* for a Room forthat Porpose, and I will haue hit hanged, and Lyned for him, with Stoof from hens"). Even where their actions are not parallel, as where Lady Sidney asserts her opinions and makes decisions about what Molyneux must do, the rhythm of the pronoun alternations implies the mutuality of the undertaking ("*I beleue* he will make what Shyft he cann; *you must assure him* hit is but for the Day Tyme for his Besines"). The softening of Lady Sidney's commands by means of indirection is the more obvious politeness strategy employed: the attenuated prolixity of "I thoght good to put you in Remembrance to moue my Lord Chamberlein," where her sons might say "I pray thee moue my Lord Chamberlain"; the double-negative redundancy of "I wish you not to be vnmyndfull hear of"; the conditional phrasing of the directives "yf you go to my Lord *Howard*" and "yf you go to Mr. *Bowyer*, the Gentelman Vsher, and tell him." But most surprising in the language the Lady Mary Sidney addresses to her own and her husband's servant are the jocularly familiar – even intimate – tones of the second letter's conclusion:

But when the woorst is knowne, old Lord *Hary* and his old *Moll*, will do as well as the cann in partinge lyck good Frends, the small Porsion alotted our longe Servis in Courght; which, as lytle as hit is, seams somethynge to mooche. And this beinge all I cann say to the Matter. Farewell, Mr. *Ned*.

Not only does she employ the affectionate diminutive "*Ned*" for Molyneux, but she makes him privy to the similar forms of endearment which in her language communicates a shared bond of affection in adversity between herself and her husband.

Critics such as Catherine Belsey, Alice Friedman, and Judith Weil have led us to recognize "the cultural ambiguity of the wife's position *vis-a-vis* the servant,"⁴³ but nothing affords us (to use Pierre Bourdieu's words quoted earlier) such a "practical, immediate recognition" of a wife's and a servant's relative positioning as Mary Sidney's politeness strategies. The subject position of the mistress in relation to the master's servingman is acted out in her style of solidarity, in her leisurely and patient unfolding of her mind to Molyneux. Hers is more the voice of a social equal than the voice of a remote superior, and yet the strategies of identification are conditioned by a prevailing directiveness that maintains her measure of authority over him. It is important to see that Mary Sidney's intermediate – and potentially ambiguous, or even contradictory – positioning is a place of opportunity for verbal invention as well as a place of constraint. This middle and perhaps difficult place is also a motive to amplify the circumstances of her discourse and to formulate reasons and arguments – to develop a fairly complex process of thought and to test it out in dialogue with another. To issue a direct command affords no comparable exercise in developing complex social interaction or a correspondingly variegated subjectivity.

As Mary Sidney's example suggests, Belsey's influential and curious denial of "determinate subject-position[s]" or even of "subjectivity" to early modern women has to be questioned. To be a proto-modern "subject" in Belsey's terms requires access to discourse, a modicum of agency whereby subjects can "'work by themselves' to produce and reproduce the social formations of which they are a product," and a complicated interiority we can recognize as mental or emotional activity.⁴⁴ What I am suggesting in this chapter is that it is in the more problematic subject positions occupied by a Mary Sidney or an Edmund Molyneux that complex forms of subjectivity are in the making and not in uncontested positions of power. Indeed, Shakespeare's sonnet 94 seems to comment on the paradoxical lack of what Belsey might call "subjectivity" in men with power like the aristocratic beloved:

> They that have power to hurt and will do none,
> That do not do the thing they most do show,
> Who, moving others, are themselves as stone,
> Unmovèd, cold, and to temptation slow . . .   (1–4)

Even when these men say and "do" nothing, their nothing has an effect, particularly on social inferiors who are closely associated with them. In relation to the poet-lover, or to a character like Helena in *All's Well That Ends Well*, an unthinking and insensitive aristocratic youth is imagined as eliciting complex, baroque, self-searching, and self-conflicted discourses.

By imagining in sonnet 94 the paradoxical nullity, or non-agency, of those with "power to hurt," Shakespeare seems to be recognizing that the power relation has greater forcefulness than the powerful person and that discursive complexity is linked to the subordinate place.

NEGATIVE POLITENESS AND SHAKESPEARE'S SONNETS

Let us turn now to Molyneux's rhetoric of "negative politeness" and its link with Shakespeare's sonnets. Negative politeness in its extreme forms is a rhetoric of contradictions, for it works in such a way as to simultaneously do and undo the speech actions it undertakes. This is especially evident if we consider the case of a subordinate issuing a directive couched in negative politeness. In such a case, politeness dictates making no assumptions about the wishes (in Elizabethan terms, "the pleasure") of the other and it also dictates avoiding coercing or controlling the action of the other. But, for Molyneux to protest his injury and to try to affect Sidney's actions is inevitably to presume. What makes Molyneux's rhetoric so interesting is the enactment of these contradictions in its highly conflicted discourse.

The negative-politeness principles of non-presumption and non-coercion clearly guide Molyneux's risk-filled answer to Sidney's rebuke. Strategic non-presumption explains his inclusion, for example, of the parenthetical conditional clause, "yf it may soe lyke you," to mitigate even a highly deferential assertion about Sidney's power to command him (something one might have thought it was safe to make assumptions about). Again varying the conventional expression, "If it please your lordship [or other title]," Molyneux later "crave[s] yt maye lyke [Sidney] to accept" his vow of obedience. The injured Molyneux goes to even greater extremes to unmake apparently unavoidable assumptions about Sidney's "pleasure" when he acknowledges Sidney's harsh letter as "a speciall Note of your lovinge Favour, that it wold please you to write vnto me." This formulation seems entirely in contradiction with the general aim of this letter of protest, but its contradiction fits the overall pattern of negative politeness. Again, it asserts the writer's non-presumption: by registering even Sidney's act in writing to him as something Molyneux does not take for granted, he signals how far he is from making assumptions about Sidney's "pleasure."

To mitigate the risk involved in answering back, Molyneux also takes great pains to establish that his speech action is not coercive. He does this by repeatedly making explicit the large power difference between them:

you have ... full Power and good Warrant to commaund me.

I have neither Will nor Power to hurt in this Case if I wolde, havinge onlie to walke in the Pathe I am directed:

For assure your selfe, you and yours have, and ever shall have, that vndowbted Interest in me, as I will obey your Commaundement, as farre as in Dewtie and Credit I may.

Elizabethan practices for asserting non-coercion include not only strategies like those Molyneux uses here for elevating the status of the hearer; they also include strategies for humbling the status of the speaker. William Cecil having offended Queen Elizabeth, for example, writes as her "poore servant and most lowlye subject, an unworthy Secretary," beseeching her pardon for "this my lowlye suite."[45] Although Molyneux does choose the verbs "crave" and "beseche" to signal his humble self-positioning relative to Sidney, nonetheless he does not employ in any profusion the self-deprecating rhetorical practices that usually mark Elizabethan "negative politeness." The very frequent testimonies to Sidney's great power seem calculated to offset this omission of testimonies about his servant's worthlessness and to keep Molyneux's language within the boundaries of subordination even while he manages through this omission a quiet assertion of his own dignity and worth.

If self-deprecation plays no significant role in Molyneux's risk-mitigating politeness, nonetheless a related strategy that is self-reflecting in its expression deserves notice. Molyneux writes: "yf I showld soe forgett my selfe (yf it were only in Respect that you esteeme Mr. *Gryvell* as your deere and entier Frend), I showld justlie condemne my selfe of vnadvised and twoe great inconsiderat Dealinge." Strikingly modern as the ideas of self-forgetting and self-condemnation may sound, to "forgett" himself, for Molyneux, would not likely mean to forget his own individual inner principles; it would mean to forget his station relative to Sidney, to step out of his social place. Here we are in the territory Anne Ferry explored in part when she explained that the "inward selves" represented in Elizabethan sonnets are not the "inward selves" of our present-day experience.[46] Nonetheless, however different from the modern-day "self" the "selfe" constructed within the social rhetoric in which Molyneux negotiates his differences with Sidney, this self bears striking resemblances to the "self" mentioned in some of Shakespeare's sonnets.

If, Molyneux claims, Sidney indeed had just cause to blame or speak against him, Molyneux would himself speak against himself – would "condemne my selfe." This proffered self-condemnation, while not a politeness strategy explicitly described by Brown and Levinson, works like the other procedures of Molyneux's socially positioned rhetoric to repair the risk Molyneux takes in answering Sidney back. Nonetheless, its congruity with negative-politeness forms is not the only warrant for identifying the gesture at self-condemnation as a specific effect of the social relation being enacted. In *The English Secretary*, Angel Day provides his readers with interaction scripts for negotiating typical situations and relations: his script for a social inferior seeking reconciliation with a superior also proffers self-blame in response to the displeasure of the superior:

. . . For mine owne parte (so much doe I stande on the reuerent regarde and account I beare vnto your L.) as were it not I rest perswaded that vpon the equall deliuerance conceiued of my willing mind vnto your seruice, you would againe bee reconciled in fauourable and good opinion towards me, *I should so farre foorth bee discontented in my selfe, as neuer could I bee at attonement with mine actions*, wherein by the least sparke of negligence whatsoeuer, I might thinke to haue ouerslipped anie thing that shoulde become displeasing, or otherwise offensiue vnto your honourable liking.[47]

It should by now be clear that some compelling strategies of complex self-presentation displayed in such Shakespeare sonnets as 57, 58, 88, or 89 resemble very closely the socially conditioned strategies we have found in Molyneux's letter. Just as Molyneux proposes self-condemning in response to the fault-finding of the other, so the Poet in sonnet 89 writes of how "For thee, against myself I'll vow debate" and in sonnet 88 of how "for thy right myself will bear all wrong." What seems so distinctive in its frequent variations in Shakespeare's sonnets – the speaker's impulse when blamed to contribute his own self-blaming "comment upon that offence" (sonnet 89), his reflection that "I against myself with thee partake" (sonnet 149): can it perhaps be said that this self-fashioning through proposing self-blame is as much a part of "Molyneux's moment" as it is part of "the Shakespearean moment"?

Shakespeare's sonnet 58 I would read as a poem that gives some new twists to the negatively polite strategies of non-presumption and non-coercion which Molyneux deploys selectively in the self-asserting subservience of his letter.

> That god forbid that made me first your slave
> I should in thought control your times of pleasure,
> Or at your hand th'account of hours to crave,
> Being your vassal bound to stay your leisure.
> O, let me suffer, being at your beck,
> Th'imprisoned absence of your liberty,
> And, patience-tame to sufferance, bide each check
> Without accusing you of injury.
> Be where you list, your charter is so strong
> That you yourself may privilege your time
> To what you will; to you it doth belong
> Yourself to pardon of self-doing crime.
> I am to wait, though waiting so be hell,
> Not blame your pleasure, be it ill or well.

It is a sonnet that deals explicitly with the underling's chafing at his duty to "bide each check / Without accusing you [the superior] of injury" (lines 7–8). In the Poet's handling of this speech problem, we can recognize his foregrounding of standard politeness maneuvers. First, we have non-presumption – "god forbid . . . I should in thought control your times of pleasure" (1–2). (The primary meaning in this context and in line 14 of the word "pleasure" arises, I would suggest, from its relation to the servingman's phrase – "If it please your lordship" – which becomes conflated with the more usually noted sexual overtones.[48]) And second, we have non-coercion – compare Molyneux's "haveinge onlie to walke in the Pathe I am directed" to the Poet's "Being your vassal bound to stay your leisure" and "being at your beck" (4, 5). What makes the poem so rich is the imaginative apprehension it offers of what it would be like to be constrained, as many proud servingmen injured by their superiors in Shakespeare's day must have been, by the contradictory pulls of a negatively polite speech repertoire. What has often been read as a psychological state figured in the language is rather (or, as I shall argue later, is also) a historically specific social relation figured in language.

Let us consider briefly how the contours of this reading compare with a psychological approach. Catherine R. Lewis argues that "the sonnets' rich psychological detail about the perceiving, writing Poet" expresses a personality – the "character structure" or "inner reality" of "a predominantly self-effacing person with highly idealized standards for a love relationship."[49] By this account, the language of subjection I have been analyzing arises not as an effect of the relationship but instead as a fulfillment of "the Poet's self-effacing needs":

The Poet does not seem to see himself as having a choice among subordination, equality, and superiority; he only swings between experiencing his subordination as noble and religious and experiencing it as degrading. For the predominantly self-effacing person, these are indeed the options.[50]

To suggest, as Lewis does, that the Poet's subordinate stance in relation to the Young Man is constrained only by his character pathology is to ignore the strong imprint that the hierarchical arrangement of Elizabethan society routinely made on the language of social exchange.

Nonetheless, it is important to see that, as in Molyneux's case, the servingman's position from which the sonnet speaker "answers back" is not simply one of subservience: forms of symbolic capital other than social rank, while they do not entirely release the speaker from the discursive repertoire of subjection, nonetheless modify his relative status and speech power. Given that the speaker and his male partner exist only as constructs of discourse, we cannot, as in Molyneux's case, compare the power relation as practically and immediately recognized in politeness forms to the power relation as reconstructed from historical evidence about material conditions. At the same time, insofar as the sonnets build up in their discourse the "details" of their characters' lives, they do so less in terms of individual qualities than in terms of oppositional pairs denoting typical social or power relationships – lower/higher class, writer/patron, actor-as-liveried-servingman/aristocratic master, old/young, talented poet/object of praise, and, in readings that interpret the homoerotic desire as consummated,[51] penetrator/penetrated. Some of these oppositions are parallel and reinforce the power differential of inferior to superior. That the homoerotic desire of the sonnets should take shape across this power axis is consistent with Alan Bray's influential argument about the hierarchical social institutions – especially the household, schools, and universities – that fostered homosexual practice in early modern England.[52] But the sonnets also structure the relationship through pairings that invert and complicate this power axis, such as older to younger, experienced to untried, talented writer to recipient of praise. Furthermore, Meredith Anne Skura has recently brought to our attention the profound contradictions internal to the typical power relationships an Elizabethan player entered into in the paradoxes of the proud beggar or of the "player king as beggar in great men's houses."[53] In sonnet 58, these complexities of evaluation make for a Molyneux-like element of self-assertion in the servant who answers back.

Margreta de Grazia has made the fascinating argument that "the exclusive interiority that Shakespearean criticism has assumed is not a given of the Shakespearean text at its inception" but arose, in the case of the sonnets, in 1780 when Edmond Malone "reinstated the 1609 quarto and encased the sonnets in a full textual apparatus that explicitly identified the first person of the sonnets with the proper name 'Shakespeare' on the quarto title page."[54] Insofar as I locate the motive for the Poet's language in sonnets 57 and 58 in the social situation rather than the character's inner being, my argument is consistent with hers, but I think that to argue for an exclusive exteriority in reading the sonnets would be as misleading as to argue for what de Grazia calls "the exclusive interiority" of "traditional Shakespeare criticism."[55] Lewis's psychological interpretation of the Poet's "self-effacing needs" does not adequately explain why the language is self-blaming or why it eschews presumption – and yet it is difficult to imagine a person habitually adopting such deferential language without the language coming to affect his feelings and predispositions. To emphasize the outward determination or the social orientation of utterances need not be to deny them any relation to inward states or individual psychology. Indeed, V. N. Vološinov argues for a close relationship between the organization of social relationships and and the articulation of inward experience: "The stronger, the more organized, the more differentiated the collective in which an individual orients himself, the more vivid and complex his inner world will be." The inner world, he suggests, accommodates "itself to the potentialities of our [outward] expression, its possible routes and directions": "What is usually called 'creative individuality' is nothing but the expression of a particular person's basic, firmly grounded, and consistent line of social orientation."[56]

Vološinov's account can help us to see how the highly stabilized forms of a negative-politeness repertoire available to a complaining servant could be internalized and reaccented as inner speech in sonnet 58. For, despite the replication of the proud servingman's inventory for complaint, despite the speech-like intonations and the apparently direct address to the "you" of the sonnet, it seems unlikely that the sonnet is intended to represent outward speech to a superior. Exaggerated though the disclaimers of self-assertion or interference throughout the entire sonnet may sound today, the language nonetheless *almost* entirely conforms to the sayable of Molyneux's situation or the Poet's, to the tensions of the outward speech forms. Yet a few words and phrases set within the properly ostentatious show of deference nonetheless set it apart from what is permissible to speak. At certain tense moments, Queen Elizabeth's courtiers may have styled themselves her "slaves" without arousing the suspicion of insolent irony, but, addressed by an esquire to a gentleman of Sidney's status or even by a play-actor to an indulgent earl, the word "slave" would betray irony. Furthermore, the direct mention of the superior's "self-doing crime," even mitigated by the Poet's disclaimer of right to judge or pardon, goes beyond the bounds of the speakable if the speech situation we are imagining is a complaint made by a servant to his superior. The Poet's articulated reservation about his obligation "to wait" – "though waiting so be hell" – goes beyond decorum in indulging the expressed contrast between his own misery and his superior's socially authorized "pleasure." Finally, the interjected "O" of enthusiastic wonderment undercuts the speaker's obligatory acceptance of the servant's lot – the "let me suffer, being at your beck." Of course, few twentieth-century readers could miss the ironic tone of this sonnet. It is too easy, on the other hand, to read more irony and exaggeration into it than its historical situation readily supplies. For example, when the Poet disclaims that "god forbid . . . I should in thought control your times of pleasure," it is easy to imagine that the expectation that a servant conform even his thinking to the master's "pleasure" is a creative exaggeration of an expected conformity in deed. But consider how the translator George Pettie "englishes" Steven Guazzo's precepts on the basic condition of the servant: "Let the servaunte also conforme *all his thoughtes and doinges to the will and pleasure* of his Mayster, and to tye the Asse (as they say) where his maister will have him tyed, without any contradiction."[57] The syntactic positioning of the phrase "in thought" may slightly foreground and hence emphasize the extremity of what is expected of the Poet-Servant, but that extremity is already a given of the early modern social discourse that figures service. The poem's irony is, paradoxically, more delicate than it might appear on first encounter.

Hence we can read sonnet 58 historically not merely as the outward expression of a social relation but as the inner speech of the Poet-Servant. Its structure of feeling originates in and is circumscribed by the tension-ridden forms of a specific socially situated outward expression, and yet its differences – its verbal play just beyond the boundary of what is speakable in the given circumstances, creating a space of mental reservation – represent a creative adjustment of the external social discourse. Shakespeare takes the contradiction-ridden tensions between the servant's self-assertive answering back and the obligatory repair strategies, and he stages the internalized emotional experience of these specific tensions. What Shakespeare communicates specifically is an intense apprehension of how miserable it can be when one's own intensely felt needs and urgencies are subordinated, not to another's needs and urgencies, but to the other's casual whims, to the master's "will and pleasure." Taking the outward contours of the service relation as his base, Shakespeare articulates the inward emotional contours of proud subservience. Centuries later – or moments in the *longue durée* of modern subjectivity – the gentleman servingman's relation to his master forgotten, it is still nonetheless possible for Shakespeare's readers to match this discourse and emotional set to the unequal relations that continue to be productive of erotic desire.

PART II

Eloquent relations in letters

CHAPTER 3

Scripting social relations in Erasmus and Day

In the preceding chapters, I have proposed a modern rhetoric derived from discourse pragmatics as a heuristic tool for reading social exchange and interaction styles in letters, plays, and sonnets. Elizabethan letter-writers and others interested in the protocols of written exchange had several contemporary epistolary manuals available to instruct them, including Erasmus's "On the Writing of Letters" (*De conscribendis epistolis* – 1522), William Fulwood's *The Enimie of Idlenesse* (1568), Angel Day's *The English Secretary* (1586; part II, 1592), and John Browne's *The Marchants Avizo* (1590).[1] Focusing on Erasmus and Day, this chapter examines how these sixteenth-century rhetorics map out, script, and play a significant role in the dissemination of both typical and novel social interactions. Denouncing the existing hierarchical arrangement of human relations, Erasmus provides models and instruction in how to perform horizontal relations of reciprocal friendship; these alternative scripts fashion homosocial relations as he wishes them to be – and, at least to some extent, as he succeeds in determining them – among communities of learned men, or between boys and their tutors. At variance with the idealistic Erasmus in relishing both the eloquent cultural "poetry" that gives discursive shape to hierarchic relations and the space of opportunity that polite exchanges can open up for ambition, performance, and advancement, Day scripts elaborate discursive models for enacting vertical as well as horizontal relations.

The sixteenth-century manuals are all shaped to some extent by the medieval *ars dictaminis*, which made letter-writing a distinct rhetorical art and presented formulaic models for official letters, figuring social difference in ornate terms of address, and by a humanist reaction to it, which adapted some new categories from classical oratory while emphasizing not the public but instead the familiar letter.[2] The sixteenth-century manuals tend either to stage an explicit contest between the medieval and humanist influences (as does Erasmus) or to exhibit some curious and undigested inconsistencies arising from their contradictory outlooks. But however dependent the sixteenth-century manuals may have been on these antecedents, they were nonetheless offered as practical guides to help their targeted audiences negotiate specific writing situations arising in their daily lives. This pragmatic purpose means that manuals anchor the inherited theories in everyday practices and so can provide significant insights into the microencounters of Elizabethan society.

Addressing different social groups, the handbooks I will focus on here and in chapter 5 configure social relations in different ways and address different interactional needs. Erasmus's 1522 revision of his Latin treatise on letter-writing, the version he authorized for publication, is written for an international learned community.[3] This widely influential teaching manual, "On the Writing of Letters," is addressed specifically to schoolmasters and proposes detailed methods for teaching Latin letter-writing to boys. An extremely successful book, it was widely used for students in the upper forms at English grammar schools.[4] Even though it actively discourages the attention to relative social status of writer and addressee that Angel Day's manual encourages, nonetheless it strongly influenced *The English Secretary*. Day's target audience consists of people in or aspiring to the upper ranks of Elizabethan society. In his revised and enlarged 1599 edition, he dedicates his efforts to Edward de Vere, the Earl of Oxford and addresses his "learned and courteous" general readers as "gentlemen."[5] Reinforcing social discriminations, *The English Secretary* has very close affinities to the letters actually circulating among Elizabethan courtiers and gentry. Two handbooks I will consider in detail in chapter 5 explicitly address another important group that is somewhat more ambiguously positioned in contemporary accounts of the social order: merchants, their sons, and apprentices. The earlier volume, William Fulwood's *Enimie of Idlenesse,* gives less insight into the actual practices of the merchant community, drawing heavily for its models on Cicero's familiar letters, but John Browne, in *The Marchants Avizo,* adapts letters and business forms from those in use among the Bristol merchants trading overseas, a group including many important civic officials. Given the limits on literacy in the sixteenth century, neither the existing letters nor the letter manuals can give a comprehensive view of the microstructures of verbal interaction in early modern England, but the handbooks provide crucial insight into the verbal interaction of those who had power and those who aspired to that power.

RHETORICAL FORM AND "THE LIVING MODEL OF THE LETTER"

As one begins to read Erasmus's treatise, one cannot help feeling a bit lost. Suddenly, you find yourself in the midst of a heated conversation or argument: told that it is "absurd" to "impose a narrow and inflexible definition" on what is "capable of almost infinite variation"; asked what is meant by saying a letter should be brief; urged to recognize the stupidity of arguing, based on Cicero's practice, that the diction of a letter "should stay close to everyday speech," when Cicero's letter to Octavian obviously "rises to storms of oratory and even ends on a note of tragedy."[6] And later you wonder whose idiocy Erasmus is heaping such scorn upon when he denounces "that absurd practice . . . of addressing a single person in the plural" (45) or using epithets like "Most holy lord of ours" (61) for the Pope. In "Erasmus on the Art of Letter-Writing," Judith Rice Henderson expertly situates Erasmus's vehement reactions as a two-fold rejection of formulaic prescriptions, both from the new humanist epistolography and from the medieval *ars dictaminis*: the former invectives, she demonstrates, are directed against a too rigid ideal of Ciceronian imitation emerging in humanist prescript and practice, while the latter are addressed against practices encouraged by the medieval formulary handbooks.[7]

Henderson shows how Erasmus joins such humanist colleagues as his German contemporary Heinrich Bebel in rejecting the medieval idea of the letter as an official communication in a high oratorical style, the five-part structure required by the medieval formula of *salutatio*, *exordium* or *captatio benevolentiae*, *narratio*, *petitio*, and *conclusio*, and the numerous and elaborate formulas for the *salutatio*, each one marking precise discriminations between the social station of writer and recipient.[8] The humanist epistolography condemns this public and hierarchical rhetoric and adopts instead the classical definition of the letter as a "mutual conversation between absent friends" (20). The humanist preference is to imitate Cicero's simpler modes of salutation – to position the writer's name before the addressee's, to address a single person in the singular form, to extend a simple greeting, and to add only an unembellished title to the addressee's name.[9] Nonetheless, Erasmus apparently regards humanist predecessors as too rigid in their prescriptions of set forms and styles for the letters, whether as templates or as guidelines: "it is foolish to bind utterance to fixed laws" (19). Keeping open a wide range of possibilities for the letter, he resists confining all letters to the "familiar" mode, and instead classifies the familiar as a category supplementing a three-fold division, adapted from classical oration, of letters into demonstrative, deliberative, and judicial kinds.[10]

Equally rejecting the ornate style of the medieval tradition and the everyday style of humanist prescriptions, Erasmus insists that a different speech or writing style must be addressed to different persons in different situations. In other words – despite his vehement condemnations of distinctions based on rank – Erasmus nonetheless emphasizes above all how language must vary with relative social position. At the heart of his objection, when schoolmasters "pester [him] for a set of abridged rules for correct writing" (6), is his resistance to the teaching of language use in the abstract; he promotes, instead, a sophisticated approach to situated speech and writing. Decorum is offered as the flexible principle that is to guide the style, the length, the arguments, and the progression of the letter: "whatever would not have escaped criticism in other forms of writing can be defended here either in consideration of the topic, or the person of the writer, or the character, condition, or age of the recipient" (20). Age, temperament, degree of friendship – rather than relative power or status of writer and recipient – are the main functional categories Erasmus proposes as affecting interaction style. A chosen subject "will present itself in one guise to the old, in another to the young; its aspect will vary according as the person addressed is stern and forbidding, or of a more jovial nature; a courtier or a philosopher; an intimate acquaintance or a total stranger; a man of leisure or one engaged in active pursuits; a faithful companion or a false friend and ill-wisher" (19). From "the accurate examination of these things," Erasmus proposes, his students "should derive, so to speak, *the living model of the letter*" (74; emphasis added).

Instead of rules or examples, Erasmus devises detailed exercise plans to "incite energetic young men" to an "assiduous practice" (23) through which they will "unconsciously assimilate" (26) this "living model." What he recommends is a form of role-playing – to take situations from classical comedies, for example, and to have the pupils write letters negotiating the requirements of those specific situations:

An example of this would be a letter from a friend of Phaedria urging him to shake off his love for Thais, stop acting foolishly and return to the settled life he used to lead, especially since keeping her involved great loss of wealth and reputation, while she did not truly love him from the heart nor did she restrict her favors to him alone. Another imaginary letter might be written to the rich man in Plautus' *Aulularia*, advising him to choose Euclio, a poor but upright man, as his son-in-law rather than the rich suitor, or, from the opposite viewpoint, urging him to give his daughter in marriage to a rich man rather than a poor man. (25)

In addition to comedies, Erasmus recommends as contexts for these improvisational exercises other forms of classical literature, histories, and imaginary situations. Through such exercises, the boys are to obtain practice in recognizing typical interaction situations and in responding with a language that can be accepted by others as the language of that situation.

What is implicit in Erasmus's instructions is a concept of rhetorical form that researchers in pragmatics and rhetorical studies are even today striving to theorize. Charles Bazerman, for example, in his book on the genre of the scientific article reaches towards an adequate definition of rhetorical genre: "Genre, then, is not simply a linguistic category defined by a structured arrangement of textual features. Genre is a sociopsychological category which we use to recognize and construct typified actions within typified situations."[11] Indeed, as Bazerman reflects on how "the reduction of any genre to a few formal items that must be followed for the sake of propriety (decorum in its most restricted sense) misses the life that is embodied in the generically shaped moment," and on the "unreflecting slavery" that teachers offer students if they fail to grant the "means to understand the forms of life embodied in current symbolic practice,"[12] he sounds uncannily like Erasmus. How "forms of life" are "embodied in . . . symbolic practice" is exactly what preoccupies Erasmus in a lengthy portion of the treatise which seems to digress from the business of teaching letter-writing to a more general theory of communication. Underlying the apparent digression is a recognition that the genres in which the boys need most practice in order to write letters well are distinct from the letter genre itself: they are genres embodied in comedies, in fictional dialogues, and in everyday speech interactions as well as in letters. We may conveniently follow Bakhtin's practice in naming these dynamic genres of everyday social intercourse "speech genres."[13] While Erasmus does not immediately classify and name the situational types and their corresponding speech genres that the boys are encouraged by his dialogic pedagogy to recognize and answer, his eventual classification of letters – into conciliation, reconciliation, encouragement, persuasion, consolation, petition, recommendation, admonition, accusation, complaint, defense, protest, justification, reproach, threat, invective, entreaty, etc. – suggests that they are closely related to speech-act categories.

"TO SHARE SPEECH IN COMMON WITH OTHERS":
SCRIPTING LIFE ROLES

Teaching boys how to derive "living model[s]" for the letter through improvisation exercises in which they identify generic situations and match them with appropriate interactions styles, Erasmus offers what Kenneth Burke calls "equipment for living."[14] This method of developing speech or writing repertoires for a wide variety of script situations replicates the socialization processes by which complex verbal competences are acquired and by which the tacit knowledge that frames one's social world is built up. When he imagines the elementary teacher objecting against the difficulties of this manner of instruction, he reminds him, first, invoking the theatrical conception of life implicit in his pedagogy, that "this is the play he had undertaken to put on" (34) and, second, that it can have enormous benefits for the students by promoting distinguished performance in many different social arenas: "From these exercises they will go on to preach fluently in churches, to guide the senate with wise eloquence, to serve with credit on missions of public importance, and lastly to be competent on any matter both in judgment and in speech" (34). Erasmus's recommendations strongly confirm the theatricality and self-consciousness of humanist identity construction, to which Stephen Greenblatt's work has given vivid testimony.[15] In the vigor with which he promotes role-playing practices for the assimilation of speech genres, we can see how Erasmus seems to understand these interactive speech genres as the ideological building blocks of identity, with identity being conceived not only as the discursive construct Greenblatt understands it to be, but also the dialogic construct Bakhtin understands it to be, always situated in the encounter with "someone else's word."[16]

There are startling contradictions between Erasmus's practical program for instilling communicative competence and his idealistic vision of communicative exchange as speech shared "in common with others" (47).[17] Erasmus suggests that when students "are more mature they must be guided gradually" from script situations from classical authors "to subjects closer to real life" (28). But if a boy were to address another in the deferential accents with which an Elizabethan courtier might address the queen, Erasmus could be expected to expostulate, as he does in a related context: "If anyone does not see the absurdity of this language, he must be completely illiterate; if he hears it and does not repudiate it, he must be very long-suffering; if he drinks in such ridiculous flattery with willing ears, he must be the victim of vainglory. Would the ears of any prince put up with such hideous expressions?" (48). To speak or to accept the language of deference is, in Erasmus's view, to "disdain to share speech in common with others" (47). And yet, with status among the chief determinants of interaction in the hierarchic society of Erasmus's time, students endeavoring to derive their living models for the letter from observation of real-life interaction would write letters in the styles Erasmus condemns as absurd. If instead they were to adopt his recommendations for greetings, as illustrated by "Pierre Tartaret sends greeting to Henri Béda, theologian" (54), they could well, as Erasmus recognizes, be heard as insulting rather than greeting. Erasmus is fully aware that in omitting the category of relative status he removes his recommended speech styles from current practices of communication. Despite his admission in other contexts that "usage" is the "arbiter of speech," Erasmus sets up "correct" use against "current" use, and looks forward to a time when "the preferences of the educated will be commonly accepted" (50).

In his pedagogy, Erasmus must negotiate the contradiction between learning through imitation and the imperfect relations available for imitation. For this reason, despite his initial disclaimers of the need for patterns and formulas to imitate when one can work to derive instead the "living model," the second half of his treatise is copious in its provision of practical patterns for his democratic ideal of communication as speech shared "in common with others." Far from merely imagining his better world, he takes an extraordinary step towards its realization by postulating – partly inventing, partly adapting – the languages of its interactions. To create the discursive forms for relations is also to create new relations. In Erasmus's ample provision of scripts for intimate homosocial relations, we encounter not so much the workings of social reproduction that we find in Angel Day as a conscious labor of ideological transformation and innovation.

SCRIPTS FOR POSITIVE POLITENESS

Given Erasmus's vehement and lengthy denunciations of deference forms as flattery in his treatment of greetings and salutations, we might well expect him to dismiss all forms of politeness as merely phatic – as reassuring noises having no essential role in the business of serious communication. We might expect a scholar so impatient of flattering terms and of social hierarchy to search out patterns of dialogic exchange which emphasize pure argumentation and do away altogether with social ingratiation. But while he certainly tries to minimize social asymmetries in the exchange patterns he promotes, Erasmus, always the thoroughgoing rhetorician, by no means discards strategies of ingratiation. Indeed, as he develops his instructions for beginning a letter, the amount of attention he devotes to winning "over the good will of the person to whom we are writing" (76) is astonishing.[18] If, for the rhetorician, persuasion requires the rhetorical construction of *ethos* to shape the writer's image and *pathos* to shape the reader's response, for Erasmus, whose thinking is all the more bound up in dialogic exchange, persuasion requires the self-conscious construction of relationships. Friendship and intimate relations are immediately treated, in a surprisingly calculating way, not as pre-existent conditions that can be referred to in the letter but as discursive constructions that are to be built up according to alternative sets of strategies. If one's ancestors had relations in common, for example, "[w]e must say that there was the deepest affection and the closest intimacy between our ancestors and his, and that very many services were rendered on both sides; that this good will has been handed on to us in a hereditary succession and has never been neglected; that true affection, which we imbibed with our nurse's milk, as it were, has increased with years" (76), and so on. But if no ancestral ties existed, "we shall say that it is those linked by no ties of friendship who like to recall the close bonds that existed between their ancestors" and trace how "at first . . . similarity of abilities and interests brought young minds together in a unique atmosphere of warmth and affection," then "close comradeship and mutual kindnesses," and "finally . . . admiration of each other's good qualities" made friendship take root, "so that now nothing could be added to the store of benefits or the measure of affection attained" (77). So copious is the store of praise and compliments that Erasmus proffers to assist in the construction of friendly relations that any adequate sampling of its alternative strategies would overflow the boundaries of this chapter.

Erasmus denounces flattery, on the one hand, and provides his students, on the other hand, with prolific inventories for ingratiation. Noticing the contradiction, Alexander Dalzell tries to explain it by distinguishing between the salutation and body of the letter:

First, Erasmus makes a distinction between what one can say in the salutation and what is appropriate in the body of the letter. Apparently it was much more offensive to use flattering terms in the heading than in the letter itself. This conforms to the practice of Erasmus himself, who is generally fairly reserved about the salutation, but is quite prepared to pour on the flattery in the text if the occasion demands it.[19]

The distinction Dalzell makes is true to Erasmus's practice, but it only adds to the puzzle. The distinction Brown and Levinson make between positive and negative politeness can account more adequately for Erasmus's procedures here. Implicit in Erasmus's practice is a qualitative distinction between the "flattery" that he recommends and the "flattery" he condemns: Erasmus's selected flatteries are all recognizable as positive politeness strategies, which Brown and Levinson consider the building blocks of friendship and intimacy; and Erasmus is consistent, then, in his omission of negative politeness, that is, of the ingratiations that typically build up hierarchic relations.

As I have already indicated, Erasmus divides letters first according to the branches of classical oratory into the deliberative, the demonstrative, and the judicial classes, supplementing this division with a class of familiar letters; second, he subdivides these classes into speech-act genres. What emerges in his treatment of these different speech-act genres is a social logic of politeness consistent with the Brown and Levinson principle whereby politeness strategies are deployed to mitigate speech-act threats to a speaker's or hearer's face. Consider, for example, Erasmus's account of how style must vary in making requests:

First, since the nature of the things we ask for varies, and since there is a great variety in the persons who make and receive the requests, the method of asking should vary too. For certain things we ask of a person are likely to inspire favour, such as advice; there are other things which make the asker blush with shame, as when we ask for a loan or something dishonourable. Thus in general the method of asking will be twofold in form, direct and indirect. (173)

Whether the direct or indirect approach is taken, Erasmus recommends using "every means to secure the good will of the person of whom we make a difficult request" (173). Similarly, when Erasmus offers instructions on letters of advice, he emphasizes the logic of repairing what is potentially threatening in advice-giving: "Since hardly anyone is pleased to learn of his own faults, we shall mitigate the harshness of criticism with praise" (189). This logic of speech-act threat and mitigation helps further to account for Erasmus's puzzling distinction between acceptable flattery and reprehensible flattery. For example, surprisingly for someone who so robustly condemns flattery directed at kings, Erasmus accepts the strategy of giving tacit advice to a ruler or king "through false praise": "I suspect that panegyrics of princes were invented for this very purpose, that under the semblance of praise they should, without offence or shame, be reminded of their faults. Otherwise what would be more repulsive than such flattery?" (189). In other words, the "flattery" that is acceptable to Erasmus is not simply the ingratiation that conforms to an idealized model of equal communication; the further feature that makes "flattery" of a kind acceptable is its important role in speech-act mitigation. This second requirement can help us to account for the oddity Dalzell has noted: if Erasmus dislikes flattering greetings but accepts certain forms of ingratiation in the body of a letter, it may be because the body of the letter is where its business is transacted in risk-filled speech-acts requiring mitigation and repair.

Erasmus encourages schoolmasters and pupils alike to conceive of friendships and same-sex intimacies as performative and strategic: specific forms of affection are produced and maintained through writing letters, and their accents vary with the business at hand in the letter because they are transparently deployed to facilitate that business. It is fascinating to observe to what extent these elaborate written intimacies take shape, by no means as expressions of bodily desire or sexual longing (though they may potentially produce such affects), but instead within a dynamic of rebuke and repair, as disciplinary techniques to frame the dedicated scholar. Consider how the copious instructions for mitigating "the harshness of criticism with praise" systematically deploy the key strategies of positive politeness – including claiming common ground, conveying that speaker and hearer are cooperators, and fulfilling some want of the hearer – to shape an intrusive but sustainable pedagogic relation:

We shall say that since he has many outstanding qualities, we cannot suffer so many virtues to be darkened by the blemish of a single fault or allow for any reservations in the praise of such a good friend. Next we shall make light of the fault itself, either blaming his age of indiscretion, or showing that it has been found even in the greatest of men, or that, while it certainly needs correction, it springs from his generosity or some other virtue and can be corrected without much difficulty. We shall say that we write in this way out of special affection for him, and would not do the same for others. (189)

Here Erasmus delineates what are familiar pedagogical methods even today for negotiating criticism by separating one's estimation of the fault from one's estimation of the person, although the effusiveness of the reparative affection, most evident here in the claim to exclusivity, would usually be restricted in modern pedagogical discourse to relations with children.

To identify Erasmus's rhetorical strategies as positive politeness is not to capture completely their distinctive inflection, an inflection evident in his "own collection" of materials for making difficult requests:

'I would seem quite shameless to importune you in the midst of your affairs with my daily requests if I were not aware that your character is such that once you have offered your patronage to anyone, you do not rest until you have confirmed him in his position.'

'Nothing is so difficult that I am not confident of gaining it with the help of your patronage.'
'Nothing is too great for me to dare ask it of you, or for you to be unable to grant it.'
'As it is easily within your power, so is my desire stronger.'
'One who employs too many words in making a reasonable request of you betrays little understanding of your generosity.'

'The matter is so just and honourable that a fair-minded man would not even refuse it to an enemy. Our acquaintance is so close that there is nothing so unfair that the one should not obtain it from the other.'

'The matter is of such a nature that if you consider what I am asking of you, you should be asking it of me.' (180)

These examples – some situated within the client–patron relation usually conceived in terms of subordination and deference – are marked by the writer's extraordinary optimism about the outcome of his request, by boldly asserted assumptions about the recipient's concern for the hearer's needs and wants, and by further insistences about the recipient's ability to perform the request. In the last two examples, we can also see how Erasmus rewrites the implicit power relation between giver and receiver as a mutual and equal relation. Presumption, above all, marks this interaction style, a presumption strongly emphasizing, to use Erasmus's own terms for the speech he favors, what is "shared in common" between the interlocutors. That presumption should figure so prominently in Erasmus's rhetorical construction of relationship is particularly significant in that non-presumption is among the strongest markers of the discourse Erasmus rejects – the subordinate's language of negative politeness. To speak with special care to avoid assumptions about the hearer's ability to perform a request or willingness to consider the request is to keep one's distance and to reassure by affirming the hearer's superiority. Erasmus's strategic recommendation of presumption instead strongly affirms the hearer's equal status, even in the process of performing a speech act which would usually give over power to the hearer. But a style that tacitly assumes the speaker's right to frame in words the thoughts and obligations of the other goes further than affirming equal status. It interferes. And it figures a relation postulated on the right to interfere.

Thus Erasmus's scripts for that "mutual conversation between absent friends" (20) which he defines letter-writing to be inflect positive politeness in a particular way, foregrounding presumption. At times the presumptive style takes forms that go well beyond what we imagine as "politeness," even in Brown and Levinson's extended definition as speech-act mitigation. Consider, for example, the strangely hybrid speech act Erasmus names "friendly consolation with reprimand" and scripts thus:

'Fancy you being in such anguish and so depressed! What is the good of tormenting yourself and wearing yourself out with tears? Is all that going to make the trouble lighter, or will it not rather make it worse? What is the good of lamenting so pitifully what cannot be changed? What has now become of your steadfastness of mind and your learning, by which you used to relieve the distress of others? You were able to heal others, but are of no help to yourself. You must now be your own physician. Why do you exhaust yourself with tears, and your friends with your laments, all to no avail? What is the meaning of this lack of self-control and faintness of heart? Surely you have not forgotten that you are a man . . .' (170)[20]

Here, in a speech genre Erasmus elsewhere calls "salutary reproof" (85), the logic of minimizing speech-act risk seems almost to be reversed, with the construction of friendship the motive rather than the mitigator of admonition or rebuke. Given Erasmus's chief recommendation for composing letters of a flexible decorum that varies style with situation and relation, it is surprising how consistently Erasmus's collected examples exhibit the presumptive style. Furthermore, the style is specifically gendered masculine, and not only by the omission of women among his imagined letter-writers: if we take Erasmus's specific recommendation of a style for letters of encouragement, as characteristic of his presumptive style in general, he himself terms it a style "masculine and, if I may say so, robust, impressive, and vigorous" (90).

Erasmus remarks in a discussion about comparisons that "It will take art to make unequal in words what is naturally equal" (85). In his discursive construction of relationship, Erasmus uses art to make equal in words what the surrounding culture inscribes as unequal. His discursive fashioning of equality is not merely a fashioning of the speaker or writer but also a fashioning of the recipient, for an interaction style prefigures its own response. Negative politeness prefigures a non-symmetrical response, but positive politeness prefigures – or summons – a symmetrical or matched response. If Erasmus is serious about speech shared in common, his style of presumption must also grant his interlocutors the reciprocal right to presume, to interfere in turn. Of course, in one sense to summon a matched response is also to coerce response: no style of discourse can entirely escape the interplay of one speaker's shaping advantage over the other. Furthermore, the will and ability of Erasmus's own interlocutors to answer him back cannot but be affected by the power dynamics already inscribed in social relations. As teachers today interested in a non-authoritarian classroom have often found, they cannot lay aside their authority simply by sharing in common the language of their students. As Pierre Bourdieu has demonstrated, the credit or value attributed to a particular speech or written discourse varies with a person's power or authority within the specific context.[21] If a teacher or tutor by virtue of his position has greater power than a pupil, his presumptive speech style and the boy's matching style have different weight and credit; thus, they may not share "speech in common" even if they use the same words. This difficulty with Erasmus's ideal may, paradoxically, not have surfaced in instances where a boy's aristocratic status offset his tutor's authoritative positioning. Yet even such an arrangement does not dissociate issues of discourse from issues of power, as Erasmus's humanist ideal would have it, even if it does occlude the operations of power and the potential for an apparently open and democratic system of communication to reproduce inequality.

Erasmus's treatise offers a radical experiment in communication. He hoped for a time when to greet a great man simply would be recognized as respectful: "It will cease to be offensive when it ceases to be arrogant, and in time the preferences of the educated will be commonly accepted" (50). Although Erasmus's treatise was widely read and used to teach letter-writing in sixteenth-century England and, together with the imitation of Cicero's familiar letters, certainly shaped the Latin letters exchanged among scholars and between tutors and pupils, it is hard to measure the effect its promotion of a familiar style might have had among the general population. In early seventeenth-century England, a "sociable" or "familiar" letter style develops that is in strong contrast to the status-marked language of Elizabethan court and administrative letters, and it becomes available to a much wider population of letter-writers than we find in Elizabeth's reign, but this development is well in the future when Erasmus writes. During Elizabeth's reign, although negative politeness is the dominant key, we shall see that familiar styles do nonetheless exist for negotiating relations among equals, with presumptive habits that bear at least a limited resemblance to Erasmus's style. However, it may be most fruitful to see Erasmus's innovations in communication as contributing not so much to the general language community as to a specialized and highly influential discourse community. In his own letters as in his handbook, he certainly sets a standard for epistolary communication among the scholars of his and the next generation – even if the interpersonal letter will come to be displaced as a main instrument for scholarly communication as Francis Bacon and a scientific revolution begin, in Charles Bazerman's words, to reshape "written knowledge." Erasmus sets, however, a more long-lasting standard for those he addresses directly in his handbook – for teachers and schoolmasters. Their professional language, to this day, foregrounds interpersonal exchange, including the speech acts of encouragement and criticism so important in Erasmus. The language of pedagogy remains a language marked by strategic presumption. Very often it is also a language that conceals power relations – speech that only equivocally claims to be "shared in common," gaining thereby the "double profit" for the speaker both of the acknowledgment of superior place and the appearance of freedom from considerations of place.[22]

ANGEL DAY: REPRODUCING SOCIAL RELATIONS

Whereas Erasmus's letter manual offers readers both the equipment to replicate and the equipment to critique and alter existing social relations, Angel Day, in *The English Secretary*, provides no social criticism or program for systemic change. Instead, like the Renaissance courtesy books Frank Whigham examines in *Ambition and Privilege*, *The English Secretary* promotes social maintenance and reproduction, while at the same time making room for individual mobility. Whigham argues that the courtesy books provided readers with "equipment for living," but equipment that could be put to opposite uses by different social groups. For the ruling elite, the articulations of aristocratic and gentlemanly behavioral repertoires could preserve and mystify social differences. Nonetheless, in presenting these behavioral competences as rule-governed, the courtesy manuals also offered talented people aspiring to higher station skills they could acquire to facilitate their advancement.[23]

Angel Day's letter-writing handbook has this double agenda. On the one hand, Day presents an interactional rhetoric inscribing social discriminations in subtler ways than the highly status-conscious handbooks of the medieval *ars dictaminis*. By promoting this rhetoric that reinforces the place of the superior, even in the invisible grain of the language, Day might hope to please noblemen like the Earl of Oxford, to whom he dedicates his book. For his less exalted readers, Day offers the skills requisite to write and speak like the Earl of Oxford and lesser gentlemen, or – perhaps more important – the skills to write *to* or speak *with* those of importance. The dedicatory letter to the readers shows that Day is conscious of a double constituency for his work. He promotes the book both for those already skilled in the "well ordering and deliuerie" of "our daylie speech" (pt. II, p. 76) and for those aspiring to communication skills, "to the end that they who . . . haue heretofore vnknowing done well, may see how with skill and discretion hereafter to pursue the same, & the ignorant also hereof whose reach hath not been so ample as others, may be therefore informed what vnto well doing is most consonant and agreeing" (A4r).

Clearly Angel Day sees *The English Secretary* as "a tool for 'making places' in the social order"[24] – not only for his readers but also for himself. Day was neither peer nor gentleman: a minor writer, he was the son of Thomas Day, a parish clerk of London, and had served in his youth for twelve years from 1563 as an apprentice to the stationer Thomas Duxwell. He recommends *himself* as well as his book to the Earl of Oxford, emphasizing the "will I have to do unto your Lordship *any acceptable service*" (A2; emphasis added). Furthermore, in addressing his second letter to "gentlemen" readers rather than the wider potential readership of aspirants to gentle status, Day may be aiming at benefits he thinks they can dispense to him. "[T]hey shall doo no more then belongeth to good mindes," Day puts his optimistic hopes, "and encourage me by whatsoever other meanes hereafter, to gratifie their fauours" (A4v). Even Day's choice of title may be a place-seeking strategy. "Truth is," he writes in the specialized 1599 supplement "Of the partes, place and Office of a Secretary," "that . . . I am none of those that maie vaunt my selfe of any furniture sufficient to so speciall an end & purpose" (pt. II, p. 101). *The English Secretary* names not an office Day has attained but an office to which he aspires. In explaining "the name of *The Secretary*," he reports himself "nothing ignorant what great perfection is to be required in such a one . . . neither supposing the matter herein contained to appeare so sufficient, as perfectly thereby to enable what in the same function is to bee required" (A4r–v). He uses the title, he claims, not because the handbook will fashion a secretary of its reader, but "because the orderly writing of Letters, being a principall part belonging to a Secretorie, is by the Method hereof delivered to any Learners capacitie" (A4v). In this way, Day elevates and mystifies the competence required of a secretary, putting it outside the reach of most readers, at the same time as he displays (despite the modest disclaimer) his own capacity to take on this important office.[25]

Day has usually been classified as a "figurist rhetorician," with his handbook treated as a resource for literary writers wishing to increase their store of verbal ornaments.[26] In what follows I will treat Day's handbook, instead, as a practical guide to the language of typical social interactions, an Elizabethan's map of lived relations. This is not to deny Day's considerable interest in displaying his literary aptitude. Some of Day's sample letters are certainly modeled more on fiction than on life. For example, the stylistic embellishments of his letters "descriptorie" and "laudatorie" suit them more to prose romance than to practical communication, while the copious variations on themes like the love of learning to be found among the letters "hortatorie" turn them into moral essays rather than casual exchanges. Furthermore, Day's marginal identification of figures of speech in his sample letters, supplemented by a "declaration of . . . Tropes, Figures, and Schemes," appears to elevate and aestheticize the letter-writing enterprise, removing it from everyday communication. Nonetheless, Day makes it clear that his purpose in naming and classifying figures is not to add on extra ornaments to everyday speech or writing but rather "to set foorth vnto the learner, how much the phrase of our daylie speech by well ordering and deliuerie is graced with Figures and other ornaments of Art" (pt. II, p. 76). In other words, the art Day analyzes into tropes and figures is what he considers normal to the practice of daily speech and conversation. Nonetheless, while it is misleading to assimilate letter-writing in general or Day's epistolary handbook in particular to the literary tradition, it may be equally misleading to make too absolute a distinction between them. As Jonathan Goldberg has usefully observed, "letter manuals serve to instruct on the socially countenanced modes for a self-production that can never be separated from the fictive simulations that structure the real."[27] Furthermore, the circulation in Day of a wide-ranging repertoire of social interaction scripts would certainly have been an invaluable resource for dramatists, like Shakespeare, who sought to simulate the situated discourse of people of all ranks.

The distinctively practical orientation of Day's handbook – its provision of real-life repertoires for the interactive self-production of letter writing – shows itself in how Day adjusts material he borrows from Erasmus. Day's handbook is heavily indebted to Erasmus's manual: he echoes Erasmus in his definition of the epistle as "the familiar and mutuall talke of one absent friende to another" (8); in his division of epistles into "Demonstratiue, Deliberatiue, Iudiciall, and Familiar" kinds (20); both in his naming of the *exordium*, the *narratio* or *propositio*, the *confirmatio*, the *confutatio*, and the *peroratio* as parts of the letter and in his qualification that "These are not altogither at all times vsed" (11). But there is a remarkable disjunction between the Erasmian theory and the contemporary social practices that Day recommends. Repeatedly Day proffers and then undermines Erasmian precepts. For example, in writing about "superscriptions and directions," he follows Erasmus at first by characterizing and praising the practices of the ancient Romans, but then he adds: "But that custome according to the antiquity of the time, is long since worne out, and these daies and seasons have induced vnto us for euerie estate of calling, a more statelie reuerence according to the dignitie and worthines of the same" (18). As in the medieval formulary handbooks, Day then proceeds to offer his readers hundreds of formulas for address, each one precisely adjusted to the "estate" of the recipient, as in these examples:

To the right honourable and my especial good L. the Lorde Chauncellor, or Lord high Treasurer of England . . . To the right honorable and my singular good Lord and father, or ladie mother, the Earle or Countesse of N . . . To the most noble and towardlie yong Gentleman G. L. esquire, if hee be a noble mans sonne under the degree of a Baron . . . To the right worshipfull his especiall good maister, M. K. Marchant and Alderman of L. (18–19)

Day's chief point of variance with Erasmus is to emphasize relative social status as the main determinant of style: when Day introduces his model letters, his usual method is to distinguish whether an inferior is writing to a superior, a superior to an inferior, or one social equal to another.

While the attention to social rank as a determinant of style strongly links Day's handbook to the medieval dictaminal handbooks, their different handling of socially situated language is revealing. In "The Medieval Art of Letter Writing," Les Perelman explains how "the rhetorical theory of the *ars dictaminis*," unlike classical rhetoric, "seems to recognize hierarchical social relationships as the principal element of communication." Perelman argues that the "dictaminal obsession with social rank" reflects the bureaucratic structures out of whose communication requirements the letter-writing art arose – the medieval "chanceries, both imperial and papal, [which] owed their very existence to the respective secular and ecclesiastical hierarchies in which they existed."[28] What the medieval handbooks deliver, then, is a formulaic rhetoric for negotiating hierarchical differences, a rhetoric notably focused, despite its primarily administrative applications, not on argument and persuasion but instead on "personal relationship."[29] While Day's handbook retains from the medieval tradition the orientation towards the interpersonal, what is remarkable in *The English Secretary* is the astonishing deepening and complicating of the rhetoric of relationship. The dictaminal handbooks develop prescriptive formulas for salutations, for the "Securing of Good Will," and for farewells; some of them go little beyond this, giving the body of the letter only the most cursory attention. Perelman singles out *The Practice and Exercise of Letter Writing*, written around 1300 by Lawrence of Aquilegia, as a treatise which, by providing the letter-writer with a menu of choices for all parts of the letter, "brought to its logical conclusion the tendency in the genre of making the act of writing a letter an automatic procedure."[30] Although early on in *The English Secretary* Day does invite his readers to pick and choose from among his enormous inventory of salutations and greetings, subscriptions and superscriptions appropriate "for everie estate of calling," the handbook on the whole does not encourage formulaic or automatic writing. Day does not theorize a "living model of the letter," as Erasmus does, but the rhetoric of social relation he delineates is no less reliant on a writer's inventiveness and capacity to apply a flexible decorum. Day accents the creative invention that is customarily deployed in the everyday prosaics of letter-writing, an artistry by no means limited to figurative ornamentation. Instead, it is on display in the eloquent elaboration of social relationship, or – to borrow Jonathan Goldberg's terms – in how "the space of writing" is made to serve as "an index of social relations."[31] Day's reluctance to tie social relation to particular formulas or parts of the letter is evident in his statements about negotiating equal or symmetrical relations: "And being in familiaritie is to no place tied, but beginning, middle, or ending of the Letter, all is one, as seemeth most consonant to the vaine & disposition of the partie, and these also at all times not delivered in the selfe worde of greeting or commendations, but by diverse Epithets, and fine conveiances, as falleth out to the matter of the Epistle, and the conditions of the partie to be handled" (13). In *The*

Scripting social relations 79

English Secretary, as in the complicated practice, at least among the ruling elite, of Elizabethan letter-writing, not only "familiaritie" but social relation in general "is to no place tied."

Day's extended treatment of request-making exemplifies this more subtle figuring of social relation. As with Erasmus, Day's epistolary rhetoric resembles Brown and Levinson's politeness theory in its classification of letter types into speech-act categories. A deeper resemblance to Brown and Levinson's theory of how social relations are constructed in language emerges as Day suggests that style should vary not only with the correspondents' relative power but also with the riskiness of verbal actions undertaken:

And in asmuch as these Epistles are so named, for the earnest petition or requests in everie of them contained, and that the variety of thinges are such to be demanded, and mens conditions so divers, at whose handes or from whom the same are to be received: It therefore falleth out by consequence that according thereunto the maner of the Epistle must needs also be divers and variable. For some things ther are which favorably and with great indifferencie, are oftentimes to be graunted, required or obtained, as counsell, aid, patronage, good speeches, natural care and regard, & such other like. Some also and such semblable persons, as for which, or to whom, to ask or sue a certain kind of shame, is in a maner tied, viz. in craving, borrowing, importuning, charging, or to vehement troubling. The stile, order, and delivery therefore appertaining to either of these must needly be different. (91)

Day's attribution of "indifferencie" to certain requests for patronage and "shame" to "borrowing" in certain circumstances could be said to reflect the culture-specific ranking of these particular "face-threatening acts" – the former as of slight risk and the latter as of considerable risk. For Day, as for Brown and Levinson, the variable risk levels of different requests (that is, their cultural ranking) go hand in hand with "mens conditions so divers" (that is, relative power) to determine style.[32]

For Day, how profoundly relative power can shape verbal actions is apparent in his division of request-making into "epistles petitorie" and "epistles commendatorie." Having offered examples of how a person might make a request of his or her social equal, Day reflects on how the request-making usual to a superior is business of so different an order as to require a separate title:

Now, besides these hereby alreadie delivered, there are letters also that might be suted under this [petitorie] forme, which from Noble men or others, are many times written in favor of sundrie persons, containing requests in their behalfs to be performed, which not withstanding the difference of estates in that the same doe for the most part passe unto their inferiours, yet seemeth the nature thereof to be *petitorie*, but in a different order of these to be altogether pursued. Insomuch as neither agreeeth it, to use like circumstances of humilitie and entreatie, nor of pleasures or curteu[si]e, as in the other are required: but rather a necessarie supposall and assurance of their demandes to be hearkened unto, in respect that of their honours, reputations, or credites, it is intended they will require nothing, but that with reasonable toleration may be liked of. But the use of such kinde of directions in choise of both, I rather hold pertinent to the title *Commendatorie*, for that whatsoever is therein written, in favour eyther of the person or of the cause, may in respect of the honour or reputation of those from whome they come, bee better deemed in sorte of a curteous recommendation, then otherwise by or under anie title of humilitie or submission: for these causes I have thought meete to adjoine immediatelie hereunto, the same Epistles *Commendatorie*, beeing so nearelie combined with those of *Petitorie* as they are. (100–01)

To vary the relative power of speaker and hearer, then, can be to change the very name and nature of the verbal action. Far from being on display only in salutations and farewells, power can enter into any space of the writing and alter the very substance of the communication.

INTERACTION SCRIPTS

By considering the three different interaction styles Day proposes for requests, we can explore in detail his understanding of how relative power shapes discourse. Day characterizes a style "of pleasures or curteu[si]e," for letters among equals; a style of "humilitie and entreatie," for letters from inferiors to superiors; and a style marked by "a necessarie supposall and assurance," for letters from superiors to inferiors.

First, the "pleasures" style, an interaction script suited to "friends" or "familiars." To reinforce his readers' grasp of this script for horizontal relations, Day offers two examples of petition, of which I quote the first in full, together with a letter of response:

An Epistle Petitorie, wherein is craved travell and counsell to be assistant upon urgent occasion

As one greatlie emboldned by the forwardnesse of *your woonted courtesie* and liking ever bent towards me, I have *dared* (Sir) once againe *upon presumption of the like*, hereby to intreate you, wherein you may see *in what degree of affection I do intertaine you, in that not contented, I have alreadie so manie and so often times used you, I doe by such meanes endevour solie to make my selfe wholy and to none other so much as beholding unto you*. My man hath returned me from London, how by more then common celeritie I have in my suite beene prevented by my adversarie, whereby it is like, my cause standing upon so great a hazard, it will goe verie hard with mee. Nowe if your woonted counsell, and friendly assistance bee not speedilie ayding, both the hope of benefit, charge and expense thereof will be lost utterly. In regard whereof, these may bee in as earnest maner as is possible to intreate you, that upon the attendance of my man, I may (as woontedlie) use you. Your counsell ioyned with a little travell may greatlie profite me, and now more then at any time else, *exceedinglie pleasure mee*. Wherein if it may please you to yoke mee further unto you by the waight of your courtesie: I shall not onelie endevour by all possibilitie to requite it, but also *your selfe shall not faile at anie time to finde such a one of mee, as of whose travaile, industrie, or what other abilitie to pleasure you*, you may account of assuredlie. I have by certaine other Letters mooved my L. to have favourable consideration touching mee, which as I am informed, his L. hath receyved. What els to bee performed heerein, my man shall make knowne unto you. And thus *doubting as little of your friendship herein, as of mine owne thankfull disposition*, prest always to the uttermost to requite you, I doe heartilie bid you farewell, D. of this, &c. (96–97; emphasis added)

A Letter responsorie to the same

Good M.C. needelesse were it you should entreate mee in that, wherein you have founde mee alwayes most willing, and such whome with small perswasions you may induce to a farre greater purpose then what in your last letter is required. The Messenger I have appointed to morrow morning to returne againe to my lodging, at which time I will not faile to finish, what in the best sort I can conceive to bee unto your occasions furthering. Hard will it bee for mee to accomplish that, wherein your selfe seeme so unperfect, for that the dullest conceyte forged from the most distempered of your imaginations, cannot but sounde farre better tunes then the ripest of my invention is anie wayes able to deliver. Neverthelesse, such as it is, or so much as (by dislike of your owne) you have will to account of, that will I prepare to your view, and put forward to your good speed, thinking it better by deliverie of a grosse devise to satisfie the demaunde of a friend, then by concealing the simplicitie therof to bee censured as uncourteous. In conclusion, *it is (sir) lawfull for you to use mee to the uttermost*, and fittest to our confirmed league of amitie, that (in whatsoever) you should imploy mee, wherein I desire you conceive no more, then such as I intend to become, and you shall assuredly find me, viz yours, &c. (97–98; emphasis added)

Striking here is the degree of elaboration that goes into the "politeness," or relational maintenance work, though our earlier examples of Elizabethan correspondence would suggest that this extravagant courtesy is widely used. These letters between "familiars" elaborate a rhetoric of association, or of insistent approach: the "pleasures" style, like Erasmus's familiar style, is remarkably presumptuous. The first petitioner, for example, "dare[s]" to make his request "upon presumption" of his friend's "woonted courtesie," and ends optimistically "doubting as little of your friendship" as of his own thankfulness. Day's second petitioner entreats "under assurance of your forwardnes to do me good" and states baldly that "it is in you to doe me good," though he states only conditionally his expectation of how he "may so farre foorth presume of your fidelitie" (97). One of the words that Day singles out to characterize this style also bespeaks presumption – that is the transitive verb "to pleasure," a distinctive usage evidently arising in the sixteenth century and not surviving much beyond it. Thus the first petitioner offers his friend the opportunity to "exceedinglie pleasure mee" in a manner that assumes the offer will be welcome.

The interaction style here exhibited, however, differs from Erasmus's presumptive style in the meticulous care taken to construct in words a reciprocal framework for the presumptive rhetoric. Balanced against the first petitioner's expectation that his friend will "pleasure mee" is his promise that "your selfe shall not faile at anie time to finde such a one of mee, as of whose travaile, industrie, or what other abilitie to pleasure you, you may account of assuredlie." In the second petition, we find the assurance of mutuality in the writer's promise on attaining liberty from prison "to none so much as to you" to "be yoked in courtesie" (97). In Day's terms, the style is one of "pleasures or courtesie," and that characterization establishes the foundation of reciprocal generosity on which the style rests: the principle that courteous friends will "pleasure" one another. While the vocabulary of this style is full of monetary overtones in its key words – including "use," "assurance," "requite," etc. – the calculus of relationship worked out is not a straightforward one of debt and corresponding obligation. This is evident in the key word "use": the first petitioner urges his friend to see from his boldness in making the request "in what degree of affection I do intertaine you, in that not contented, I have alreadie so manie and so often times used you, I doe by such meanes endevour solie to make my selfe wholy and to none other so much as beholding unto you." The argument that affection is enhanced by this form of persistent "use" certainly gives a different accent to familiarity than we are accustomed to today, when "being used" by a friend has an exclusively negative connotation.

The large and demanding claims of the "pleasures" style could only be sustained in a community that recognized, sanctioned, and maintained such a logic of relationship. The petitioner's rhetoric anticipates and depends upon the return of courtesy in its answer, as in the example of Day's "letter responsorie": "it is (sir) lawfull for you to use mee to the uttermost." Without a strong expectation of such response fostered by a social milieu that could maintain and reproduce this ethos of liberal courtesy, a speaker venturing to prove affection by the frequency of his demands would make himself extraordinarily vulnerable to rebuff and to shame, or loss of face.

It is well understood that vertical relations of deference and patronage played a large role in the stratified society of early modern England, but the distribution and qualities of horizontal relations are perhaps less fully understood. Historian Keith Wrightson discusses "neighbourliness" as a characteristic social formation in local rural communities making for relations "between *effective*, if not actual, equals."[33] This type of relationship, "established on the basis of . . . residential propinquity," Wrightson characterizes as follows:

it involved a mutual recognition of reciprocal obligations of a practical kind and a degree of normative consensus as to the nature of proper behaviour between neighbours. Finally, and crucially, it was essentially a horizontal relationship, one which implied a degree of equality and mutuality between partners to the relationship . . . The reciprocity of neighbourliness was a reciprocity in equal obligations, the exchange of comparable services between *effective*, if not actual, equals.[34]

By looking at the organization of debt and credit in local communities, Wrightson tries to specify in material terms how far the "tacit assumption" between neighbors "of reciprocal aid in time of need" might have extended. He points to a widespread lending of money without interest among local people, but also establishes that the "willingness to forgo interest" had limits: "both interest and the drawing up of formal bonds becomes apparent in the case of substantial sums of money."[35]

There is an obvious tension between the unlimited promises of "use" in the "pleasures" style scripted by Day and the tacit assumption of relatively clear limits on "neighbourliness." Wrightson's further explorations of the possibilities open for horizontal relations do not take us very far in finding a perfect match or local situation for the "pleasures" style. He regards it as "an open question . . . [w]hether urban society was . . . markedly less structured and impersonal than rural society."[36] And concerning the local contexts and discursive structures of "friendship," which he separates from "neighbourliness," Wrightson is far more vague: "Beyond the boundaries of mere neighbourly duty, any heightened positive content in either practical or emotional support carried a relationship to a higher plane; that of friendship . . . 'Friends' was, of course, a term which could be used to denote kinsfolk, but it was at least as often employed to indicate friendship in the modern sense."[37] It would be naive to imagine that Elizabethan "friendship" had only one or a few discursive scripts, but it is equally problematic, I think, to separate out and historicize "neighbourliness" while proposing a modern cast for "higher" relations of friendship. We may be tempted to read the effusiveness of the "pleasures" style as the sort of "heightened positive content" that would match it to a "higher" relation of "friendship" in preference to "neighbourliness," especially since Day's interlocutors address one another as "friends." And yet effusiveness does not always signal intimacy in relations; it can, instead, be a way of creating and sustaining boundaries. Before we assume that "pleasuring" friends was a discourse limited to intimates, it is important to see how it might be more congruent with the material practices of "neighbourliness" than at first appears: the rhetorical elaboration, rather than serving as a transparent index of intimacy, could just as well serve to do part of the cultural work needed to sustain and reproduce "neighbourliness" as a viable social formation. The Elizabethan contexts of use for the "pleasures" style will be discussed further in relation to merchant discourse and Shakespeare's plays in chapter 5.

Day's chapters on request-making also offer sample scripts for negotiating vertical relations, especially relations between suitors and noblemen, clients and patrons. The section on commendatory letters focuses on requests for the preferment of a third party. This kind of verbal action on the behalf of another is standard business fare in Elizabethan court circles, as Frank Whigham has demonstrated in his analysis of suitors' letters in the *Letter Book* of Sir Christopher Hatton and as Day's moderate ranking of the face threat involved in pressing for the preferment of a servant, friend, or relative also suggests.[38] Day's examples make us privy to the different inflections obtaining depending upon whether the message ascends or descends the social scale, and this relative positioning of commendatory acts is something Whigham's analysis does not take explicitly into account. Though Day explains that "petitory" letters go under too great a title of "humilitie or submission" to apply to noblemen and superiors, "commendatory" letters both ascend and descend the social scale. For an inferior to press for the preferment of another, then, was a normal circumstance, and the inflections of such a request, according to Day, might sound like this:

... And thus much by your pardon and allowance dare I assure unto you, if it may please you in credit of my simple knowledge and opinion to imploy him, you shal find that besides he is by parentage discended from such, as of whome I knowe your Lordship will verie well accompt of, hee is also learned, discreete, sober, wise, and moderate in all this actions, of great secrecie and most assured trust, governed in all companies accordinglie: finallie, a man so meete, and to this present turne so apt and necessarie, as I cannot easilie imagine howe you may be served better. Pleaseth your L. the rather for the great good will I beare him, and humble duetie I owe unto you, to accepte, imploie, and accompt of him, I nothing doubt but your L. having by such means given credit to my choice, shall finde him such, as for whose good service, you shall have further occasion to thinke well of mee for him . . . (102)

The rhetorical strategies for mitigating the speech-act risk in this letter follow a familiar pattern for humility and deference: the writer makes explicit the trespass implicit in his request and makes explicit his boldness in anticipating the other's pardon for the imposition ("thus much by your pardon and allowance dare I assure unto you"); he further mitigates his request with a conventional formula indicating non-coercion ("if it may please you"); and he deprecates his own knowledge and capacities ("my simple knowledge and opinion").

By contrast, the style of a superior making a recommendation to an inferior is marked by "a necessarie supposall and assurance of [the writer's] demandes to be hearkened unto" (100) in Day's example:

After my verie heartie Commendations unto you, where I am given to understande, that you are in election, and it is also verie likelie you shall bee pricked by her Maiestie, high Sheriffe for this yeare, of the Countyes of Sussex and Surrey. This Gent. the bearer hereof, beeing one whom for manie respectes, I doe greatly favour, and for his learning, skill, and honest usage, have long time used and reputed of, I have thought good by these (if it so happen you shall this yeare bee named thereunto) to recommend to your good allowance to bee receyved as your under-sheriffe for that time, putting unto you such good and reasonable securitie as appertaineth, for discharge of the sayde office. And hereby also to pray you, that the rather for my sake, and for the especiall choice and reckoning I have made of him, you will nowe before hand make certaine acceptance of his skill, by refusall of whatsoever other that may bee recommended unto you for the exercise of the same office, assuring you, for that I have well knowne and prooved to be in him, you shall be so well furnished, as you would wish. And besides, in that you shall gratifie me herein, I will not faile in anie sort I may to requite you. And even so I bid you heartily farewell. (104–5)

The forms in which the recommendation is made in large measure presuppose its acceptance: "This Gent. . . . I have thought good by these (if it so happen you shall this yeare bee named thereunto) to recommend to your good allowance to bee receyved as your under-sheriffe for that time"; "And hereby also to pray you . . . you will nowe before hand make certaine acceptance of his skill, by refusall of whatsoever other that may bee recommended unto you for the exercise of the same office." The addressee's "receipt" of the gentleman as under-sheriff is represented as actual, not as hypothetical: the parenthetical condition attaches to the addressee's future election as sheriff, not to his choice of under-sheriff. Even stranger, while future recommendations of other candidates are cast only as contingent possibilities ("whatsoever other . . . *may* bee recommended"), the addressee's anticipated response to them is cast as a certainty, an action to occur in the immediate future ("you *will nowe before hand make certaine* acceptance"). And even though the writer promises that he "will not faile . . . to requite" his addressee's anticipated cooperation, this aristocratic rhetoric of "supposall and assurance" does not share the linguistic patterns of reciprocity marking the rhetoric of "pleasures and courtesy" examined above.

In sum, a baroque and complicated tentativeness and a direct and self-possessed assurance are the discursive markers of the respective knowledge claims of inferior and superior regarding the future actions of their addressees. We can identify other surprising contrasts between the letters if we attend to what discourse analysts Wallace Chafe and Johanna Nichols call "evidentiality," that is, "the linguistic coding of epistemology."[39] To analyze this coding, Chafe recommends "a taxonomy of evidential phenomena" that includes discursive markers of "the reliability of knowledge, the mode of knowing, the source of knowledge, nd the matching of knowledge" against available "verbal resources" or "prior expectations."[40] The concept of "evidentiality," even without the deployment of a fully developed taxonomy of evidential phenomena, offers a helpful perspective for recognizing how differently knowledge is constructed in the verbal details of the two "commendatory" letters.

One difference concerns the knowledge claims that give rise to the recommendations. "*I know* your Lordship *to be now presentlie disfurnished* of such a one," writes the subordinate; "*I am given to understande, that you are in election, and it is* also *verie likelie* you *shall bee* pricked by her Maiestie, high Sheriffe for this yeare" (emphasis added), writes the superior, inferring from this likelihood that the addressee may in future require an under-sheriff. So, whereas the superior expresses the outcome of his request as certainty and the subordinate expresses his only as likelihood, it is, in fact, the subordinate who initiates his request on certain knowledge and the superior on likelihoods. In other words, relative power bears a clear relation to knowledge construction and to the knowledge–action nexus.

Furthermore, in the contrast between the subordinate's "I know" and the superior's "I am given to understande," the letters construct different relations between the person and his knowing: the more complex passive construction of the superior lends an element of mystification, both with regard to the source of his knowledge and to the mode of his knowing. In a similar vein throughout the letter, the superior's knowledge claims about the person recommended tend to be cast as the outcome of his own complex acts of judgment: whereas the subordinate speaks directly of how his friend "is learned," the superior speaks of the "reckoning I have made of him," of what "I have well knowne and prooved to be in him." The ponderous phrasing, "I have thought good by these . . . to recommend," also demonstrates the superior's habit of complicating and foregrounding his own acts of meditation and judgement, stretching knowing out of a simple present condition into a deliberative process extended in time. In this regard, the asymmetrical language of superior and subordinate, like the symmetrical "pleasures" language exchanged between friends, is interdependent: the mystified knowing of the superior is not constructed by his voice alone but instead as a collaboration between the self-complication of his own "assured" style and the other-complication of his respondent's necessarily deferential style.

A final point in comparing evidential features concerns the nature and extent of the evidence the writers offer to support their claims about the recommended person's qualifications for a post. The subordinate offers three kinds of evidence: descent, personal qualities, and "the great good will I beare him." Personal qualities are specified and seem to be given the most weight. The category of descent is offered as a qualification expected to be held in particular account by the nobleman addressed. The superior offers his own judgment and preference for the candidate as the main evidence of qualification, and he makes only a brief mention of personal qualities – "his learning, skill, and honest usage." We get fewer specifics in the superior's letter, but, of course, neither letter, by today's standards, says much of qualities pertinent to the job. Along similar lines, Whigham has noted in his analysis of Doctor Toby Mathew's suit for the deanery of Durham in the early 1580s "the dearth of objective arguments" and, in particular, how little discussion is offered of what we would recognize as "qualifications for the office."[41] The insights into positioned style that Day's handbook encourages enable us to go beyond Whigham's generalization to suggest how the relative power of the correspondents bears a significant relation to the quantity and kind of evidence offered.

Thus we see, in the deep structures of knowledge construction, how relative power is figured in the grain of the discourse. Indeed, it may well be that what we observe in the limited example of letter-writing from Day's handbook has wider implications for how relative social status regulated knowing in early modern England, since even state business and scholarly communication regularly took the form of letters: indeed, the discursive instruments for communicating knowledge and information, on the one hand, and negotiating interpersonal relations, on the other hand, had yet to be separated and specialized.

In the latter half of this chapter, we have used Day as our guide to map out three socially positioned interaction styles – "humility and entreaty," "pleasures and courtesy," and "supposal and assurance." *The English Secretary* gives us insight into interaction repertoires for Elizabethan culture, including scripts available for enacting hierarchic relations and reinforcing social distinction and scripts that posit relations of effective equality. As with Erasmus, Day's logic of social practice understands risk mitigation, or repair work, as bound up in fundamental ways with the discursive articulation of social relations. Relations are not static things: their scriptings shift and change with the business at hand, so that while set forms to be imitated and assimilated can be provided for typical speech-acts occurring in typical relations, nonetheless the negotiation of a friendship or of a client–patron relation always requires some element of improvisational ingenuity in the particular instance. Furthermore, in this logic of social practice, the connection between risk management and relational articulation provides a motive for rhetorical copiousness in verbal interaction: repeat performances and improvisatory amplification are needed to accomplish the requisite relational maintenance work, work that also tends to make for the reproduction of existing relations and power structures. Nonetheless, this social logic available in the epistolary handbooks also highlights relations as enactments or performances and so opens up the ideology reinforced by repetition to an apprehension of alternative possibilities for performance. Setting Erasmus's scripting of relations beside Day's, we can see how such a performative understanding of social relation could make competing ideologies of relationship available to Elizabethans, and in this way perhaps even make social change thinkable.

As a coda to this chapter, let us consider the improvisational ingenuity with which Shakespeare performs the eloquent relation of client to patron in his only surviving "letters," the dedicatory epistles prefacing

Venus and Adonis and *The Rape of Lucrece*, both addressed "To the Right Honourable Henry Wriothesley, Earl of Southampton, and Baron of Titchfield":

Right Honourable, *I know not how* I shall offend in dedicating my unpolished lines to your lordship, nor how the world will censure me for choosing so strong a prop to support so weak a burden. Only, *if your honour seem but pleased, I account myself highly praised*, and vow to take advantage of all idle hours till I have honoured you with some graver labor. *But if* the first heir of my invention prove deformed, I shall be sorry it had so noble a godfather, and never after ear so barren a land for fear it yield me still so bad a harvest. *I leave it to your honourable survey*, and your honour to your heart's content, which *I wish* may always *answer your own wish* and the world's hopeful expectation.

Your honour's in all duty,
William Shakespeare

The love I dedicate to your lordship is without end, whereof this pamphlet without beginning is but a superfluous moiety. *The warrant I have* of your honourable disposition, not the worth of my untutored lines, *makes it assured of acceptance. What I have done is yours*; what I have to do *is yours*, being part in all I have, devoted yours. Were my worth greater my duty would show greater, meantime, as it is, it is bound to your lordship, *to whom I wish long life* still lengthened with all happiness.

Your lordship's in all duty,
William Shakespeare[42]

The obligatory performance of deference and self-abasement by a Shakespeare to an anyone is an obvious and a startling feature of both letters. But there is a remarkable contrast in how the letters encode epistemology: in the first letter, knowledge is in the control of the addressee; in the second letter, knowledge is controlled by the writer. The *Venus and Adonis* dedication pays the full deference of non-presumption to the patron. Writing to a nobleman whose own letters customarily foreground his access to knowledge ("Whereas I am gyven to understand," Southampton begins a 1592 letter to Mr. Hicks regarding repairs required to his manor house at Beaulye),[43] Shakespeare foregrounds his own disclaimer of knowledge about how Southampton will receive his gesture of dedication ("I know not how"). The two "if" clauses open up alternative possibilities, casting Shakespeare's own acts of deliberation as merely hypothetical. Yet, even the imagined possibility that the patron might make so small a gesture as to "seem but pleased" rates the fervent promise of the writer's further toils on his behalf – a division of pleasure and labor that anticipates the asymmetrical master–servant relation we have analyzed in sonnet 58. The action of judgment in Shakespeare's first dedicatory letter is cast entirely as the action of the other – the writer's efforts subject "to your honourable survey."

With early works such as *Love's Labor's Lost*, criticism has often noted Shakespeare's rehearsal of set rhetorical figures and forms – his apprenticeship in linguistic virtuosity. No less important to Shakespeare's rhetorical development, I would argue, is his rehearsal in the dedication to *Venus and Adonis* of a life form in words – of the social action of deferential address to a patron. Prince Hal in *1 Henry IV* takes pride in having the language to talk with the drawers in an Eastcheap tavern. The implication, as in Erasmus, is that linguistic and rhetorical mastery is not a matter of dazzling words, but of situated intercourse. Would Shakespeare then have taken less pride in his competent address to an earl? At the same time, Shakespeare's linguistic practice is almost always an art of variation. And in Shakespeare's dedicatory epistle prefacing *The Rape of Lucrece* the language of deference is rewritten, creating a hybrid script that combines linguistic acts of humility and assurance.

In the second commendatory letter Shakespeare gives his patron the visible deference of explicit assertions – his full due in praise ("of your honourable disposition") and in self-deprecation ("my untutored lines," "Were my worth greater"). But in the less visible construction of power relations in terms of knowledge claims, the letter complicates its rehearsal of the client–patron relation. It takes only a few bold strokes. The letter makes unequivocal assumptions about the addressee's reception of the writer's offerings ("The warrant I have of your honourable disposition . . . makes it assured of acceptance"). The letter raises no doubts or hypothetical imaginings concerning the acceptability of the dedication; nor does it premise the writer's own actions on the reactions of the other. The writer "dedicates," professes his deeds "yours," wishes his patron "long life" – all without hedging or qualification. He makes himself a full participant in the act of giving as well as in the act of knowing. Shakespeare's subtle revisions in his second published dedication to his patron register, as do the sonnets, a complex discursive recognition that he possesses forms of capital which complicate the power relation designated by social rank. While he owes duty and pays out his obligation, with his hybrid epistolary style, he also makes his own subtle and mildly subversive claim to recognition.

CHAPTER 4

Reading courtly and administrative letters

The field of cultural poetics has alerted scholars of the early modern period to the textuality of documents such as letters that were formerly treated merely as contexts for literature – it has alerted them to these documents' rhetorical performances and the cultural work they do, to the permeability of the boundaries between non-literary genres like the letter and literary genres like tragedy, comedy, or epic. Nonetheless, while individual scholars have produced brilliant textual analyses of particular social documents (including letters), these readings have often been informed more by epideictic ingenuity and a scattershot of reading strategies drawn from formalist habits, deconstructive practices, or figurist rhetoric than by reading practices more appropriate to the genre, that is, practices that can open up the particular eloquence of the Elizabethan courtly letter to rigorous close analysis. An exception is to be found in Frank Whigham's 1981 study, which brings contemporary sociology and historical rhetoric to bear on reading Elizabethan suitors' letters. Whigham regards the virtuosity of courtly letters as motivated by "courtly alienation" and insecurity, by a stress-filled environment where competition for scarce resources and status required competitive self-display and where the shoring up of a hierarchical social world required "repeatable assertions of relation."[1] The demands of insecure self-consciousness and competitive self-interest, on the one hand, and of societal maintenance, on the other hand, relate dialectically, in this view, to motivate the rhetorical copiousness of epistolary (and presumably also conversational) exchange. Whigham underlines the "*reciprocity* of courtesy,"[2] even if the individual letter-writer remains very much at the center of his study of Doctor Toby Mathew's petitionary letters, and he gestures toward an understanding of the co-construction of social world and subject in the practices of letter-writing and also toward the co-construction of addresser and addressee. Nonetheless, the method he offers for analyzing "the interior tactics of the letter," drawing on

"Aristotle's analytic divisions of oratory" to categorize in turn the strategies depicting the suitor, the strategies depicting the patron, and the objective arguments brought to bear,[3] are not fully answerable either to his ideas about the dialectic construction of the social world or to my conception of how radically positionality affects style.

No one has, to my knowledge, taken up Whigham's challenge to develop a more richly delineated practical methodology for the close analysis of early modern letters. The combined resources of current politeness theory and Elizabethan epistolary theory can provide what is needed to move forward from Whigham's inaugural insights and to develop a hermeneutics of the letter, including interpretive concepts and tools that may equally serve for epistolary discourse situated outside the "anxious" circuit of the court. Indeed, given the massive collections of correspondences preserved as the "state papers" that historians draw so frequently upon, to restrict attention to those letters we may style "courtly" and to exempt from consideration the administrative letters is, in effect, to reinscribe the boundary between the literary critic's "texts" and the historian's "documents." The early modern state transacted its administrative business, for the most part, in personal letters – letters out of which "history" has been constructed without regard for the rhetoricity of letter-writing – making the case for the rhetorical reading of administrative letters all the more critical and compelling. Whereas Whigham attributes the copious rhetorical performances of suitors' letters to the local anxieties of Elizabethan courtly interaction, the politeness theory and the epistolary handbooks both suggest that risk mitigation, or repair work, is integral to all verbal interaction with claims to civility; while the need to mitigate risk arises in all interaction, risk mitigation work will be at its most copious in a hierarchical or deference society. If the concept of repair work in epistolary interaction provides a crucial perspective on the rhetoricity of the letter, the related understanding of repair as conditioned jointly by the relative positioning of the correspondents and the risk level of the business at hand enables us to negotiate the complex dynamics of the letter's flexible decorum. To make the detailed discriminations among available repertoires of repair strategies we require for effective close reading of Elizabethan letters, we can draw on the complementary tools that politeness theory and epistolary theory have to offer, as the preceding chapters have suggested.

To conceive of politeness as repair and maintenance is also to understand the link Whigham's essay gestures towards between the enacted courtesy of letter-writing and social maintenance. Given the interactive logic of speech-act mitigation, what satisfies the imperative towards interpersonal repair work also satisfies the imperative towards social maintenance and the reproduction of existing hierarchical arrangements. "Politeness," as Pierre Bourdieu writes, "contains a politics, a practical, immediate recognition of social classifications and hierarchies, between the sexes, the generations, the classes, etc."[4] In their efforts to describe the Elizabethan social order, cultural historians have generally relied heavily on the contemporary descriptions of William Harrison, Sir Thomas Smith, and others to arrive at pertinent divisions of the population into large groups,[5] but, for the most part, they have disregarded the practical enactment of social organization in the politeness forms displayed in such everyday documents as letters. Without Brown and Levinson's insight into how politeness co-varies both with relation and speech action, even a theoretician like Bourdieu has lacked the equipment to read this politics of politeness with any great precision. Elizabethan politeness, as enacted in letter-writing, does inscribe "a practical, immediate recognition of social classifications," but, as I suggested in chapter 2, that recognition cannot be read in abstraction from its correlation to the speech-act business in hand. The politeness model makes resources available for mapping the microdynamics of the Elizabethan social order in terms attentive both to its typical relational dyads and its typical situations. Given what Keith Wrightson calls a graduated social hierarchy rather than a class society, power differences usually typify the interactional dyad, with negative politeness the characteristic pattern and with most exchanges asymmetrical in their styles. Furthermore, given a graduated social hierarchy, most speakers or writers will find themselves negotiating different power relations in their different interactions: hence, the social demeanor of an individual or group will not be marked by a single style but instead by a trajectory or repertoire of the several styles suited to the contexts repeatedly encountered.

This chapter analyzes the situated rhetoric of specimen letters by examining how their interaction schemes and variations construct and coordinate social relation and speech-act business. Given the prevalence and spectacular complicatedness of negative politeness in Elizabethan letters, I will analyze the variations to be found in two administrative letters: a letter by Sir Ralph Sadler and Sir James Croft to Sir William Cecil reporting on affairs in Scotland and a letter by Sir Henry Sidney to Queen Elizabeth giving an account of the cess tax in Ireland. In the first instance I will demonstrate how difficult it is to untangle the business enacted from the power relation enacted, and propose some consequences for our understanding of administrative letters. In the second instance I will identify some typical interaction schemes and explore the elaborate imaginative variations that can be played on them and the complex significances that can attach to them. In a culture characterized by its vertical relations and their extravagant rhetorical display, it is nonetheless interesting to identify situations in which language figures horizontal, or ostensibly equal relations. To this end, I will conclude the chapter by analyzing a friendly letter of request sent by Sir Edward Warner to Cecil, a letter in which the significance of the "friendship" rhetoric can only be deciphered in relation to the letter's "business" – to request the costly goods and furnishings left in the Tower after an important prisoner's release.

THE PERSONAL LETTER AS ADMINISTRATIVE INSTRUMENT

On 27 October 1559, Ralph Sadler and James Croft write to William Cecil from Berwick, the fortress town on the border of Scotland, advising him of the urgent need for Queen Elizabeth's assistance and open support of the Scottish Protestants in their efforts to expel the French powers from Scotland and requesting instructions on how to proceed in negotiating with the Protestant lords. Despite peace agreements signed in April 1559 both with Scotland and France, many developments from the outset of Elizabeth's reign exerted pressure on her to assist the Scottish Lords of the Congregation against the French encroachment in Scottish government and affairs. On the death of Mary Tudor in 1558, Mary Queen of Scots, wife to the French dauphin, was proclaimed Queen of England by her father-in-law, Henri II of France; during her absence in France, her mother, Mary of Lorraine, sister of the influential French noblemen the Duke of Guise and Cardinal Lorraine, governed Scotland as Queen Regent with her French supporters; in May 1559, John Knox returned to Scotland from Geneva, where he had fled during Mary Tudor's reign, and he inflamed the Protestant lords to take action to advance the Reformation cause and release Scotland from the French yoke.[6] The Scottish lords had opened up negotiations with the English by making contact with Sir Henry Percy, commander of Norham Castle, and with Sir James Croft, governor of Berwick. The English had reasons to consider giving support besides the advantages to be gained by Protestant self-rule in Scotland, for William Cecil and others had cause to fear that the French might invade Scotland en route to an English invasion. In response to this difficult situation, Elizabeth had sent Ralph Sadler to engage in negotiations with the Protestant lords and to distribute £3,000 to assist them; he was directed to maintain such "discretion and secrecy" that "no parte of your doings maye empayre the treatyes of peace lately concluded betwixt us and Scotland."[7] It is as this situation escalates that Ralph Sadler and James Croft write this letter of advice to William Cecil:

Sir R. Sadler and Sir J. Croft to Sir W. Cecil
   Yesternight we receyved letters in cipher from Randall, with others from th'erle of Arrayn, alias Beaufort, to the Quene's Majestie, to you and to us, and also certen other writings which we send you here enclosed, prayenge you that uppon consideration of the same, we may be directed from thence with spede, how we shall answer their desires in such sorte as to your wisedomes ther shal be thought convenyent, for now you may see great lykelihood what this mater woll growe unto.
   We have in the meane season thought good to put them in some hope of suche reliefe as with honor and secresie may be ministered unto them, and also have given them such advise as you shall perceyve by the copie of our letters presently written in cipher to Randall, which you shall receyve herewith. But surely we thinke if they be not relieved and supported by the Quene's Majestie, their povertie being suche as they alledge, they must of force desiste and leave of their enterprise to their owne confusion. And if by her Highnes ayde they may prosper and achieve the same, yet in th'ende, as far as we can see, her Highnes must either manifest herself on that syde, or els they shall not be able to stryve and wrastle with the power of Fraunce. Wherin we be bolde to say our poore mynds as men which from the bottom of our herts do wyshe and desyre th'establishement of this ileland in perpetuall unitie and concord, the lyke oportunitye whereof, that is now offered, we thinke we shall not lyve to see, if this be pretermitted, the consideration whereof we referre to the wisedom and depe iudgement of those to whom it chiefelie appertayneth, which can more depely wey it, and decerne and see further in the same then our poore witts can arreche. So we ende, commytting you to God, who directeth all to his pleasure. From Berwyck, the 27th of October, 1559.
Your assured poore frends,
R. SADLER.
JAMES CROFT.[8]

Even though this is a missive undertaking state business in urgent circumstances, the letter is nonetheless remarkable for its extravagant performance of negative politeness. The characteristic contradictions of negative politeness are played out, not in superficial forms of greeting and address, but in the critical construction of the information and advice that is at the heart of their important business. As with Day's commendatory letters, knowledge construction is intricately caught up in the politics of politeness. The see-saw of assertion and qualification emerging in such representative details as the writers' "surely we thinke" takes shape first in the opening request for direction as their urgent need for a speedy response is qualified by their strategies for asserting non-coercion and non-presumption: "prayenge you," they write, "that *uppon consideration of the same*, we may be directed from thence with spede, how we shall answer their desires *in such sorte as to your wisedomes ther shal be thought convenyent*, for now you *may* see great *lykelihood* what this mater woll growe unto" (emphasis added). Despite the pressing circumstances of the writers, the language opens up a large discursive space for the meditations, "wise" consideration, and convenience of the addressee; and, despite the information the writers have to offer about "what this mater woll growe unto," they open up room with the modal auxiliary "may" for other possible "lykelihood[s]" their addressee may choose to "see."

While they await further instructions, the writers offer a hedging report of the actions they are undertaking before an answer arrives: they have "*thought good* to put them in *some* hope of *suche* reliefe *as with honor and secresie may* be ministered" (emphasis added). But the full performance of politeness emerges as they urge their opinions and advice on the course of action to be taken by the Queen. While a careful reading of the letter suggests that a single course of action is being urged upon the Queen, a course without viable alternatives – that is, her public support of and alignment with the Protestant lords against the French in Scotland – it is presented as a complex construction of alternative possibilities. The two key sentences are cast in the conditional, the indirect manner reinforced by the consideration first of the negative alternative, with a passive construction displacing any imagination of the Queen's direct agency ("But surely we thinke if they be not relieved and supported by the Quene's Majestie . . . they must of force desiste . . ."). Having disposed of the negative alternative, this still permits a more positive course of action to be opened up as one of two alternative possibilities ("And if by her Highnes ayde they may prosper . . ."), but Sadler and Croft are arguing that secret aid is not enough, and they move towards their main point by way of a temporal qualifier ("yet in th'ende") and a qualification of their own powers of prediction ("as far as we can see"). "[H]er Highnes *must*," they finally venture, only to mitigate the force of their directive by a syntax branching off alternatives ("*either* manifest herself . . . *or els* they shall not . . ." [emphasis added]). Of course, the provision and closing off of alternative possibilities works in one way to build an argument for their position. Nonetheless, the strategies of argumentation are motivated by the politics of politeness, by the requirement to avoid presumption in advising the powerful. Within the situated rhetoric of the letter, even while the two advisors are those best placed to have the requisite knowledge, they must not presume to know what they know, or to do what they do. The contradictions come out in full force when, having carefully considered and weighed the wisdom of their recommendation, as confirmed by the syntax of conditions and alternatives, Sadler and Croft then refer the "consideration" of the matter "to the wisedom and depe iudgement of those to whom it chiefelie appertayneth, which can more depely wey it, and decerne and see further in the same then our poore witts can arreche."

Thus, we can see how the framing logic of the letter's paradoxical turns is socially directed. Furthermore, we can find out more about what typical interaction schemes these experienced diplomats are drawing upon by comparing letters written in similar situations. Indeed, the two main rhetorical patterns occurring in Sadler and Croft's letter – the provision of alternative possibilities and the assertion of the superior wisdom of the addressees even in the matter under advisement – appear (albeit in more perfunctory form) in advice given on the issue of Scottish fortification ten years earlier during the first Protectorship in the reign of Edward VI. William, Lord Paget of Beaudesert, a chief councillor, advises the Duke of Somerset and other members of Council against expenditure on fortifications in Scotland:

Then *yf warre with Scotlande bringe warre with Fraunce*, yt is good to consider whider we be hable to maintayne warre with Fraunce so many yeres as we shall make them wery to take parte with Scotlande. And yf we be, then maye we be the bolder to contynewe our conquest and fortifications in Scotlande. *But if we be not (as vnder correction) I thincke we are not then* to take more and fortefie more and *in thende* to be enforced to leave it over to your enemie, *albeit the first parte viz.* takinge, hath a visage of honor: yet the other parte . . . ys a certayne and inevitable dishonour in the judgment of the worlde . . .
. . . Wherfore myne opinion (which I declare simplie without entent to contende with your grace or my lordes therein *submittinge the same to your consideracions and wisedomes*) is to abandone Hadington as sone as youe can . . .[9]

Clearly, the syntax of alternatives and the deferring to a superior's ability to judge could both be recognized as practical markers of social difference, as part of an available repertoire of rhetorical behaviors that facilitate copious discourse and – at the same time – discipline it to the structures of authority.

In trying to situate the complicated rhetoric of Sadler and Croft's advice-giving, we still need a more adequate account of the positioning of the correspondents. For, if we consider the writers' status in relation to William Cecil, the measures of deference seem out of proportion. Both men had been knighted, and they held high offices in previous reigns: Sadler as one of two principal secretaries of state to Henry VIII and as an important statesman in Scottish affairs; Croft as Lord Deputy of Ireland in 1551–52.[10] The lords of Elizabeth's privy council address Sadler and Croft in their correspondence not only by their degree but also as "our very loving Frends," signing themselves, in return, as "Your loving frends."[11] Sadler, at least, shared a close bond of trust and friendship with Cecil: Conyers Read emphasizes that they "had fought together, twelve years earlier, at Pinkie Cleugh," and their extensive correspondence is marked both by frank disclosures and by cryptic suggestions that the one is to infer the other's meaning.[12] And even once Croft has joined in the secret commission at Sadler's choice and urging to Cecil that all letters "in this matier, may be addressed and directed to him and me ioyntly," Cecil writes to them as "myn honourable frends," signing himself "Your assured frend to command."[13] Certainly, this is not a relation in which the expression of advice or opinion would require the self-contradictory repair work displayed in the letter analyzed above. Why then do we find such elaborate politeness forms? The most likely explanation is that the letter was written with a double audience in mind. Offering as it does advice on the Queen's course of action, it may very well have been intended for her hearing and persuasion. Indeed, Cecil – writing to Sadler and Croft three days after their letter was sent but before he had actually received it – comments on the Queen's wavering determinations on the issues under debate and seems to urge Sadler to send letters that will counter the views in circulation against Scottish support:

At this present ye shall perceive hir majesties contentation, and as that shall prove well expended, so wer it necessary to bestowe more; to which purpose it were requisite that you Mr Sadler, if ye thynk it not unmete, shuld wryte hither. For here be many more lettres than ye wold thynk. Some not lyking the progress of relligion; some not so angry with the French good fortunes as I am, some douting other successes, as in marriadg, and such lyke, if prosperitie shuld follow there; and so with some more difficulte ayde is granted then semeth convenient. *In any wise, hasten them as ye have done, for so shall they fynd there worke easyer.*[14]

The repair work of the letter, this would suggest, may not even be intended for Cecil, who is known by Sadler and Croft to share the opinions they express in it. Instead, it may well be that the letter works indirectly, as a solicitation of an authority not directly addressed at all, an authority meant nonetheless to overhear and to "depely wey it" in her "wisedom and depe iudgement" so as to reach the determination being urged not only by the letter-writers but also by the nominal addressee.

The Sadler and Croft letter aptly demonstrates how complicated discursive procedures can be an index to social relation and to the risk level of the speech-act "business," even when the positioning of correspondents is complicated by secondary audiences, but it also suggests that the maintenance work done by the politeness forms in Elizabethan letters is not confined to the interpersonal level of relational repair. The letter is one of more than 241 letters and dispatches dating from August 1559 to April 1560 passing between the Queen's principal secretary and her agents on the Scottish border, or among the other principal actors in the negotiations.[15] Unlike the suitors' letters analyzed by Frank Whigham, in which the interpersonal repair work of the letters is clearly motivated by an individual suitor's wish to advance, secure, and maintain both position and relative status, the letters that pass between the Scottish borders and the secretary's office – letters that so eloquently enact interpersonal relation – are administrative instruments and enact state business. The important role of the personal letter in transacting the state's business in sixteenth-century England has often been noted, and – most recently – emphasized in Jonathan Goldberg's work on handwriting, signatures, and secretaries.[16] With the increased authority under Henry VIII of the principal secretary, Sir Hilary Jenkinson commented, "went the rise of a new administrative instrument – the informal letter in English"; and G. R. Elton argued that, from Cromwell's time as secretary, "every aspect of the government of England is reflected in the correspondence of the king's principal secretary."[17] Jonathan Goldberg quotes Gervase Markham's letter manual of 1618, *Conceyted Letters, Newly Layde Open,* to demonstrate in what "transparently ideological terms" the importance of letter-writing to government was understood by that time. Letters and other writings are there imagined as "soules" or "substances" by which "even the whole state of the world is sustained": "how shall Kings know and communicate their great actions, enlarge their bounds, redresse their peoples iniuries, how shal the noble, know intelligence to serve his Countrie, the Merchant trade ... or any or all sorts of people speake at a farre distance, but by the helpe of Letters only."[18]

If the vernacular letter is a chief instrument in early modern England of state government, then the practices of government must be closely caught up with the practices of letter-writing. Jonathan Goldberg has written about the empowerment of a state bureaucracy through the material practices of handwriting and through the material arrangements of the secretary's office, but the interconnection between the interpersonal rhetoric of the letter and the practices of government has not been extensively explored. Considered from the viewpoint of a central administration's need for accurate information from the most distant portions of the realm, the personal letter so oriented to the status of the addressee that it may characteristically shape an urgent message into an indirect suggestion – or certain knowledge into qualified opinion – may seem very far from an ideal state instrument. At the same time, considered as a mechanism for the gentle control of the state's servants "at a farre distance," the polite personal letter was, perhaps, the ideal instrument, for every word in the elaborate politeness regime of the Elizabethan epistolary style provided a means to shape and reinforce the reciprocal relation and cooperation of the correspondents, even more strongly in situations of disagreement, and so to extend and sustain the far-flung network of relations constituting the government service. In the politeness forms of state papers like Sadler and Croft's letter, in other words, we have access to the microstructures of an early modern state apparatus that is clearly an ideological state apparatus.

TROUBLE-MAKING AND TROUBLE-TAKING

On 20 May 1577, Sir Henry Sidney, on his second tour of duty as Lord Deputy of Ireland, writes to Queen Elizabeth to answer serious complaints against his enforcing of the "Cess," whereby the landholders of the Pale are required to contribute a portion out of every "Plough Lande" or "Acre" towards the feeding and maintenance of the soldiers garrisoned there.[19] Delivered to the court together with letters to the privy council by Edward Waterhouse, who also has written instructions to forward Sidney's causes in person,[20] the long letter constitutes, in part, the Lord Deputy's defense and counter-attack against attacks being made to the Queen against him by Barnaby Scurlocke, Richard Newterville, and Henry Burnell, who have traveled to the court to complain in person. Sidney's letter undertakes a second serious business in informing the Queen of a threatened invasion by James Fitzmorrice "and dyvers principall Gentlemen of *Fraunce*" and requesting from her two thousand foot soldiers, three ships, "a large Masse of Powder, Lead, Matche, and Peeces," and "20000 *l.* to mainteine that Warre" – the ammunition and money to "lye safe, vntouched in your Officers Custodye, as a dead Threasure, not to be issued, but for that Service onelye."[21] Given the grave business and high station of the addressee, there is nothing ambiguous about the rhetorical situation of the letter. It calls for and displays a negative politeness incorporating extreme forms of deference, as excerpts from the first and final paragraphs make apparent:

In the lowliest Manner I can, I most humblye beseache youer most excellent Majestie, to pardon me that I have so seldome written to your Highnes: So bad a Delyverie of my Minde I have by Pen, and so illeagible it is when I do it my selfe, as I rather thought it necessarye for me, to addresse that which I had to write to the Lordes of your Majesties Councell, and to pray theim to relate the same to your Highnes, then convenient to trouble your selfe with it. But nowe hearinge from some of my private Freindes there, that I am complayned of to youer Majestie, do presume in Defense of my selfe, to write thus rudelye. As I am enformed theyr Complainte is for that they are chardged with *Cesse*, and annoyed with Disorder of the Soldiours: And for that your Majestie may the better knowe, what that *Cesse* is, it may like the same to understand, that it is a Quantitie of Vittell, and a Prisage sett vpon the same, necessarie for soch Soldiors as here youer Majestie is contented, to be at Chardge with for their Defence, and of so moche as is thought competent for the Expence of your Deputies Howse . . .

. . .

Most deare Sovereigne, in the Beginninge of this my rude and evell digested Lettre, as their was Cawse, I besaught your Majestie to pardone me for so seldome Writinge to the same; and nowe have I greater Cawse: And so do I beseache your Highnes for Encombringe the same, with so many ill written Lynes, which I had once donne with myne owne Hand; but when I beheld theim, they seamed to me so evell favored, as I thought theim not worthy to comme into your Sight, but made theim to be written out agayne, by one that can better do it then I.

And thus, prayinge the Almightie God to contynewe with Encrease your Majesties Felicitie, with a greater Number of Yeares then ever Prince reigned in this World, and to crowne you after with a celestiall Diademe, I most humblye kisse the Feete of your sacred Majestie. From your Highnes Howse of *Kilmaynghame*, the xxth of *Maij*, 1577.

Your Majesties most humble and
obedient Servaunt,
H. Sydney[22]

From the opening plea to her "excellent Majestie" made in his "lowliest Manner" to the closing gesture to "most humblye kisse the Feete of your sacred Majestie," Sidney's letter is replete with familiar deference forms whereby he elevates Elizabeth's status and abases his own. Indeed, it resembles Sadler and Croft's letter in both displaying and denying a personal competence: in a well-written letter, Sidney presents himself as an incompetent letter-writer, scarcely able to produce the letter he is producing. His repeated representation of his own letter as "rude and evell digested" is, of course, a variation on self-deprecation: not only is the letter-writer "most humble" in comparison to her "excellent Majestie" but even the productions of his pen further signal his inferiority.

This letter brings into focus two pivotal themes of Elizabethan politeness – what I call "trouble-making" and "trouble-taking" – and illustrates how the practice of politeness could involve the playing out of imaginative variations on these standard rhetorical themes. The theme of "trouble-making" emerges as Sidney begs pardon for the infrequency of his letters addressed directly to the Queen: he had "rather thought it necessarye . . . to address that which I had to write," he claims, "to the Lordes of your Majesties Councell, and to pray theim to relate the same to your Highnes, then *convenient to trouble your selfe with it*" (emphasis added). It recurs at the close of the letter when he craves pardon "for Encombringe" the Queen "with so many ill written Lynes." The theme of "trouble-taking" emerges in the contradictory pull of the letter towards amplification and copiousness, especially in the elaboration of its civilities. The entire Elizabethan dance of civility may be said to turn on this opposition between the imperative to take trouble – to dance attendance – and the imperative to avoid making trouble – to respect distance. While the tropes of trouble-making and trouble-taking tend to be most prominent and exaggerated in situations calling for negative politeness, as in Sidney's letter, they shape the rhetoric even of the most commonplace and trifling of messages, those which Frank Whigham has associated with "checking in" or "keeping in touch."[23] Just this antithesis, for example, structures the contentless letter that Anne (Dacre) Howard, Countess of Arundel, writes to Sir Christopher Hatton on 20 August 1582:

Good Mr. Vice-Chamberlain, Having at this time so convenient a messenger, and never wanting at any time cause to remember how much I am beholding unto you, I was loath either to omit the opportunity of the one, or to show myself unthankful for the other; and therefore, since I found that writing was the best mean to satisfy me in either, I desired to recommend my letters to this bearer, and myself by them to your good opinion; which, as I have often said, and now must needs repeat, is one of the greatest comforts I have, and the greater, because I rest assured that the constancy of your friendship, and the goodness of your nature, is such as I shall never lose it without desert; and I know myself so well, as, by the Grace of God, I never mean willingly in the least respect to deserve the contrary. *I am loath to trouble you with long letters, and the less careful to enlarge the good-will I owe you*, because, as I hope, it is sufficiently known unto you; and therefore will here conclude, wishing you all good hap. From Arundell Castle, the 20th of August 1582. Your most assuredly ever,

A. Arundell.[24]

The Countess of Arundel requests nothing of Sir Christopher Hatton and tells him nothing that is not already "sufficiently known unto" him: the only explicit business of the letter is to sustain the good repair of the relationship through repetitive assurances – to say what she has "often said, and now must needs repeat." The balanced style of the Countess's letter rehearses the contrary pulls at the heart of civility, pulls that make for brevity, on the one hand, and for amplification, on the other hand: "loath to trouble [Hatton] with long letters," she is also heedful of the need "to enlarge the good-will" between them. This hesitation between reserve and approach – between the conflicting decencies of maintaining distance and assuring attention – is what the "trouble-making" and the "trouble-taking" tropes so common in Elizabethan letter-writing enact.[25]

So common is the trouble-making trope that it regularly provides the entrance into and closing off of reports and other business matters in state letters, as in the following examples:

. . . I am so bold as to trouble your Lordship with my opinion therin, as also to advertise your Lordship of some doings here in Skotland . . .

. . . Thus have I troubled your Lordship over longe with these matters . . . (Lord Hunsdon to Lord Burghley, from Berwick, 24 August 1575)

I am bolde to trouble your Lordship with these my letters, not for any greate matter that I have to certefye you, but in acknowledging my dutye and assured good will, which I wold be lothe to be conceived oblyvious of, as also being required by Mr. Wakeleye to write unto your Lordship in his behalfe concerninge his suytes . . . (Sir George Stanley to the Earl of Sussex, from Tryme, February 1560)

I besech your Lordship to pardon me yf thus I shal becom troblesome unto you to know some certenty of the [Queen's] Progres, yf it may possibly be. The time of provision is so short, and the desire I have to do all thinges in such sort as appertaineth so great, as I can not but thus importune your Lordship to procure her H. to grow to some resolucion both of the time when her Ma. wilbe at Lewis, and how long her H. will tary theare. (Thomas Sackville Lord Buckhurst to the Earl of Sussex, 4 July 1577)

And thus I wil (troblinge your Maiestie I fere) ende with my most humble thankes. (The Princess Elizabeth to King Edward VI, n.d. [15 May])

And so I leave to trouble you, although the poor tenants trouble me daily with their continual pitiful complaints, as being deceived in their opinions in laying out their money to have purchased their quietness, where, by this accident, they are with their own made subject to a charge unreasonable. (Lord Burghley to Sir Christopher Hatton, 1 September 1582)[26]

In these letters, the excusing of trouble-making, while by no means perfunctory, might nonetheless be read merely as a gesture at conventional decorum that does not affect reports of information in any substantial way, but in other instances it becomes clear that it plays a significant role in regulating and controlling the dissemination of information. Hesitation at "over-troublesome" intrusion in reporting information, in the two examples that follow, leads Archbishop Sandys to leave to his addressee's discretion the hearing or not hearing of his serious business and William Fletewood to impart serious news to Secretary Walsingham while at the same time requesting his mediation in troubling Lord Burghley with it:

Sir, I had in mind to have imparted unto you, ere this, the disordered and scornful submission made here at York by the insolent Knight and his godless confederates; but I forbear so to do, for fear lest I should be over-troublesome unto you. Yet now this bringer, my son, passing by London to Oxford, who was *auritus testis*, I have commanded him to attend upon you, and to declare unto you how the matter was here used, if it shall please you to hear him. (Archbishop Sandys to Sir Christopher Hatton, 17 August 1583)

May it please your Honor, I am bolder of you than doth become me, and specyally in wryting of matters unpleasant. The truthe is that within these two dayes Mr. Norton's mother hath drowned herself . . .
. . . I beseeche your Honor to make my Lord Treasurer acquaynted with this unfortunate cause, for surely I am loathe to trouble his Honor with such unpleasant matters. (William Fletewood to Mr. Secretary, n.d.)[27]

In these examples, the hesitation engendered by politeness motives connected with troubling someone of importance constrains the behavior of subordinates, just as Sir Henry Sidney claims it had prevented him from making his report about the cess tax directly to the Queen. Here we can begin to see how the personal letter as administrative instrument of the early modern state created ambiguities which could, on the one hand, cause confusion and contribute to incompetence, but could also, on the other hand, provide some of the Queen's servants with opportunities to control access to information and hence power. The prevalence of the "trouble-making" trope means that there is always an excuse available for withholding information from superiors, and it must have provided one important means by which Queen Elizabeth's councillors and commissioners could shield aspects of their activities from the royal gaze.

For William Cecil as the Queen's principal secretary, however, concerned to manage or superintend the government of far-distant parts of the realm, the interference between the trouble-making trope and the requirement for accurate and detailed reporting could create obstacles. Cecil's letters are full of complaints and rebukes directed at correspondents whose reports he judges to be too sparse or too confused. He exempts neither peers nor friends from these rebukes, as the following excerpts from letters to the Earl of Sussex (as Lord Deputy of Ireland) or his friend Sir Thomas Smith on embassy to France suggest:

Good my lord, lett your letters hyther conteyne more specialletie of your proceedings, for the shortnes thereof doth not so well content her Majestie. And so I take my leave of your good Lordship. (William Cecil to the Earl of Sussex, 7 October 1561)

I never thought so long to here from ambassadors. For God's sake hereafter devise some shyfts to let us know somewhat, though you send by Flanders by some merchaunts. But herin I ask your pardon, for I am assured your lott is over great, and so I take my leave. (William Cecil to Sir Thomas Smith, 13 November 1562)

Sir, although my leasur be small, that I am constrayned not onely to wryte to you the Quene's Majestie's letters, but also to all other parts, yet I will not leave to thank you for your private letters, praying you so to continew. That which my Lords here do fynd lack in, is that you kepe not a contynuation in the order of your newes; as by your letters of the 29th of November, it appered that the prince lay in sege at Corbell, and by those of the seventh of this moneth it appereth that he was nere Pariss: but how he left Corbell is not wrytten. And we here have reports that Monsieur D'Aubmale was taken prisoner, but beyng not wrytten by you I do not beleve it . . .
. . . You wryte of three thousand Spaniards newly arryved at Pariss; but from

whence they cam appereth not. So as you see how in playne manner I wryte to you, praying you to interprete me to the best; for though I thus wryte to yourself, yet I doo not leave you unexcused here . . . (William Cecil to Sir Thomas Smith, 14 December 1562)[28]

The conflict between adequate reporting and the "trouble-making" trope is made explicit when Thomas Randolph, writing of Scottish affairs, defends himself against Cecil's complaint:

Your Honour, as in the beginninge of your laste letter, greeved that you had no knowledge from me of the Quene's arrival, but from Berwick. I assure your Honour, yf you had not two lettres that bore date the 19th of August, both you and I are deceaved . . . This I thought good to wryte, that your Honour maye knowe that I feare rather that I trouble you too oft, then that I leave anye thinge unwrytten that I judge my dutie chargeth me to make you privie of. (7 September 1561)[29]

Given Cecil's elaborate efforts to regulate the reporting practices of his correspondents, one might wonder why the personal letter nonetheless survived throughout Elizabeth's reign as the main instrument of her chief minister's labors and why Cecil did not endeavor to separate out reporting forms from politeness forms. It seems plausible to suggest that Cecil's own identity and self-esteem may have been closely caught up in the epistolary rhetoric of trouble-making and trouble-taking: that the troublesomeness of his life and occupations is a defining theme for him. When Cecil describes himself to his friend, as he often does to his correspondents, as being continuously troubled with his affairs, as having "leasur . . . small" for private matters, he is not merely stating facts. His words are also a register of his increasing power and authority, an acknowledgment of his status as the powerful person correspondents hesitate to "trouble." Hence it may have been that even Cecil profited from the interferences between the polite excuse of "trouble-making" and the accurate and objective construction of information.

The "trouble-making" theme then, which Sir Henry Sidney's letter to Queen Elizabeth has opened up to our more general exploration in Elizabethan state letters, can interfere with reporting, but it also offers subordinates opportunities to shape information to their own advantages at the same time as it contributes to a different empowerment of their addressees. Let us turn briefly now to the compensatory theme of "trouble-taking" as Sidney's letter develops it. Sidney's "trouble-taking" in recognition of the superior status of his addressee takes the form, of course, of his copious and elegant performance. But its most distinctive manifestation involves the material practices of handwriting and the symbolic significance that becomes attached to his writing in his own hand.

It was Sidney's usual practice, as deputy in Ireland, to employ a secretary for his correspondence. In a memorial written of his old master, Edmund Molyneux reports that "At ech seuerall time he was sent deputie into Ireland, he was . . . furnished with a new secretarie": first Edward Waterhouse, second Edmund Tremaine, and third Molyneux himself. Molyneux was well placed to describe Sidney's usual composing practice in letter-writing: "Such ample instructions," he writes, "he would giue for the framing and writing of his letters, or anie other thing he committed to be conceiued and put downe in writing, and dispose the same in so good order and fine method, as a verie simple man, if he reteined and remembred but a part of that he said and deliuered, might supplie himselfe with matter inough to the purpose to write of."[30] In writing to Elizabeth, then, Sidney departs from his usual procedure of writing through the mediation of another's hand despite his claims about how "bad a Delyverie of my Minde I have by Pen" and how "illeagible it is when I do it my selfe." We need not suppose that this altered procedure occurs because no competent secretary was available: indeed, Sidney makes the remarkable revelation at the end of the letter that the letter Elizabeth is actually to see, despite its repeated insistences on the rudeness displayed in his handwriting, has been "written out agayne, by one that can better do it then I." It would seem instead that Sidney's painstaking in writing in his own hand is a marker of his "trouble-taking," a sophisticated and imaginative deference strategy: this would explain his decision not to excise the mentions of his own illegible hand even when the letter is recopied so that the Queen sees no material signs (the signature excepted) of his own hand. In fact, this curious practice permits Sidney to signal his trouble-taking with his letter to the Queen at two levels: both by writing it out himself at first and then by taking the trouble to have it recopied.

The theme of writing in one's own hand (where one has the recognized option, that is, of writing in the hand of another) is a recurrent one in Elizabethan courtly and administrative letters, and, while it can be prompted by other motives (haste, secrecy, convenience, for example), it often contributes to the delineation of social relation inscribed in the eloquence of these letters. Nonetheless, while the material practice of writing in one's own hand generally does signify the trouble-taking of the letter-writer, it does not invariably signify the relation of deference inscribed in Sidney's letter. More usually, when it is noted by the recipient, it is recognized as a special gesture at friendship or favor made by a superior – an act of condescension rather than an act of deference. This is often the case, for example, when Lord Burghley's correspondents express appreciation for his special attention to them, as in these examples from Sir Nicholas White and Sir Walter Mildmay:

My deare good Lord, I received by my nephew your loving letters, all written with your owne hande, which were more comfortable to me than I can expresse.
   I find in them a rule to direct me, and a pillar whereon to stay me, whom yourself hathe lifted up from stumbling downe, wherof I and my posteritie shall always carry a loving memory. (30 September 1576)

I humblie thanke you, my very good Lord, that it pleased you to bestow so large a letter uppon me of your hand, and therby to let me understand how thyngs passe above, and specially the King of Spaine's sending to entertayne assured amyty with her Majestie, which I will hope is so meant. (27 July 1574)[31]

The significance of writing in one's own hand may, of course, be variable in different contexts like any rhetorical trope, but it often seems to demarcate a private moment – to gesture at intimacy. In general, although the early modern state's business was conducted by means of personal letters emphasizing social relationship, the letters were nonetheless fairly public in nature: they were often meant to be seen by and shown to others, sometimes to specific secondary audiences, and they were delivered by bearers instructed to amplify or explain particular matters. To include with other official letters a letter in one's own hand, then, could serve to mark a special relation, or a moment of exclusive attention. It may be that the recopying of the letter that Henry Sidney sends to Queen Elizabeth not only demarcates an extra layer of trouble-taking but also re-establishes a prudent distance so that the letter can at once signal special attention and avoid presuming that attention to be acceptable. It may, in other words, dance in handwriting the often repeated motions of Elizabethan courtesy – approach, but not too near, withdraw, but not too far.

THE PROFITS OF FRIENDSHIP

We can understand the courtesy rhetoric of the letters analyzed above not merely as expressing or constructing a power relation but instead as effectively managing the coordination of a power relation with the speech-act risk of the business undertaken. The fact that politeness registers, at one and the same time, both social relation and discourse task opens up a space of ambiguity which the practical rhetorician can potentially exploit as a place of opportunity. We can see how this works in a letter written to Sir William Cecil by Sir Edward Warner, Lieutenant of the Tower, shortly after Lady Katherine Grey's release from an imprisonment in the Tower that was occasioned by the Queen's distress at the unauthorized marriage and pregnancy of a potential successor. The first half of the letter, taken alone, encourages a reader to link rhetorical strategies exclusively to the articulation of relationship:

Sir, I most hartily thank you for your gentyl letter of late sent me by my servant. I have therby good occasion to thynk your frendship passeth not away with myne absence; the which to my power I wil ever be redy to acquyt. Sir, the loss of Newhaven so sodenly, and in such sort, as it semeth, I am sorry for, to the bottome of my hart. But ageynst God's ordynance no man can stand: and not deming otherwise than by the proclamation, I leve it, many tymes thynkyng of you, of the last word that ever ye said to mee: which was, that you envyed my felicitie. And truly I thank God, I lyve here, though poorly, yet very quietly, and the countrie presently, thanks be to God! very clear of al syckness, or other penurys other then now and then a shyp taken by the French. God continue the one, and send sum spedy order for defence of the other. And now I say to you, that with all my hart I pity your burdene and travelsome lyf.

You know I have often wyshed you to seke som relefe. Ye shal therby avoyd both envye and danger. But now perchance ye wil thynk I am too busy; and therfore I wold no furder in these matters. But this I say, and you shal trust to it, if I were able eyther with counsel or otherwise to pleasure you, ye shuld be sure of it.[32]

The relationship articulated is not one of deference: the letter does not establish distance between the writer and recipient like the two letters we analyzed in detail earlier in this chapter. Here, although Sir Edward Warner makes a clear distinction between his own quiet life and Sir William Cecil's troublesome lot, nonetheless we encounter at the outset not a rhetoric of division but instead a rhetoric of identification. The language gestures toward a reciprocity in the relationship: Warner matches up Cecil's actions and dispositions with his own – for Cecil's "gentyl letter" he returns his hearty thanks; for Cecil's assurance of enduring friendship he offers his in exchange. His use of the verb "to pleasure" signals Warner's discursive construction of the relation as one between effective equals as does the presumptuousness of his manner. Warner presumes to know something of how Cecil feels (i.e. inward grief of heart at the loss of Newhaven); he also presumes that his own sustained mental focus on Cecil's situation and on Cecil's words ("the last word that ever ye said to mee") will be welcome to his friend. Above all, Warner presumes to pity Cecil, and to pity someone who might not recognize a relation as close or as equal can be to presume very far.

Warner's choice of positive rather than negative politeness in his address to Cecil is somewhat surprising. It would seem more suited to a writer of very high social status, as is the case when Sir Henry Percy, the Earl of Northumberland, addresses Cecil (then Lord Burghley) in 1576 with similar inflections:

Right Honorable and my very good Lorde, I have hearde of late that your Lordship hath not been well, and that you have kepte your chamber, which I am hartyly sory for; and being desirous to knowe in what case your Lordship is, I have sent to understand the same, wishing to your Lordship not only helthe, but also comforte and harte's desire to you and all yours. I live here lyke a rustyke, and yet I assure your Lordship very well contente therewith, for altho' it be solitary, yet is it quiett. I do nowe finde what delyte and pleasure your Lordship hath had in buylding; for in reforming but a fewe windows and making a seller, and some other lyttell necessaries, I finde contentation. But if I were able and had suche workes as your Lordship hathe, I shoulde take too muche delyte therein. Of all humours it is the moste pleasante, I must confesse. And thus, being desirous to hear howe your Lordship dothe, *I wishe unto you as to myself*, with my wyfe's harty commendations, and myne to my Lady of Oxforthe and my Lady your wyfe, and God's blessing to the lyttell Lady. From my house at Pettworth, this 22nd of March, 1576.

Your Lordship's cossen ever assured,
H. Northumberland.[33]

Assuming Warner is generally acknowledged to have less status than Cecil, if both rank and administrative position are taken into account, one wonders that he shares the discourse strategies of an earl in addressing the Queen's principal secretary. Can it be that the forms of affection and familiarity deployed by Warner reflect or acknowledge an existing level of intimacy between the two men? Or is it more likely that they capitalize on the opportunity afforded by some kind words in Cecil's "gentyl letter" (quite possibly kind words meant as sympathetic condescension) to refashion the relation – to strengthen what must have been a very useful bond or alliance? The status of a man like Cecil in 1563, increasingly powerful though still not created a peer, would not have been fixed and invariable in its degree: it would have been susceptible to interpretation, and Warner's friendship rhetoric, co-constructing his own status and Cecil's as relatively equal, represents just such an act of interpretation. Thus, we can see how politeness forms could be made to function as vehicles for self-promotion and social mobility.

Once the chief business of Warner's letter finally emerges in its third and final paragraph, however, we must adjust our interpretation of Warner's advantage-taking:

> Sir, my Lady Kateyrine is, as ye know, delyvered; and the stuff that she had, I wysh it were sene, it was delyvered by the Quene's commandement, and she hath worn it now two yere's ful, most of it so torn and tattyred with her monkies and dogs, as wyl serve to smal purpose. Besydes, that she had one other chamber, furnished with stuf of myn, the which is almost all mard also. Now, Sir, I wold be lothe to have now any more busynes with my Lord Chamberlayn, if it please you to move a word to hym, that I may quyetly enjoy it; for that it was delyvered by the Quene's pleasure, I trust he wyl be so content. If I have it not, sum of it is fytter to be gyven away, otherwyse then to be restored to the wardrobe agayn: and that I justify with my hand. If he lyke not that I shal have the bed of down, I shal be content to forbear it. I send you here inclosed a bill of the parcels, with some notes in the margent truly written. If it please you to let me know your pleasure herin by two or three lynes, Sir William Wodhouse wyl se it sent unto me, and whatsoever it is, I shal, as becometh me, take it in good part. And I pray you, bere with me that I trobyl you with such a trifle. And thus I wysh you prosperous felicitie, with increase of godliness. From my poor house at Plumsted, nere Northwych. This 8th of Sept. 1563.
>
> Yours most assured to command,
> Ed. Warner[34]

Warner's business, it turns out, is not merely to commiserate with Cecil; it is also to request the used furnishings from Lady Katherine's rooms in the Tower. This turn of affairs suggests that Warner pursues in this case a more concrete advantage than social advancement with his politeness strategies. Capitalizing on an available opportunity to construct the relationship as close and familiar, given the politeness logic that keys the level of speech-act risk to relationship, permits him to construct the request itself as a trifling one: Cecil is to move but "a word" with the Lord Chamberlain to gain for Warner furnishings that "wyl serve" but "to smal purpose" and needs to write only "two or three lynes" by way of answer to Warner. Reading the inventory that accompanies the letter, it is hard to reconcile the luxury items with Warner's minimalist request: it includes – together with the bed of down – tapestry hangings, silk quilts, turkish carpets, a chair of velvet and cloth of gold, and many other items – although with marginal annotations attesting individual items to be worth "Stark naught" or to be "An owld cast thyng."[35] Like so many of the letters between "friends" to be found among the Elizabethan state papers, Warner's is grasping and self-seeking, taking small risks at the interpersonal level in pursuit of substantial material gains.

Warner's letter provides a fairly crude and transparent example of how a writer can coordinate the rhetorical construction of social relation and discourse task not merely to recognize and maintain existing social structures but to gain advantage and to move ahead. In this chapter, we have seen how the complex social rhetoric of the Elizabethan courtly and administrative letter figures social relation and inscribes relative social status, so that these written exchanges open up to close reading the microstructures of Elizabethan society – or at least its upper reaches. At the same time, we have seen how the stylistic complexity depends both on social relation and on discourse task, opening up a space of interpretive ambiguity that the skilled rhetorician can exploit to his or her own advantage to re-rank either relationships or discursive undertakings.

It would be fascinating to consider as well how the intended readers of these complicated early modern administrative letters negotiated the ambiguous space between social relation and discourse task, for competence in social discourse must involve not only discourse production but also reception and interpretation. Practice in reading thousands of such letters must have made William Cecil, for example, an expert interpreter. To glance in closing from actual letters to letters as represented in dramatic literature is to discover Shakespeare's attention to precisely this issue of interpretive competence. The comparison in *1 Henry IV* between Prince Hal and Hotspur turns to a large measure on the contrast between Hal's interest in and mastery of socially situated language and Hotspur's impatience with and incompetence in social exchange. Not only is Hotspur incompetent in face-to-face communication and mocking or dismissive of others, as is demonstrated in the missed opportunities for negotiation with the king's perfumed messenger at Holmedon and with Owen Glendower in Wales, he is also represented as an unskillful reader of letters, which the play foregrounds as critical to the enterprise of the widely dispersed rebel forces. Shakespeare's portrait of Hotspur as letter-reader focuses on Hotspur's direct quotation of two sentences from an unnamed lord's letter, interspersed with a running commentary that fully unfolds his reading process:

"But, for mine own part, my lord, I could be well contented to be there, in respect of the love I bear your house." He could be contented; why is he not, then? In respect of the love he bears our house! He shows in this he loves his own barn better than he loves our house. Let me see some more. "The purpose you undertake is dangerous" – why that's certain. 'Tis dangerous to take a cold, to sleep, to drink; but I tell you my lord fool, out of this nettle, danger, we pluck this flower, safety. "The purpose you undertake is dangerous, the friends you have named uncertain, the time itself unsorted, and your whole plot too light for the counterpoise of so great an opposition." Say you so, say you so? I say unto you again, you are a shallow, cowardly hind, and you lie. (2.3.1–15)[36]

Hotspur may be able to identify a formal stylistic choice made by the letter-writer ("*could be* contented; why *is* he not, then?" [emphasis added]), but the complexity of interpretation demanded by the strategic interplay between the assurances of personal relation and the cautionary or critical speech acts is entirely lost upon him. Where linguistic contradictions seem to arise as the letter-writer coordinates relation and discourse task (as is common in Elizabethan business letters), Hotspur simply concludes that the writer must be a liar, his profession of love mere flattery, and his message unworthy of serious consideration. A reader more attentive to the social rhetoric of the early modern letter would perhaps not have been able to sift all ambiguity out of the lord's letter, and yet he or she would nonetheless have been better positioned to hear the friendship and the criticism as compatible and to judge the counsel worth heeding.

CHAPTER 5

Linguistic stratification, merchant discourse, and social change

In *The English Secretary*, Angel Day seems to map out a full range of interaction styles, offering a letter suited to every situation and purpose. Nonetheless, he writes for those in the upper ranges of English society and hence the social relationships and interactions he maps out give only a very partial perspective on the complex and dynamic social reality of early modern England. Two other sixteenth-century handbooks in English respond explicitly to the communication needs of other social groups: William Fulwood's *The Enimie of Idlenesse*, the first letter-writing manual in English, appeared in 1568 and was sufficiently popular to run through nine further editions by 1621; and John Browne's *The Marchants Avizo*, which has been described as the first business-writing manual in English, appeared in 1590 and had gone through three further editions by 1640.[1] Dedicating his handbook not to a nobleman but to "Master Anthonie Radcliffe, Master of the worshipfull Companie of the Merchant Tailors of London" (p. 3, sig. A2), Fulwood is explicit about the social group he addresses as "equals" – that is, "merchants, burgesses, citizens, &c." (p. 11, sig. B2).[2] John Browne, himself a leading member of the Bristol Society of Merchant Venturers, a group also holding the key civic offices in that city, dedicates his volume to "Maister Thomas Aldworth Marchant of the Citie of Bristowe: and to all the Worshipfull companie of the Marchants of the saide Citie" (sig. A2). In David Cressy's tentative scheme of the social strata of English society, those addressed by these handbooks correspond to his third group of merchants, tradesmen, and craftsmen, coming after the gentlemen who comprise a first group and the clergy and professions who make the second. Yet Cressy comments that this grouping does not so much constitute "an homogenous social group" as "a handling category" which "unfortunately conceals differences of wealth and effective status."[3] Fulwood, nonetheless, addresses the range of this urban group, encompassing the high-status merchant groups and the lesser craftsmen and other citizens. Browne, on the other hand, focuses on the special communication requirements of a particular community and occupational group: he writes for the sons and apprentices of the elite Bristol merchants trading overseas in the Iberian peninsula.

In this chapter I consider the extent to which *The Enimie of Idlenesse* and *The Marchants Avizo* can provide insights into the social discourse of the "middling sort," and I suggest some intersections between the interaction types of these handbooks and the socially stratified language of Shakespeare's plays, including *Love's Labour's Lost, A Midsummer Night's Dream, The Merchant of Venice,* and *Timon of Athens.* This examination opens up perspectives on social conflict and on social change as we see these social dynamics enacted in the microcosms of verbal encounters between and within groups of different status.

SOCIAL STRATIFICATION AND LINGUISTIC DOMINATION

William Fulwood's early English handbook is in fact a translation, with minor changes, of the 1566 edition of a French letter-writing manual entitled *Le Stile et manière de composer, dicter, et escrire toute sorte d'epistre, ou lettres missiues, tant par response, que autrement.*[4] In four books, its first part sets forth "the necessarie precepts, which belong to the well composing and inditing of Epistles and Letters" (p. 34, sig. c5v), together with illustrative examples; its second part reproduces letters by learned writers taken from Politian's *Illustrium Virorum Epistolae*;[5] the third book, "containing the manner and forme how to write by answer," has a dialogic cast in its models for imitation, pairing a father's reproof, for example, with a son's response to it; and the fourth book treats love letters and includes some English examples in verse not taken directly from *Le Stile et manière*. Given that it is a translation, *The Enimie of Idlenesse* cannot be considered as a record, faithful or otherwise, of the typical interaction scripts of the London citizenry. It may nonetheless be helpful to ask what its readers could hope to learn and then reproduce in their own practice from this manual.

The "necessarie precepts" strongly accent issues of decorum: decorum of time, decorum of place, but above all social decorum. Although the handbook depends heavily on advice from Erasmus and the Latin formulary manuals and does eventually come around to the usual classification of letters as demonstrative, deliberative, and judicial (p. 56, sig. D8v), it gives priority to a classification of letters according to the social group to be addressed:

> Of epistles or letters there be three principall sorts, for some are addressed to our Superiors as to Emperors, kings, princes, &c. Some to our equals, as to merchants, burgesses, citizens, &c. Some to our inferiors, as to servants, labourers, &c. If wee speake or write of or to our superiors, we must doe it with all honour, humilitie & reverence, using to their personages superlative and comparative termes: as, Most high, most mighty, right honorable, most redoubted, most loyal, most woorthie, most renowned: and so of the rest altogether according to the qualitie of their personages: and it is to bee noted that of superlative, comparative, positive, or diminutive termes, wee must use but three at once at the most. (p. 11, sig. B2)

Here, the "we" of solidarity suggests a strong identification with one's own group or "sort": there is far less emphasis than in *The English Secretary* on a finely graduated hierarchy within which one's daily interactions are always situating the self slightly above or slightly below the other. Instead interactions are imagined as taking place on the one hand within one's own status group or on the other hand in relation to one's social betters or inferiors. The purpose of the manual emerges as two-fold: to offer the writer the equipment to take a relaxed pleasure in written communication with his friends and to offer the writer the equipment to negotiate what are treated as more tense and dangerous interactions across social groups. Fulwood writes of composing "without danger . . . both amply and eloquently" to friends, but warns, for example, of how in writing to "the spiritualitie" his readers must strike a fine balance to avoid offending:

> we must reverence them, and that by right . . . and if wee request any thing at their handes, wee must humble ourselves, giving them that honour and reverence which is justly due unto them. Yet wee must warily take heede that wee exalt them not too much and more than reason would permit, for so might we be noted of flatterie and adulation, and they themselves also might there withall justly be offended; therefore let us take heede that we write not rashly or unadvisedly. (p. 16, sig. B4v)

The handbook is full of this sort of advice to be heedful of risks and to take wary precautions in interacting with social superiors or in treating of "higher matters, than our knowledge or capacitie doth comprehend: for thereby are fooles knowen and manifested" (p. 17, sig. B5). As for the craftsmen in *A Midsummer Night's Dream* or the countrymen and scholars performing the Worthies in *Love's Labour's Lost*, for Fulwood's addressees the danger of giving offence by indecorums and the consequence of being judged stupid or foolish for indecorums are emphasized.[6]

At the same time that *The Enimie of Idlenesse* fosters a strong awareness of the need to attain a decorous standard of discourse, its reader is very unlikely to succeed in acquiring that competence through its instruction. Certainly there is some explicit advice on speech behavior together with the provision of examples:

It is to be noted, that it becommeth not an inferiour person, writing or addressing his wordes to his superior, to speake or write, by the imperative or commanding moode, as if one should say thus: *Soveraigne king, beholde a valiaunt man make him a knight: Beholde such a one, who is a good Clarke, give him a benefice:* But with all humilitie wee must say: *Worthie soveraigne, I assure your majestie that he is an expert man, pleaseth it you to have him in remembraunce. Such a one seemeth unto me to be verie learned and skilfull, it were a charitable deede of your majestie, to provide for him, and therefore I am bolde to commit him to your remembraunce.* (p. 14, sig. B3v)

The difficulty is that while the treatise makes strong warnings against indecorum and abuses of language, especially advising against "rare and diffused phrases, or inckhorne termes skummed from the Latine, not [*sic*] of too base termes and barbarous, or termes unknowen" (p. 18, sig. B5v), nonetheless it is almost impossible to distinguish between the examples of indecorum and the model letters. Consider, for example, the opening sentences of two recommended letters, the first to a king recommending a candidate for knighthood and the second to a judge recommending leniency towards an offender:

It behooveth me not (most Christian king) to write familiarlie to your sacred Majestie, for so might I be noted of presumption and foolish hardinesse, but considering that great benignitie and humanitie, whereby you give favour and supportation not onely unto them that have well deserved it, but even also unto strangers: for this cause therefore I have taken audacitie to write unto you, under hope to obtaine that which I earnestlie and most humblie require. (p. 36, sig. c6v)

I knowe for certaintie (most uncorruptible Judge) that you have alwaies hated, abhorred, and had in abhomination all sorts of malefactors and evill persons, correcting them and ministring upright justice ... (p. 42, sig. D1v)

Imitating such models, the writer will sound a little like Armado or Holofernes in *Love's Labour's Lost*, exposing his pretension and indecorum in the choice of the rare over the usual word ("I have taken audacitie" for "I am bold", in the unnecessary heaping up of synonyms, or in the use of figures of sound repetition ("hated, abhorred, and had in abhomination"); or, if he imitates without a sure sense of a rarified vocabulary, he risks sounding like Dogberry in *Much Ado About Nothing*, his arrogance made foolish by the malapropisms coloring his *synonymia*.[7]

In addition to the general resemblances I have been gesturing towards between Fulwood's manual and Shakespeare's depiction of linguistic stratification in some of his early comedies, there are enough small thematic and verbal links with *Love's Labour's Lost* to suggest the possibility of direct borrowing. With new editions of *The Enimie of Idlenesse* published in London in 1586, 1593, and 1598, it would have been readily available to Shakespeare when he was composing *Love's Labour's Lost* and *A Midsummer Night's Dream* (*c.* 1594), both of which rely for comic effect on the linguistic indecorum of the non-elite or the "meaner sort." Furthermore, the repeated use in *Love's Labour's Lost* of the letter as the vehicle of linguistic pretension makes it all the more likely that Shakespeare would have turned to the few available epistolary handbooks in English for ideas on how to develop this material.[8] In the introduction in *Love's Labour's Lost* of its central theme – that is, precisely, linguistic decorum – Berowne first raises decorum as a measure of his own linguistic performances ("Fit in his place and time" [1.1.98]) and then, when criticized by the other lords, deploys a sequence of vivid analogies to suggest that the King's prescriptions for study are unreasonable because they violate the decorum of time:

> Why should proud summer boast
> Before the birds have any cause to sing?
> Why should I joy in any abortive birth?
> At Christmas I no more desire a rose
> Than wish a snow in May's new-fangled shows,
> But like of each thing that in season grows.
> So you, to study now it is too late,
> Climb o'er the house to unlock the little gate.
>
> (1.1.102–09)[9]

In *The Enimie of Idlenesse*, a similar set of analogies illustrates how indecorum of time or place might make a demand too unreasonable to be granted:

The second is the time: as to demaund ice in Summer, or that one shoulde pay an oblation, or rent, before the time be expired.

The third is the place: as if my debter should owe me x. pound, to bee paide in the Royall Exchange, and I shoulde demaund it in Westminster Hall. (pp. 33–34, sig. c5r–v)

When Costard delivers Armado's pompous letter to the assembled lords, he anticipates his answer to the charges it bears against him in an elaborate excursion on the expression "in manner and form following":

COSTARD The matter is to me, sir, as concerning Jaquenetta. The manner of it is, I was taken with the manner.
BIRON In what manner?
COSTARD In manner and form following, sir, all those three. I was seen with her in the manor-house, sitting with her upon the form, and taken following her into the park, which, put together, is 'in manner and form following' ... (1.1.199–208)

The full humor depends on recognition of the phrase being varied: it is recognizable as the phrase consistently used by Fulwood to introduce a letter of response – "An aunswere to the same in like maner and forme" (p. 32, sig. C4v).[10] Similarly, a number of the learned or pretentious words upon which the linguistic ballet of the play turns also make an appearance in *The Enimie of Idlenesse*, including "remuneration," "abhominable" or "abhomination," and "condign."[11] Furthermore, it is possible that Bottom's frustrated effort in *A Midsummer Night's Dream* to express what "eye of man hath not heard, the ear of man hath not seen, man's hand is not able to taste, his tongue to conceive, nor his heart to report" (4.1.209–11) was suggested by the mismatched words concerning inexpressibility that open a letter of consolation in Fulwood – "It is not possible for me to write unto you neither is the heart of man able to thinke, (my singular and perfect friend) what sorrow and grief I had, when it was reported unto mee, that you were greevously sicke" (p. 94, sig. G2v).

More important for this study than possible echoes and borrowings, however, is how the strange amalgam in *The Enimie of Idlenesse* of decorous standards and incompetent performance helps to illuminate Shakespeare's analysis of socially based linguistic stratification in these comedies. Although Fulwood writes quite explicitly of how a middle-ranking status group should act out suitable forms of deference in their interactions with their social betters, social analysts in Shakespeare's own time often bifurcated these groups into the "meaner" and the "better" sort.[12] Plays like *A Midsummer Night's Dream* and *Much Ado About Nothing* clearly fall into this pattern in bifurcating social groups, with even the variegated cast of *Love's Labour's Lost* becoming dichotomized into the commoners and the nobility in the final act.

The important role that linguistic incompetence plays in these comedies in the representation of deference by the lower-status group can be only partially understood in terms of the Brown and Levinson politeness model that has proved so helpful for analyzing deference behavior among the privileged. It is fascinating to consider how the model constructs as "strategically selected" discourse even extreme forms of speech behavior that resemble the "tongue-tied simplicity" in *A Midsummer Night's Dream* of the "great clerks" who, having "purposèd / To greet [Theseus] with premeditated welcomes," instead "shiver and look pale, / Make periods in the midst of sentences, / Throttle their practiced accent in their fears, / And . . . dumbly have broke off" (5.1.93–98):

> In societies all over the world members of dominated groups or lower strata express deference to dominant members by bumbling, by the kinesics, prosodics and language of slow-wittedness or buffoonery . . . For instance, in front of a landlord, a Harijan [low-caste speaker in a Tamil village] when reprimanded may giggle like an English child; when given instructions he may appear slow to comprehend; when speaking he may mumble and speak in unfinished sentences as if shy to express foolish thoughts; and when walking he may shuffle along. All this contrasts with the same man bargaining with less powerful but still high-caste persons, and there can be no doubt that this bumbling is a strategically selected style.[13]

When Brown and Levinson analyze even these performances of stupidity and bumbling as the competent enactment of politeness, their analysis certainly brings the politics of politeness into perspective, for it demonstrates forcefully how acts of civility extend into acts of exposure, humiliation, and domination in which the disempowered subjects themselves collaborate. While the Brown and Levinson interpretation is at variance with the judgments of most of the courtiers gathered for the Pyramus and Thisbe play, who read the bumbling of the craftsmen as incompetence and innate stupidity, it is consonant with Theseus's inclination to "read" a respectful welcome in "tongue-tied simplicity" and "in the modesty of fearful duty" (5.1.100–04). Theseus, of course, constructs his own reading as an act of generosity, but it is also a self-satisfied recognition of social difference, defining his own group's full adequacy through the inadequacy of the "meaner sort."

Obviously, the performers in *Love's Labour's Lost* and in *A Midsummer Night's Dream* do not see themselves as selecting foolishness and bumbling as a deference strategy. More often, we find the speakers of the "middling" or the "meaner" sort behaving as we might imagine Fulwood's readers to behave: cognizant of a legitimate standard of competence in cross-class encounters, they aim at it as a prestige discourse in the hope that it will win them a measure of distinction or, at the very least, allow them to escape "offence"; at the same time, however, they lack the mastery to assimilate the prestige forms successfully to their actual performance. They hypercorrect, producing a different effect from what they intend. The mechanism of social stratification at work here closely resembles a pattern that Pierre Bourdieu, following William Labov, has theorized.

Bourdieu sees language as a competitive field, in which the disparity among groups between knowledge of a legitimate language and its recognition promotes a dynamic of assimilation and dissimilation that drives linguistic change within a framework of social reproduction:

> the social mechanisms of cultural transmission tend to reproduce the structural disparity between the very unequal *knowledge* of the legitimate language and the much more uniform *recognition* of this language. This disparity is one of the determinant factors in the dynamics of the linguistic field and therefore in changes in the language . . . Thus, if the linguistic strategies of the petite bourgeoisie, and in particular its tendency to hypercorrection – a very typical expression of 'cultural goodwill' which is manifested in all areas of practice – have sometimes been seen as the main factor in linguistic change, this is because the disparity between knowledge and recognition, between aspirations and the means of satisfying them – a disparity that generates tension and pretension – is greatest in the intermediate regions of the social space. This pretension, a recognition of distinction which is revealed in the very effort to deny it by appropriating it, introduces a permanent pressure into the field of competition which inevitably induces new strategies of distinction on the part of the holders of distinctive marks that are socially recognized as distinguished.[14]

Bourdieu's analysis may not be wholly adequate to classes that are only in the process of formation, as in early modern English society, and yet it provides a useful paradigm for reading the cross-group linguistic negotiations of *Love's Labour's Lost*. There the court speech is recognizable as distinguished, and outsiders to the court like Armado, Holofernes, and Nathaniel strive for assimilation to this prestige language. As is the case in later comedies with Dogberry and other over-reaching speakers, the play's thematizing accents the difference rather than the similarity of their verbal acts of emulation. Their vulgarity is an effect of their efforts to attain an elite cast of speech. In *A Midsummer Night's Dream* and in most of the other comedies representing social stratification through the mechanisms of language, the representation of linguistic domination culminates in a tense, formal situation that reasserts the distinction of the social superiors by devaluing and rendering foolish the ambitions and speech products of their inferiors. But in *Love's Labour's Lost* Shakespeare takes the analysis one stage further.

One strange effect of the overblown feast of rhetoric in that play is that, despite the continual assertion of differences, with the court parties consistently playing the arbiters of decorum, characters tend to sound very much alike. Camille Wells Slights makes this point, commenting that

> Although critics have distinguished among the characters on the basis of their attitudes towards and uses of language, for me, and I would argue for most of the theater audience – even an Elizabethan audience more familiar with subtle rhetorical patterns than we are – the primary effect is stylistic similarity rather than variety.[15]

If the efforts at assimilation made by the various social groups outside the courtly inner circle do indeed come closer to success in this play than is generally acknowledged to be the case, then it may make sense to read the final gesture of the play, the scene of the lords' second oath-taking that apparently leaves behind the negotiation between social groups to treat of the lords' reformation, as still a part of the production of status difference. To interpret the demand that the ladies make of the lords – that they abandon their "silken terms precise" for speech whose "prosperity lies in the ear / Of him that hears it" (5.2.406, 843–44) – actually requires a large measure of rationalization. It requires the hearers of the play to construct the linguistic practices of the women and the men retrospectively as differentially defined throughout the play. This cue to distinguish difference between two character groups equally obsessed with word play and rhetorical performance does often become an interpretive imperative in detailed readings of the play's languages. But it may be more important to see what it conceals: the impulse within the elite group to produce, in Bourdieu's terms, new strategies for distinction or "dissimilation" in reaction to the threat to their cultural capital from their upstart imitators – to produce "endless refinements, with constant reversals of value which tend to discourage the search for non-relational properties of linguistic styles."[16] The privileged elite react to the verbal self-display of the meaner sort, then, not merely by the direct assertion of difference in judgments about the incompetence of the upstart groups but they also react by indirection in the invention for their own group of a more mystified standard of legitimacy.

STRANGE SHORES, FAMILIAR STYLES

The Marchants Avizo can offer insights both into the actual interaction practices of the elite merchants trading overseas and into social innovation in their language use. John Browne assembled the handbook to provide discourse repertoires for the "Sonnes and Servants" of Bristol merchants like himself and his dedicatee, Thomas Aldworth, to use "when they first send them beyond the Seas, as to *Spayne and Portingale or other Countreyes*."[17] He introduces the letter collection as "a briefe forme of all such letters as you shall neede to write throughout your whole voyage. The which forme is effectual and sufficient inough, and may still be observed, untill by experience you may learne to indite better your selfe" (p. 8). In addition to model letters suited to the apprentice's specific needs on a trading voyage, this business manual also contains notes on weights, measures, and "value of monies" in Portugal, Spain, and France; descriptive notes about such wares for purchase as pepper, cloves, mace, cinnamon, calico, cochineal, oils, and wines; a complete sample account for a voyage with detailed entries for "sales" and "impliments"; and "forms" for such financial instruments as the apprentice may need to employ, including a bill of exchange, an acquittance, a bill of attorney, a bond or obligation, and a policy "or writing of assurance." The sample writings seem to be based on actual documents relating to Thomas Aldworth's trading ventures: at least Browne acknowledges the account reproduced to be "the accompt of my Master, Alderman Aldworth" and many of the letters and documents (all dated in late 1589) are signed R. A. for Thomas Aldworth's nephew and servant Robert Aldworth.[18] Clearly, Browne's book, an experienced Bristol merchant's version of a Bristol's merchant's interaction repertoire, offers much more direct insight than *The Enimie of Idlenesse* into the practices of his group.

At the same time, Browne's handbook offers insight into social invention in language, the invention through discourse of new "forms of life." If a writing handbook like *The English Secretary* reproduces established social relations, *The Marchants Avizo* has a very different agenda, one motivated by the need to provide language for new (and potentially distressing) situations, to find discourse scripts commensurate with new forms of activity and relationship. Browne is acutely aware of how the merchant's ventures take him not only into strange lands but into communication situations that are unmapped and disorienting: "by my own experience," he writes, "I knowe, how greatly myselfe and many other my countrimen, at our first going into Spayne were troubled with difficulties, for want of such a patterne as this, for ease of our tender wittes" (sig. A2). Here, for a moment, we have privileged access to how changing material conditions can promote verbal innovation and to how, in turn, discourse can renegotiate social relationships. That merchant trade was in the process of altering social relations in the sixteenth century has often been asserted in recent criticism, and Browne's handbooks allow the opportunity to test generalizations about the shape of this change against an exemplary instance. The grander narratives about change can benefit from the adjustment and fine tuning to be gained by examining the microencounters of verbal interaction. The keynotes of the usual narrative about how merchant trade and commercial practices changed social relations and affected language are impersonalization and competitive self-interest. Such a narrative is fleshed out in fascinating detail by Jean-Christophe Agnew, who argues that, between 1550 and 1750, "a volatile and placeless market" triggered a "crisis of representation" that "transfigured" social relations, a crisis in which he sees the theater as also implicated.[19] Agnew emphasizes how the "liquidity" of the money form radically changed the nature of the exchange transaction, extending the immediate exchange between two people in time and space by splitting it "into two mutually indifferent acts: exchange of commodities for money, exchange of money for commodities; purchase and sale."[20] This material condition of the market exchange, with its deferral of face-to-face negotiation, marked the merchant's relations and his emerging discourse as impersonal, and in Agnew's theatricalized reading, increasingly dissimulative: as *mis*representation, the secretive holding back of private meanings. In this narrative, the transformation occurring is unidirectional: "commodity exchange was gravitating during the sixteenth and seventeenth centuries toward a set of operative rules that fostered a formal and instrumental indifference among buyers and sellers." The market, this argument goes, has no place for reciprocity as a new "logic of mutual indifference" comes to define the exchange transaction.[21] I will not be arguing against the view that something like this change occurs over a long period of time. But "crisis" seems the wrong word. No crisis takes two centuries, and the microanalysis of change that Browne affords leads one to call into question the simple linear construction of the trajectory of change that goes with the "crisis" narrative. In particular, I will be looking at how Browne's handbook adapts and reaccents styles familiar from *The English Secretary*, specifically the styles of "humilitie and entreatie" and of "pleasures or curteu[si]e," applying them to changing contexts and new uses. By also considering two instances where the style of "pleasuring friends" is adapted, reaccented, and – in Bakhtin's special sense – "disputed" in Shakespeare's plays, *The Merchant of Venice* and *Timon of Athens*, I will explore a significant point of contact between the social invention, or "prosaic creativity," in the merchant's scripting of discourse and the artistic form of verbal innovation in Shakespeare's dramatic composition.[22]

Over recent years, social historians have developed a much fuller picture of the merchant's position in the Elizabethan social organization. In centers of commerce, merchants have been shown to be among the most substantial citizens, both in wealth and in effective social status. David Cressy's rankings of London tradesmen according to wealth and illiteracy levels in the years 1580 to 1700 produced two surprising and pertinent results in this regard: first, the merchants sampled were almost four times as wealthy as "the next-nearest tradesmen," including mercers, tanners, and maltsters; second, with illiteracy being measured by the use of a mark in the place of a signature, the merchant sample group had no illiterate members.[23] The fact that the Bristol merchants produced and circulated a business writing manual for the training of their apprentice members strongly suggests that they shared in this full possession of literacy. David Harris Sacks's invaluable study of Bristol and the Atlantic economy from 1450 to 1700 gives a more specific picture of the situation of the merchant group for whom John Browne is writing. His study shows how the overseas trade of the city moved through three major phases, from the yearly exchange in the early fifteenth century in Gascony of cloth for wine, to trade southward in the second half of the sixteenth century centered in the Iberian peninsula and driven by the import of a limited number of rare and expensive commodities, to transatlantic commerce in the seventeenth century involving a wide range of goods.[24] The special privilege and status of a prosperous group of approximately seventy-five "mere merchants," men who devoted their commercial efforts entirely to the overseas trade with the Iberian peninsula, was consolidated in 1552 with the incorporation of the Society of Merchant Venturers through letters patent granted by Edward VI. An Act of Parliament in 1566 supported their exclusive right to the overseas trade, and while this principle of specialization that denied retailers and other craftsmen rights to the foreign trade was so contentious that the other groups, led by prominent clothiers, succeeded in achieving its repeal in 1571, the establishment of the Spanish Company in 1577, a new national commercial organization with Bristol membership, effectively renewed the privileges of the mere merchants. This group dominated the civic government in the late sixteenth century: both John Browne and Thomas Aldworth belonged to the Society of Merchant Venturers and served terms as Mayor of

Bristol.[25] Despite what John Browne describes as "a long stay of the Marchants trade, to the great decay of many a one" (sig. A3) due to the war from 1585 with Spain, the Merchant Venturers were for the most part its wealthiest citizens. Sacks's analysis shows clearly that this group came to be positioned at the top of a civic hierarchy, not, as William Fulwood's grouping of the "merchants, burgesses, and citizens" of London suggested, as equals in a larger corporate body. Sacks actually demonstrates that social mobility among the citizens of Bristol declined in the late sixteenth and early seventeenth century as this tightly knit group of entrepreneurs drew increasingly on their own sons and kinsmen for apprentices and servants.[26]

As I suggested earlier, Browne accents the novelty and disorientation of the merchant apprentice's business, remembering his and his associates' troublesome "difficulties" when first venturing into Spain, "for want of such a patterne as this, for ease of our tender wittes" (sig. A2):

my chiefe purpose herein is, onely to worke a generall ease to all Marchants: whereby they may the lesse trouble themselves, either with writing, invention, or thought of these matters. And likewise that it might be some stay to young and weake wits: yeelding them thereby the more freedome of minde toward their own businesse. (A2v)

Unlike Day, Browne registers no interest in the creativity of everyday language use or in helping his readers towards eloquent rhetorical performances. His interest in providing a storehouse of interaction scripts is utilitarian. He recommends the rote practice of copying out scripts as appropriate for acquiring the essential forms of verbal competence, noting that "If this booke may not bee thought tollerable beyond the Seas: then it will be yet a good exercise and but little labor, for euerie Prentise to copie it all out in writing: and so carie it with him for his instruction" (A2v). Browne also disclaims for himself any creative invention in the making of the book: "Mine owne labour or skill I confesse, is but very little or nothing in this thing, because I myselfe doo but onely as a poore willing labourer, to helpe forwards that worke, the foundation and platforme whereof, is setled and builded alreadie" (A2v). Even while Browne's manual arises out of change-making moments of defamiliarization, he builds up a communication repertoire continuous with the apprentice's everyday practices: he works to normalize the apprentice's interactions. Hence, in his directions to the apprentice on appropriate conduct and conversation, he gives attention first and last to daily prayer: "let this bee your first and chiefest poynt in all your actions: that especiallie you omit not your duetifull service towards almightie God, but every morning and night, to pray that God will still prosper and protect you, and to give him humble thankes that hee hetherto hath alwaies mercifullie defended you" (p. 6, sig. B3v). His detailed advice for performing the prayers "you have learned by heart" (p. 6, sig. B3v) turns out to be continuous with his directions for making reports to the merchant at home, for bargaining over prices, and for negotiating encounters with Spanish countrymen and other foreigners in that Browne makes humility their main key:

Moreover be you in any wise circumspect touching your behaviour when you be in the Countrey of Spaine or else where: and shewe your selfe lowly and courteous to all people, and learne what be their Lawes and customes, and bee carefull to keepe them. If anie of the rude and common sort of people (as so it is in all Countries) will by chance offer you anie abuse or wrong, appease them againe rather by sufferance and gentlenesse, than by revenge: for so shall you best quiet your selfe, and overcome your enemie. (p. 5, sig. B3)

Deference in self-presentation is the repeated theme of Browne's instructions for personal conduct, recommended as a kind of multi-purpose style serviceable wherever there is confusion. In this recommendation, he is adapting deference to a use distinct from its courtly use as a precise acknowledgment of the social superiority of the interlocutor. Here it serves both to manage the risk involved in verbal encounters where relative status is ambiguous and to diffuse potential hostility: "in any case shew your selfe lowly, curteous, and serviceable unto everie person: for though you and many of us else may think, that too much lowlinesse bringeth contempt and disgrace unto us: yet . . . gentlenesse and humilitie . . . will both appease the anger and ill will of our enemies, and increase the good will of our friends" (p. 3, sig. B2). So serviceable and all-purpose are the forms of deference for the Bristol merchant that they find a place not only in the recommended conversational demeanor and model letters but even in the business forms, as in the "forme of a bill of exchange for the countrey of Spaine," which begins "Worshipfull: may it please you to pay upon this my first bill unto R. N. or the bearer hereof, within 15 daies after the safe arrivall of the Gabriell of Bristow to her Port of discharge, thirtie and three pounds, sixe shillings and eight pence" (p. 53, sig. H3).

Deference provides a normalizing language and a resource for negotiating unfamiliar relations, but the latter receive far less attention than do interactions among English merchants and associates. One might well expect, in reading Browne with anticipation shaped by something like Agnew's narrative of change, a concentration on the invention of scripts for negotiating cross-cultural exchanges, perhaps the depersonalized scripts Agnew predicts will be marked by calculated role-playing or dissimulation. But direct references to encounters across language and cultural barriers tend to be bypassed in the manual by advice to depend on other English merchants at critical points: "before you enterprise any thing," the apprentice is advised, "do you after curteous & gentle manner aske counsel, either of some Marchant in the Ship, or your Hoste, or of some English man" (p. 3, sig. B2); "and likewise . . . when you receive your moneys for your wares, crav[e] the paines of some Marchant your friend, as to helpe you the first time to receive it for you" (p. 4, sig. B2v). The real surprise of the manual is the model letters for communicating with and asking assistance of the apprentice's English friends and associates: here what we find is the language of gentlemen as Day represents it in *The English Secretary*. Browne's sample letters reaccent the reciprocal rhetoric of "pleasuring friends":

To be written to a friend, giving him thanks for some pleasure he hath done for you, and requesting againe some farther good turne of him.

Emanuel.

After my very hartie commendations unto you: I pray for your good health and prosperitie, &c. These are giving you most heartie thanks for your great paines & gentlenes heretofore shewed unto me: *assuring you that you shall finde me to the uttermost of my power, both gratefull and mindfull to pleasure you againe in the like and greater if I be able.* Desiring you hartily yet once more, to let me crave so much your good wil, as *to do me again this one pleasure*: which is, to deliver this letter herein closed, to master P. R. Draper, that dwelleth in Lisbon in the *Roa nova*: and that you would receave for me of him 100 Dks. which I have written to him to pay you. And when you have receaved it, that you would be so good as to imploy it all in good Pepper, and to set my masters marke on it, which is as in the margent. Praying you to agree for freyte, and to procure to have it laden in the *Pleasure*, & to write a letter unto my Master about it. I am sorie that I am driven *to make still so bold upon you: wishing that you had the like or greater occasion to trie also my good will towards you.* Little news I hear worth the writing &c. Thus taking my leave, I commit you to Almightie God. From Civel 25 day of Januarie 1589.

Your assured to my
power. R.A.
(pp. 15–16, sig. C3; emphasis added)

A Letter to be written to a friend when you would have him to pleasure you in any matter.

Emanuel.

After my very heartie commendations unto you: I pray for your good health and prosperitie, &c. These are most hartelie to desire so much your friendship and good will, to *doo me this pleasure* to receive for me out of the Gabriel when she cometh to S. Lucar, 6 tunnes of Lead, conteining 150 peeces, being marked as in the margent & to doo so much as make present sale of it, the best you can as the time serveth. And when you have made sale and received monies for it, that you would bee so good as to ride unto Sheres and buy for me 8. Buts of very good Secke the best that possible can bee gotten, though they cost a Ducket or two the more in a But: & to lade them away as soone as is possible abord the Gabriell, marking them with the former marke in the margent. And the rest of the monies that you shall have left, I pray you to passe it with all speede hither to Sivil unto me. *Herein (if without seeming over bold) I may crave your paines to pleasure me: I doo assure you that you shall finde me to the uttermost of my power, both gratefull and mindfull to pleasure you againe in the like and much greater if I can bee able* . . . (pp. 16–17, sig. c4v–d1; emphasis added)

At first glance these letters seem quite extraordinary. Here the merchant's apprentice is taught how, in the one letter, to request of a friend at a great distance the receipt of money and purchase of pepper or, in the second letter, the receipt and sale of six tons of lead, travel to purchase sack, loading of the purchase aboard ship, and transfer of money, all with the courteous rhetoric of a country gentleman requesting some pippins from a neighbor or a courtier requesting the furtherance of a suit from his friend. The gentleman's "forms of life" seem entirely incongruent with the merchant's undertaking, the personal style out of keeping with prevalent ideas about the impersonal material realities of trade. Yet all of the key words and features of the pleasuring style are brought into play, including the transitive verb "to pleasure" and the presumption of making "bold" with such a request on the assurance of the writer's "uttermost" in exchange of favors. Instead of impersonalization in the merchant's language, we find, surprisingly, not only the rhetoric of reciprocity but one of its most hyperbolic styles.

If we consider the adaptation of the "pleasuring friends" style in the light of David Sacks's interpretation of the changing environment within the merchant community over the course of the sixteenth century, it comes to seem less strange. Sacks accents how "[t]he new forms of commercial organization that emerged in Bristol during the sixteenth century depended . . . upon the existence . . . of close personal ties and the mutual trust they engendered among overseas merchants" (60). At the same time that the group of overseas traders was becoming more homogeneous, with retail shopkeepers and clothmakers closed out of overseas trade and the small elite group of Merchant Venturers consolidating ties through recruitment dependent on kinship and blood ties, trading practices were becoming increasingly complicated. As Sacks puts it, "nothing could be further from the truth" in this situation than a vision of "the mercantile profession as composed of isolated individuals, each single-handedly confronting the pitfalls of the marketplace": "Rather than plying their trades alone, Bristol's merchants habitually aided one another by dealing in partnership, by serving as factors and agents, by acting as intermediaries in the delivery and receipt of coin or goods, and by jointly transporting merchandise" (61). Given such a culture and set of material needs, the highly personal and presumptuous rhetoric of reciprocity – with its repeated assertions of solidarity, mutual obligation, and status – not only made sense but helped to effect the network of dependencies which could facilitate the complex practices of overseas trade. As discourse analyst Jay Lemke argues, "the role of discourse in society is active; it not only reconfirms and re-enacts existing social relationships and patterns of behavior, it also renegotiates social relationships and introduces new meanings and new behaviors."[27] Regardless of all Browne's disclaimers of creativity, what we find filling the discursive spaces opened in the moments of trouble and estrangement of his youthful interactions overseas is indeed a kind of "invention" in language. Bakhtin suggests how "social" or "prosaic" invention in language can occur through the recirculation in new contexts of familiar styles, and the renewed "forms of life," or interaction styles, of the merchants whose practice is recorded in *The Marchants Avizo* innovate in this way. Browne may ignore or elide the strangeness of alien "contact zones," but his language holds the surprise of making the strange world familiar by adapting and developing in-group solidarity forms. The story of change through merchant trade shapes itself differently than Agnew might lead us to expect, as we come to see how one of the first collections of business letters in English manages trading relations not by impersonalizing but by shaping the supporting community and consolidating personal relations.

DISPUTING THE "PLEASURES" STYLE

We have now seen how a culturally specific form of civility – the gentleman's exchange style of "pleasuring friends" – is adapted by merchant traders to respond to complex commercial practices across large distances that require a reliable network of dependable agents and associates. If discourse styles help to shape and reshape social relationships, then narratives about social change need to take into account how discourses themselves change. Mikhail Bakhtin suggests that they change through a "messy" dialogic process of repetition, reaccentuation, and dispute – that is, through a prosaic process of social invention. As Gary Saul Morson and Caryl Emerson paraphrase Bakhtin, "something new" – an intonation or a special accent – is imparted in every utterance of an already-used word or style by "the singularity of the dialogic situation." Where formerly separate or distinct spheres of activity come into connection in the situation of an utterance, one language is recast through another. This continuous intersection of languages shapes change:

When this happens, the value systems and worldviews in these languages come to interact; they "interanimate" each other as they enter into dialogue. To the extent that this happens, it becomes more difficult to take for granted the value system of a given language. Those values may still be felt to be right and the language may still seem adequate to its topic, but not indisputably so, because they have been, however cautiously, disputed.

In fact, this dialogizing of languages is always going on, and so when these words attract tones and meanings from the languages of heteroglossia, they are often attracting already dialogized meanings. Having participated in more than one value system, these words become dialogized, disputed, and reaccented in yet another way as they encounter yet another. This potentially endless process pertains not only to particular words but also to other elements of language – to given styles, syntactic forms, even grammatical norms. Complex interactions of this sort serve as a driving force in the history of any language.[28]

By taking a close look at repeated uses of the "pleasures" style in changing contexts in the late sixteenth and early seventeenth century – in *The English Secretary*, *The Marchants Avizo*, *The Merchant of Venice*, and *Timon of Athens* – we can see this cautious dispute of an established "form of life" repeatedly occurring. Even as the collision of worlds in *The Marchants Avizo* finds out new work, a new job of community integration for the "pleasures" style, it can also be said to open its value system to interrogation and dispute. In Browne's manual this emerges most clearly in the way that the "pleasuring friends" letters ask favors only; they are not paired with sample responses to requests received from "friends." Certainly the sample letters make assurance of mutual assistance; indeed, both letters add a mercantile variation to the promise of reciprocity, adding a mention of potential profit or increase:

> assuring you that you shall finde me to the uttermost of my power, both gratefull and mindfull to pleasure you againe in the like *and greater* if I be able... wishing that you had the like *or greater* occasion to trie also my good will towards you. (pp. 15–16, sig. C3; emphasis added)

Nonetheless, contradictions emerge in Browne's instructions to the apprentice on the conduct of his relations with friends. We have seen how the apprentice is to seek out the help of other merchants in dealing with his wares in new places. But, at the same time, we hear that the apprentice is not to be expansive in his conversation in return but should instead "be your selfe as secret and silent as is possible" (p. 3, sig. B2). Furthermore, although the apprentice is told to be "faithful & just in all your accompts with every man" and to "defraud no man willinglie," he is nonetheless sternly cautioned against getting involved in the affairs of others: "See that at no time you doo take any mans doings or dealings into your hands, without my leave and counsell: because by the trouble of other mens businesse, you may neglect & frustrate mine owne" (p. 5, sig. B3). An apprentice following Browne's advice, then, would be asking much of others but giving back little in return – employing, in other words, the "pleasures" style with little real attention to the logic of exchange upon which it depends.

Shakespeare's artistry with the "pleasures" style in *The Merchant of Venice* operates in much the same way, as he quotes it in contexts that add new accents and brings it into collision with the value systems of other languages. The trajectory of change that we have already considered – the resituation of an aristocratic or gentrified style within a mercantile context – may permit a fresh perspective on the friendship language exchanged by Bassanio and Antonio early in the play:

BASSANIO
>   To you, Antonio,
> I owe the most, in money and in love,
> And from your love I have a warranty
> To unburden all my plots and purposes
> How to get clear of all the debts I owe.

ANTONIO
>   I pray you, good Bassanio, let me know it;
> And if it stand, as you yourself still do,
> Within the eye of honor, *be assured*
> *My purse, my person, my extremest means*
> Lie all unlocked to your occasions.

BASSANIO

...

> I owe you much, and, like a willful youth,
> That which I owe is lost; but if you please
> To shoot another arrow that self way
> Which you did shoot the first, I do not doubt,
> As I will watch the aim, or to find both
> Or bring your latter hazard back again
> And thankfully rest debtor for the first.

ANTONIO

> *You know me well, and herein spend but time*
> *To winde about my love with circumstance;*
> *And out of doubt you do me now more wrong*
> *In making question of my uttermost*
> Than if you had made waste of all I have.
> (1.1.130–57; emphasis added)

"[N]eedlesse were it you should entreate mee in that, wherein you have founde mee alwayes most willing," begins the friend's distinctive answer-word in *The English Secretary* to a friend's request; and it concludes with precisely the same kind of assurances that Antonio gives Bassanio: "it is lawfull for you to use mee to the uttermost . . . and you shall assuredly find me, viz yours, &c."[29] If we come to *The Merchant of Venice* without prior experience of the "pleasuring" style, the logic whereby Bassanio points out how "beholding" he is already to Antonio "in money and in love," as if his large-scale indebtedness should assure him of Antonio's willingness to give more, sounds very strange to our ears. So strange that it prompts Lars Engle to compare the relation of Bassanio and Antonio to that between Citibank and Zaire, "whereby the creditor, by the magnitude of the investment, becomes the thrall of the debtor."[30] Furthermore, many of the most interesting readings of *The Merchant of Venice* find an extremity that calls out for interpretation in the manner of Antonio's assurance to his demanding friend: it is said to carry a "wistful homoerotic suggestion," showing Antonio as "imagining, even desiring, an 'occasion' for self-sacrifice" or behaving "like the altruists described by Anna Freud who have given up to another person, with whom they identify, the right to have their instincts gratified."[31] It should by now, however, be clear that Bassanio and Antonio's expressions of friendship correspond to a normative discursive script, an unmarked style so often repeated in the social exchanges of the Elizabethan gentry as to admit very little in the way of an "alien" accent.

Even interpretations that recognize a social rather than a psychological basis for Antonio's language may mistake the provenance of the dialogized "pleasuring" style. For Michael Ferber, for example, the "conspicuous largesse" of such gestures belongs to the ideology of the nobility and "is of course the opposite of the calculation and *curiositas* associated with the poor and especially with merchants."[32] In Ferber's interpretation, Shakespeare brings together in Antonio's portrayal a number of ideological discourses incompatible with Elizabethan realities in order to invent and celebrate an idealized version of mercantile enterprise separated from finance capital and consonant with Christian and aristocratic values.[33] On the whole I agree with Ferber's account of the ideological work performed by Shakespeare's play, but Browne's prior assimilation of the "pleasuring" style to the workaday repertoire of the merchant trader suggests that the categorical distinction between merchant calculation and aristocratic liberality is faulty. Shakespeare's verbal power derives partly from his alert awareness of the social life of discourses, and the speech forms he puts in Antonio's mouth may well signal his consciousness of how aristocratic and mercantile worldviews were already "interanimating" one another in the new uses merchant traders made of the "pleasures" style.

Shakespeare interrogates the "pleasures" style and brings it into "dispute." He does so by breaking the circle of address and answer-word when he brings Bassanio's habitual way of speech into direct collision with Shylock's "alien" language:

BASSANIO   May you stead me? *Will you pleasure me?* Shall I know your answer?
SHYLOCK   Three thousand ducats for three months and Antonio bound.
BASSANIO   Your answer to that.
SHYLOCK   Antonio is a good man.
BASSANIO   Have you heard any imputation to the contrary?
SHYLOCK   Ho, no, no, no, no! My meaning in saying he is a good man is to have you understand me that he is sufficient. Yet his means are in supposition. He hath an argosy bound to Tripolis, another to the Indies. I understand, moreover, upon the Rialto, he hath a third at Mexico, a fourth for England, and other ventures he hath squandered abroad. But ships are but boards, sailors but men. There be land rats and water rats, water thieves and land thieves – I mean pirates – and then there is the peril of waters, winds, and rocks. The man is, notwithstanding, sufficient. Three thousand ducats. I think I may take his bond.
BASSANIO   *Be assured you may.*
SHYLOCK   I will be *assured* I may; and that I may be *assured*, I will bethink me. May I speak with Antonio?

BASSANIO   *If it please you* to dine with us. (1.3.7–30; emphasis added)

What the stylistic collision before Bassanio's language and Shylock's brings out most clearly is how much the "pleasures" style takes for granted. It takes for granted – above all – an answer in kind to the request made, since its style of presumption leaves the respondent little room to improvise or to shift the direction of the interaction. For this reason, it is dependent on the like-minded group (which it also binds together), and it is caught up short by differences. It takes for granted an answer which, in the terms Antonio has used, cuts off "circumstance." To "pleasure" a friend is to agree without scrutinizing the conditions or evaluating the risk level in any detail. In Bassanio's words, it is to "[b]e assured" by the reciprocal understanding sustaining the language. Hence, Bassanio does not even hear Shylock's remarks as "answers" to his questions. Shylock's cultural difference is marked by the difference in his evidentiary procedures: before yielding his answer to the loan request, it is second nature for him to weigh and reckon the evidence of Antonio's sufficiency to guarantee the loan. In Bakhtin's terms, the "pleasures" style is cautiously "disputed" through this dialogic encounter which brings out the "alien" quality in Bassanio's language as much as it does in Shylock's.[34]

Shakespeare revisits the "pleasures" style in *Timon of Athens* and pronounces its exhausted force. Here the interrogation has the simple shape of a moral fable. Early in the play, when Lord Timon is the gift-giver surrounded by friends, the dialogue articulates the reciprocal principle upon which his generosity is predicated even though he seems unlikely to have occasion to put it to the test:

FIRST LORD   Might we but have that happiness, my lord, *that you would once use our hearts*, whereby we might express some part of our zeals, we should think ourselves for ever perfect.
TIMON   ... I have told more of you to myself than you can with modesty speak in your own behalf; and thus far I confirm you. O you gods, think I, what need we have any friends if we should ne'er have need of 'em? They were the most needless creatures living, should we ne'er *have use for 'em* ... Why, I have often wished myself poorer, that I might come nearer to you. We are born to do benefits; and what better or properer can we call our own than the riches of our friends? (1.2.84–103; emphasis added)

When Timon's steward begins to draw his attention to the desperate consequences of his prodigality, Timon voices his assurance that

> If I would broach the vessels of my love
> And try the argument of hearts by borrowing,
> *Men and men's fortunes could I frankly use*
> As I can bid thee speak.   (2.2.182–85; emphasis added)

"*Assurance* bless your thoughts!" (86) is his steward's response, and Timon's conviction that he can "use" his friends "to the uttermost" is, of course, literally what the "pleasures" style promises. Timon very soon has occasion to "try the argument of hearts," or, more specifically, the argument of the "pleasures" style. Timon's servant Flaminius approaches his friend Lucullus with an empty box, which, he explains,

> in my lord's behalf, I come to entreat your honor to supply; who, having great and instant occasion to use fifty talents, hath sent to your lordship to furnish him, *nothing doubting your present assistance therein*. (3.1.17–21; emphasis added)

Lucullus's answer treats the standard expressions of the friendship style he has repeatedly exchanged with Timon as if they were entirely alien words: "La, la, la, la! *'Nothing doubting,'* says he?" (3.1.22; emphasis added). Timon's friend Lucius similarly refuses a request communicated by the servant Servilius. Lucius also frames his answer in the words of the pleasuring style, but giving it in an entirely different tone than Lucullus:

> And tell him this from me: I count it one of my greatest afflictions, say, that *I cannot pleasure* such an honorable gentleman. Good Servilius, will you befriend me so far as to *use mine own words* to him? (3.2.56–59; emphasis added)

Lucius does not disclaim the "pleasures" style the moment its troublesome obligations are brought home to him. Instead, he makes a minor but convenient adjustment to it, speaking as if the reciprocal indebtedness implied by the style could be construed merely as a matter of words.

Critics have been sensitive to the crisis of language occurring in this play, and yet a lack of familiarity with the discourse script I am calling "pleasuring friends" together with a tendency to assume that the personal and the commercial were always already disjoined has led to important misreadings, albeit small ones. For example, in Coppelia Kahn's invaluable analysis of Timon's experience in relation to Jacobean patronage and maternal power, she rightly claims that Timon's word "use" sounds "a jarring note that soon becomes the keynote of the whole play." But, as with many discussions that interrogate how commercial practices affect personal relations, in "friend" and "use" she hears "two opposed registers of exchange" – the world of personal relations and the world of monetary or commodity exchange, friendship contaminated by getting and spending. Timon's statement

> makes the people [he] is addressing as friends seem people who have no value, no *raison d'être*, apart from what they can do for him. More important, in Shakespeare's world "use" always connotes usury, practiced widely though also disparaged as unethical.[35]

But if, as we have seen, "friendship" and "use" have throughout the sixteenth century been coupled in the same non-commercial lexicon – the style of pleasuring friends – the trajectory of change is slightly different. For it is when the "pleasures" style comes to be reiterated in commercial contexts within the changing material conditions of Shakespeare's world that its defining ideal of "using" friends is eventually brought into dispute, dividing the style's own words against themselves.

Timon of Athens is an extremely puzzling play: the hero's psychological crisis over the fickleness of his friends is central to it, and yet Timon's thinking seems too naive, his psychology too shallow, to provide the substance for a convincing play. Part of the difficulty may be that friendship seems so transparently universal a relationship that it is easy to forget how differently it was accented in Shakespeare's day and written into the Elizabethan psyche. To see how the "pleasures" style is embedded and interrogated in the dialogic exchanges of the play is at least to recognize the social basis of the crisis represented: how deeply inscribed Timon's overblown expectations are in the specific contours of an Elizabethan friendship language, how his disintegration figures the disintegration of this eloquent and fragile life-style.

PART III
A prosaics of conversation

CHAPTER 6

The pragmatics of repair in King Lear *and* Much Ado About Nothing

The sustained production of ordinary conversation is a remarkable social accomplishment. There are so many things that could go badly wrong, and yet they rarely do. The potential for trouble is always there and at virtually every level – the textual, the ideational, the experiential, and the interpersonal.[1] At the textual level, speakers in conversation regularly produce well-coordinated speech exchanges, with speaker change recurring and one member talking at a time, despite the fact that turn order, turn type, and turn size are not prespecified or governed by any obvious set of rules.[2] At the ideational level, speakers generally manage to make sense of one another's contributions, despite the fact that the interpretation of speakers' meanings draws upon complex processes of inference-making.[3] The meanings communicated are not by any means transparent, even in what we think of as rudimentary exchanges: to make sense, hearers must draw not only upon what is communicated "in" words (words which are at best ambiguous and imprecise) but also upon what text and context co-construct as shared or tacit knowledge.[4] At the experiential level, speakers are constantly managing to do things with their words – both in the sense that J. L. Austin expounded when he demonstrated that utterances themselves act upon the world and others and also in the sense that utterances can persuade or compel people to take actions that go beyond words. And finally, at the interpersonal level, talk enacts relationships – and the continuance of talk, in spite of the potential for eruptions of aggression and in spite of people's opposing impulses to assert themselves at the expense of others and to avoid the interference of others, works to cement and maintain relationships.

Seen in this light, talk is a very considerable achievement, and the mechanisms that sustain it deserve serious attention. This chapter reflects on one general type of mechanism by which this achievement of social action in the ongoing flow of conversation is sustained – that is, through the various forms of "repair." Social interaction is extended and sustained in conversation because those speaking tacitly expect the recurrence of minor forms of trouble and have resources to repair it – indeed, even resources to anticipate trouble spots and to prevent them.

I argue in this chapter that the social action of talk in general and the particular actions caught up in repairing conversational troubles bear some important connections to the shaping of social identities and to the constitution and reproduction of social structure. I argue further that Shakespeare, like his character Tranio in *The Taming of the Shrew*, urges upon his auditors the value of studying "rhetoric in your common talk" (1.1.35). The plays I will focus upon in this chapter, *King Lear* and *Much Ado About Nothing*, offer insight into the role of talk both in generating social identities and shared realities and in negotiating social change.

INTERSUBJECTIVITY AND CONVERSATION IN *KING LEAR*

King Lear highlights its characters' need for and efforts to elicit the acknowledgment of others, as Stanley Cavell and others have suggested.[5] At the outset Lear demands acknowledgment from his daughters and proffers thirds of his kingdom in exchange for it, and the play's passage toward its painful ending is marked by recognition scenes between Lear and Cordelia and Lear and Gloucester. "To be acknowledged, madam," the Earl of Kent tells Cordelia when they are reunited, "is o'erpaid" (4.7.4). Indeed, the only claim the altruistic servant Kent makes for the payment of what Albany calls "the wages of [his] virtue" takes the form of his unsatisfied efforts to be acknowledged by the dying Lear at the end of the play. The need for reciprocal acknowledgment is not restricted to those characters usually grouped among the "good" lot. It is on exhibit in Goneril's message to Edmund – "Let our reciprocal vows be remembered" (4.6.266) – and in the message the dying Edmund reads in Goneril and Regan's deaths – "Yet Edmund was beloved" (5.3.244). It is not surprising that scenes of recognition should play a role in bringing toward conclusion a play involving as many separations and disguisings as *King Lear* does: these are theatrical staples. But what is particularly striking is how often identity is reinforced or challenged through the small acts or withholdings of acknowledgment that occur in conversation: when, for example, neither Cornwall nor Regan answer Lear's repeated question in 2.4 – "Who stocked my messenger?" – their withholding of response itself speaks to the question of who Lear is. The play accents as mechanisms of reciprocal acknowledgment conversational exchanges of the most basic and everyday kind: greetings and forms of address; deference behavior and other gestures at social status; as we shall see, even the simple fact of cooperative and inclusive conversational exchange.

This prevalence of acknowledgment suggests that an intersubjective theory of identity is being worked out – something like we find in the social interaction model underlying Jessica Benjamin's psychoanalytical study, *The Bonds of Love*. In Benjamin's version, the self is constituted to a large extent by what is mirrored back in the responses of the other; and so the self must negotiate a difficult tension between its own acts of assertion and its need for the recognition of the other.[6] But one need not rely on modern formulations for a transactional conception of selfhood: in *Troilus and Cressida*, Ulysses and Achilles give explicit expression to ideas of how the self is constituted through the recognition of the other. Achilles speaks of how "eye to eye opposed / Salutes each other with each other's form" (3.3.108–09) and Ulysses of how a man does not "of himself" know his own parts "for aught / Till he behold them formed in the applause / Where they're extended" (119–21). I argue that the small acts of acknowledgment featured in the conversation or face-to-face interactions of *King Lear* contribute to a rhetoric not of individualistic self-fashioning but instead of reciprocal self-maintenance. This rhetoric of reciprocal self-maintenance constitutes and sustains the quotidian selves of the characters. The mechanisms of this rhetoric in *King Lear* emerge mainly through the play's exhibition not of its functioning but of its disfunctions.

My proposal that the dialogue of *King Lear* exhibits a rhetoric of reciprocal self-maintenance takes as its starting point some observations I adapt from discourse pragmatics – the discipline that studies how communication works within social contexts – and particularly from its branch of conversational analysis. Harvey Sacks, one of the originators in the 1960s of conversation studies, claimed that "social organization reaches 'downward' to the details of interaction" so that attention to the microstructures of conversation should illuminate social practice.[7] Nonetheless, much of the foundational work on repair structures in conversation was descriptive rather than theoretical. E. Schegloff, G. Jefferson, and H. Sacks demonstrated in detail how speakers negotiate the correction of speech errors, misunderstandings, non-hearings, and other mundane problems. They argued that conversation typically shows a bias towards "self-repair" over "other-repair": that is, when a speaker stumbles, or chooses the wrong word, or says something inaudible, the speaker will typically self-correct. Repairs in the fabric of interactive communication can be further classified as "self-initiated" or "other-initiated": "other-initiated self-repair" is a common pattern in conversation, where the speaker responds to the hearer's expression of non-comprehension or of difficulty in understanding.[8]

As conversational analysis extended the study of repair, attention was paid to remedial strategies deployed by speakers to address "perceived violations of grammatical, syntactic, conversational, and societal rules."[9] The ongoing maintenance work in conversation was shown to extend to "preventatives" as well as repairs, and some tentative links began to be made between conversational maintenance and collaborative self-construction. When J. P. Hewitt and R. Stokes looked at preventatives and repairs in conversational exchange, they developed the idea that "meaning in social encounters is organized around the *identities* of the interacting parties" and concentrated on how "breaches of social understandings may produce undesired alterations in the perceived identity of the party regarded as the author of the breach."[10] And finally, as we have already seen in previous chapters, Penelope Brown and Stephen Levinson greatly extended the possibilities for viewing conversational maintenance work as social self-construction when they adapted Erving Goffman's concept of "face-work" and defined politeness as linguistic work mitigating or counteracting modes of aggression inherent in speech interaction. The two aspects of "face" emphasized in their model, positive face relating to the "want to be approved by others" and negative face to the "want . . . that [one's] actions be unimpeded by others,"[11] roughly correspond to the two basic "needs" posited in Jessica Benjamin's general model of intersubjectivity: the need for recognition and the need for self-assertion. Politeness theory imagines social relations as continuously being repaired even as they are being constructed.

To take stock then – from discourse pragmatics comes the germ of a model for reciprocal self-maintenance in everyday interaction. If conversation can be regarded as an important arena for self-constitution, then it suggests a view of identity as a leakier vessel than, for example, what Stephen Greenblatt posited in *Renaissance Self-Fashioning*. It is a view of identity as always undergoing maintenance and repair, always being patched even in the making; and a view of that patchwork and maintenance of selves as a cooperative, or collaborative activity.

One further reflection on the quotidian self as rhetorically constructed and maintained in everyday conversation before turning to examples from *King Lear*. The idea that people or dramatic characters have stable or continuous identities usually goes together with the idea that one is what one does – that the person provides the principle that unifies his or her actions or manifestations. In their work in *The New Rhetoric* on everyday argumentation, Chaim Perelman and L. Olbrechts-Tyteca make valuable comments about the rhetorical strategies commonly used to manage the relation between a person and his or her manifestations, what they call the "act-person liaison." Their rhetorical inventory includes important techniques for *dissociating* rather than associating "acts" and identity: for example, "techniques of severance" work to separate the person from the conventional estimation of an act and "techniques of restraint" work to limit the link made.[12] In other words, if one is to consider the self as a rhetorical construct rather than a natural essence, then an important part of the rhetorical work constituting identity will turn out to be not creative fashioning but instead work that prevents and repairs threats to the continuity of the self. For this reason the reciprocal self-maintenance constantly occurring in conversation can be seen as fundamental to the discursive construction of the quotidian self.

The opening of *King Lear* – the conversation among Gloucester, Kent, and Edmund – provides a clear example of the normal workings of reciprocal self-maintenance.

KENT I thought the King had more affected the Duke of Albany than Cornwall.
GLOUCESTER It did always seem so to us; but now in the division of the kingdom it appears not which of the dukes he values most, for equalities are so weighed that curiosity in neither can make choice of either's moiety.
KENT Is not this your son, my lord?
GLOUCESTER His breeding, sir, hath been at my charge. I have so often blushed to acknowledge him that now I am brazed to 't.
KENT I cannot conceive you.
GLOUCESTER Sir, this young fellow's mother could; whereupon she grew round-wombed and had indeed, sir, a son for her cradle ere she had a husband for her bed. Do you smell a fault?
KENT I cannot wish the fault undone, the issue of it being so proper.
GLOUCESTER But I have a son, sir, by order of law, some year elder than this, who yet is no dearer in my account. Though this knave came something saucily to the world before he was sent for, yet was his mother fair, there was good sport at his making, and the whoreson must be acknowledged. – Do you know this noble gentleman, Edmund?

EDMUND   No, my lord.
GLOUCESTER   My lord of Kent. Remember him hereafter as my honorable friend.
EDMUND   My services to your lordship.
KENT   I must love you, and sue to know you better.
EDMUND   Sir, I shall study deserving.
GLOUCESTER   He hath been out nine years, and away he shall again. The King is coming. (1.1.1–33)

The acknowledgment of one person (here Edmund) by others is the central issue in this exchange: the limited acknowledgment that Gloucester affords his bastard son Edmund in the world of Lear's court is enacted in the micro-form of his conversational non-acknowledgment of his son. Kent is the most active agent in the work of conversational repair that Shakespeare is foregrounding. The damage control begins with his question to Gloucester: "Is not this your son, my lord?" (8). With this question, Kent addresses the potentially damaging fact of Edmund's non-acknowledgment and non-inclusion in the conversation. But by drawing attention to Gloucester's neglect in this matter of introduction, Kent's words (true to Brown and Levinson's idea that many speech acts threaten hearer face) themselves pose a slight threat to Gloucester's face. The threat is slight especially since Kent's question form, despite its implied criticism, nonetheless itself proposes a straightforward mechanism for repair. That is, Gloucester should introduce his son and continue the conversation with Edmund included as a participant. However, the question brings about, instead of the anticipated introduction, a disclosure potentially much more threatening to Gloucester's face. Both the indirectness and the volubility of Gloucester's responses can be understood as a mask for his embarrassment, and his jocular apologetics are clearly aimed at restraining the damage which his own admission of his "fault" threatens to Kent's estimate of him. As Bakhtin, anticipating many of the insights of discourse pragmatics, emphasized, "The word in living conversation is . . . oriented toward a future answer-word,"[13] and now it is Gloucester's manner that sets up a "preferred strategy" available to Kent for remedying Gloucester's distress: that is, to assert common ground with him, for example by voicing interest in womanizing. Kent's minimal responses ("I cannot conceive you." [12] – "I cannot wish the fault undone, the issue of it being so proper." [17–18]) convey his rejection of this proffered option, presumably because he is aware of the need to balance Gloucester's "face" requirements with Edmund's. I would read Kent's "I cannot conceive you" as an effort to drop the subject, an indirect signal to Gloucester that the damage of the anticipated disclosure of fault can still be prevented. But rather than minimizing the conversational awkwardness in this way, Gloucester amplifies. The function of repair is still most prominent in Kent's next remark – "I cannot wish the fault undone, the issue of it being so proper." – where he finds the compromise solution of approving in the "issue" of the fault each one of his interlocutors. Finally, the anticipated introduction proceeds, with Gloucester's and Edmund's contributions being exactly as prescribed by the social etiquette of Shakespeare's day. The one contribution that stands out is Kent's – "I must love you, and sue to know you better" (30); it seems excessive, its protestation of affection overstated for the ritual circumstances of a formal introduction. The exaggeration clearly marks a further instance of strategic "repair," Kent's gracious effort to redress the damaging impact of Gloucester's talk on Edmund's person.

As I have just demonstrated, the dialogue opening *King Lear* foregrounds conversation as reciprocal self-maintenance, especially in the strategies Kent deploys to maintain both Gloucester's and Edmund's face. What this normative example sets up are the spectacular departures from it that are to follow – these include, for example, Lear's unsatisfactory trial of his daughters' love in 1.1, Kent's refusal of cooperative conversational exchange with Oswald and then Cornwall in 2.2, Goneril and Regan's mirroring back to Lear in 1.4 and 2.4 of a changed self – a self unmade and remade in their speech with him. Indeed, my argument that *King Lear* puts on display the normal everyday mechanisms by which people interactively maintain one another's identities depends on this foregrounding of breakdowns in normal communication in the play. For as is also the case in conversations apart from plays, it is in circumstances of breakdown or disfunction that these social strategies, generally exchanged among people without attention being turned to them, become visible.

As we build here on the insights of discourse pragmatics towards a dialogic or interactive view of quotidian self-construction, there is an important qualification to be made. Pertinent is Pierre Bourdieu's objection in his *Outline of a Theory of Practice* against social interaction studies "that 'interpersonal' relations are never, except in appearance, *individual-to-individual* relationships and that the truth of the interaction is never entirely contained in the interaction": "In fact it is their present and past positions in the social structure that biological individuals carry with them, at all times and in all places, in the form of dispositions which are so many marks of *social position*."¹⁴ It would be misleading to suggest that the individual speakers in *King Lear* are continuously producing, through their own independent initiatives, the coordinated practices of self-maintenance. What is on display in the microencounters of acknowledgment in *King Lear* is often not so much an interplay among the styles of individual speakers as it is what we have attended to in the preceding chapters – the inscription in the conversational organization of the characters' relative social positions.

We have only to look at Cordelia's conversation in 4.7, the short scene in which she is reunited with Kent and with her father, for a clear example of how relative social position rather than personal style directs the interaction. In the first part of the scene, Cordelia speaks with Kent and the Doctor, and a Gentleman, before she addresses the sleeping Lear:

CORDELIA
O thou good Kent, how shall I live and work
To match thy goodness? My life will be too short,
And every measure fail me.
KENT
To be acknowledged, madam, is o'erpaid.
All my reports go with the modest truth,
Nor more nor clipped, but so.
CORDELIA
                                    Be better suited.
These weeds are memories of those worser hours;
I prithee, put them off.
KENT   Pardon, dear madam;
Yet to be known shortens my made intent.
My boon I make it that you know me not
Till time and I think meet.
CORDELIA
Then be 't so, my good lord. [*To the Doctor.*] How
does the King?
DOCTOR
Madam, sleeps still.
CORDELIA
O you kind gods,
Cure this great breach in his abusèd nature!
Th' untuned and jarring senses, O, wind up
Of this child-changèd father!
DOCTOR
So please Your Majesty
That we may wake the King? He hath slept long.

CORDELIA
> Be governed by your knowledge, and proceed
> I' the sway of your own will. – Is he arrayed? (4.7.1–21)

The relative positions of the speakers are most obviously displayed in the forms of address – Cordelia is addressed as "Your Majesty" (18) by the Doctor and as "madam" (4) by Kent; Cordelia uses the pronoun "thou" in her address to Kent, while he addresses her using "you." In her interactions with Kent, the Doctor, and the Gentleman, Cordelia repeatedly directs the others, as we would expect a Queen to do. She employs the imperative form for her directives, with her imperatives politely softened by indirection (for example, to Kent – "Be better suited." [6] not "Change your suit." and to the Doctor – "Be governed by your knowledge, and proceed / I' the sway of your own will" [20–21] not "Wake my father up now."). The Doctor is repeatedly required to direct the Queen, but we can clearly see how forms like "So please Your Majesty / That we may wake the King?" (18–19) bespeak his subordinate relation to her.[15] Even Cordelia's words of gratitude to Kent acknowledging his service mark her position relative to his: she follows her rhetorical question "O thou good Kent, how shall I live and work / To match thy goodness?" (1–2) with an exaggerated claim of her indebtedness actually more reminiscent of Goneril's claim in 1.1 to love Lear "no less than life" than of her own earlier words: "My life will be too short, / And every measure fail me" (2–3). Whatever we make of the strange echo of Goneril, Cordelia's words do nonetheless fit her recently acquired position. As Pierre Bourdieu remarks, to manipulate or reduce social distance in conversation, as Cordelia's generous remarks to Kent do, is the reflex of a superior.[16] As we have seen, it was Kent's own aristocratic reflex when he was introduced to Edmund at the start of *King Lear*: his words – "I must love you, and sue to know you better" – unexpectedly familiar, seemed to overstate his obligation. This strategy of acknowledging the other through reducing social distance is one that would not be available, in reverse, to Edmund speaking with Kent, or to Kent speaking with Cordelia: coming from a subordinate, it would signal presumption or insolence.

Relative position within a social structure more than individual temperament also organizes Cordelia's part in the second movement of the recognition scene when she speaks with her father. The style of Cordelia's address to Lear is foregrounded, I would argue, by a contrast Shakespeare establishes between Cordelia's speech to the sleeping king and her speech to the waking king. Cordelia addresses the sleeping Lear as "my dear Father," "poor perdu!" and "poor Father" (27, 36, 39); and she makes repeated use of the "thou" form (28, 30, 39, 40, 42). When Lear wakes, she addresses him as "Your Majesty," "my royal lord," or "Your Highness" (45, 87) – never as "father" – and she consistently uses the pronoun "you." Also puzzling is the shift from her profuse expression of concern addressed to the sleeper to the laconic style of her famous words to Lear – "And so I am! I am!"; "No cause, no cause" (72, 78). And, again in contrast to the first half of the scene, Cordelia is not the initiator of speech topics but instead she mainly responds to Lear. Within the codes of our own cultural context, it would be easy to read in Cordelia's profuse address to her sleeping father an authentic language of intimacy and closeness and to read into the formal and laconic style of her actual address some inhibition or inward conflict, a holding back, the failure to find a fully adequate expression of her acknowledgment of Lear.[17] I think this would be a misreading of the scene. What Cordelia's speech style expresses is not her personal coldness but instead a hierarchical relation intact. What she speaks are the forms of acknowledgment, or of kindness, that their relative positions make most immediately available.

It is easy to object that what I am claiming to be of considerable importance, these conversational practices of reciprocal self-maintenance, amount in this example to little more than superficial forms of social decorum. But my point is that *King Lear* insists on the extraordinary power that the banalities of conversation exert in constructing and holding in place the structures of reality that characters in *Lear* inhabit, and Cordelia's role in the recognition scene helps to bring this into the foreground. Nonetheless, I pause over the scene because I do, in fact, find Cordelia's utterances disappointing and, so, in need of explanation. I find them disappointing because in 1.1 Cordelia seemed to be an agent of change, to challenge the established forms of social recognition as inauthentic, and so it is disappointing when at the fullest moment of recognition in which Cordelia participates, she speaks in entire conformity with the established forms. In this reproduction of social forms, the play denies us the discovery or the invention of alternatives. As Queen of France, Cordelia advances in social position and power, but the voice she develops when she changes place seems to be almost entirely constrained by that place. When she speaks kindly to her father, she does not speak with the voice of the future that one might have hoped to hear from her but instead with the voice of the past.

Again, Pierre Bourdieu's work on social practice can help with this question of why the interacting voices of acknowledgment in *King Lear* tend to be voices from the past. Bourdieu developed his concept of *habitus* to deal with questions about how coordinated social practices are generated and about what mediates between an individual agent's practices and a social structure. The *habitus* is "history turned into nature," says Bourdieu: "The habitus, the durably installed generative principle of regulated improvisations, produces practices which tend to reproduce the regularities immanent in the objective conditions of the production of their generative principle."[18] The *habitus*, then, acting as "the immanent law" governing the "individual agent's practices," or as the person's "second nature," is always molded on the objective or material conditions obtaining in the past.[19] If we accept Paul Delany's and Rosalie Colie's characterization of *King Lear* as reflecting a world undergoing an enormous change in the material structures of relations – if we accept their rough characterization of that change as a transition from a feudal-aristocratic society to a commercial bourgeois state[20] – the time-lag built into Bourdieu's concept of *habitus* can help us understand why those characters in *King Lear* initially most critical of the status quo – Cordelia and Kent – end up acting nonetheless as yesterday's people. The case is almost exactly that of today's forward-looking feminists, who find themselves reproducing in their lived relations yesterday's world, even or especially – as in Cordelia's case – in their acts of kindness.

This problem is articulated most clearly in Kent's efforts to dissociate himself from established social practices, which, in the changed circumstances of the present, are carrying meanings he finds unpalatable. One such effort occurs when Kent, disguised as Caius, meets up with Oswald outside Gloucester's house. No conversation in *King Lear* is more curious:

OSWALD   Good dawning to thee, friend. Art of this house?
KENT   Ay.
OSWALD   Where may we set our horses?
KENT   I' the mire.
OSWALD   Prithee, if thou lov'st me, tell me.
KENT   I love thee not.
OSWALD   Why then, I care not for thee.
KENT   If I had thee in Lipsbury pinfold, I would make thee care for me.
OSWALD   Why dost thou use me thus? I know thee not.
KENT   Fellow, I know thee.

OSWALD What dost thou know me for?
KENT A knave, a rascal, an eater of broken meats; a base, proud, shallow, beggarly, three-suited, hundred-pound, filthy worsted-stocking knave; a lily-livered, action-taking, whoreson, glass-gazing, superserviceable, finical rogue; one-trunk-inheriting slave; one that wouldst be a bawd in way of good service, and art nothing but the composition of a knave, beggar, coward, pander, and the son and heir of a mongrel bitch; one whom I will beat into clamorous whining if thou deny'st the least syllable of thy addition. (2.2.1–24)

Here Kent seems to play out a conversational part almost exactly opposite to his part in the play's opening conversation with Gloucester and Edmund.[21] His elaborate maintenance strategies there served the acknowledgment of the others. Here Kent himself violates all the norms of cooperative conversation; he seems to be trying to remove himself altogether from the practice of reciprocal self-maintenance which is in the grain even of the most basic conversational maneuvers. One basic principle enunciated by conversation analysis is that conversation is a "cooperative endeavor." As Ronald Wardhaugh expressed it in *How Conversation Works*, to engage in polite conversation is to some extent to assent (at least conditionally) to "the other's presentation of the world."[22] I would argue that what Kent is trying to do through his non-cooperation here with Oswald is to "say" that he does *not* assent to Oswald's "presentation of the world," or in the terms we have been pursuing in this chapter, he does not agree to acknowledge Oswald through the normal repair mechanisms of conversation. Why the wish to deny Oswald the acknowledgment of normal conversation? I think we can read the situation thus. Kent hears in Oswald's mouth the established language of service, which is a well articulated language of mutual self-maintenance working across hierarchically organized relations. But while Kent hears the familiar language, he judges it to be matched in the relation between the servant Oswald and his mistress Goneril to a relation configured in a new and unpalatable way, a way that does not strike him as authentic or decent. The new relation – produced by the historical change Delany and Colie discuss – jars with the old language. It changes the meanings and the values Kent had prized in the old language, and it makes the old language no longer his own. To speak his own language with Oswald is then to produce meanings he cannot control. As Bourdieu says of all language use guided by the *habitus*, the speaker finds himself "endlessly overtaken by his own words."²³ The extremity of Kent's verbal tactics here, then, seems to be aimed at opting out of the social forms of acknowledgment that Oswald and his kind have appropriated and made their own. Shakespeare's message, however, would seem to be that there is no opting out – that to converse is itself to acknowledge and sustain the self of the other, and precisely because the mechanisms of acknowledgment – or, to put it another way, of ideology – are engraved in the most banal and automatic mechanisms of exchange – the turn-taking structure, the question/answer sequence, the pronominal choices, and even the disposition of the variously positioned speakers to take long or short turns in their talk.

Like *Timon of Athens*, in which changing forms of relation bring a specific social speech style into dispute, *King Lear* explores the role of discourse in relation to social systems undergoing large-scale change. As *King Lear* dramatizes its crisis of change, it makes visible the normal conversational mechanisms of acknowledgment, or reciprocal self-maintenance – mechanisms which usually function apart from the awareness or conscious intention of the participants. That making visible does not, however, enable characters like Cordelia or Kent to change their practices of acknowledgment or to alter their needs for acknowledgment, because these forms of acknowledgment are what make and sustain their own quotidian selves.

REPETITION AND REPAIR IN *MUCH ADO ABOUT NOTHING*

Like *King Lear* but with an altogether different accent, *Much Ado About Nothing* incorporates and highlights ordinary social uses of language prevalent in everyday conversation. I will focus on two features of social discourse brought out in the play: first, verbal reproduction – that is, the reiteration of everyday speech forms; second, verbal maintenance – those remedial strategies effecting conversational repairs which also receive attention in *King Lear*. Both the simple practice of reproduction and the more complex practice of maintenance are features of normal conversation which promote social conservation. I will argue that these practices of ordinary language shape the distinctive and – in some views – troublingly prosaic outlook of the comedy. In doing so, I will be suggesting that the unauthored art of mundane conversation itself has a complex and interesting rhetorical organization, and that the author of *Much Ado About Nothing* both recognizes and foregrounds this.

First, verbal reproduction. Repetitive speech formulas are highlighted in the conversations of *Much Ado About Nothing*. Often, utterances are represented to us not as the individual expressions of the characters but instead as revoicings of speech forms from a collective social repertoire. For example, easily recognizable forms of civility for negotiating the social relation of guest and host mark Don Pedro's entrance and exchange of greetings with Leonato:

DON PEDRO   Good Signor Leonato, are you come to meet your trouble? The fashion of the world is to avoid cost, and you encounter it.
LEONATO   Never came trouble to my house in the likeness of your grace: for trouble being gone, comfort should remain: but when you depart from me, sorrow abides, and happiness takes his leave.
DON PEDRO   You embrace your charge too willingly.   (1.1.71–76)[24]

This routine, in which the guest urges the troublesomeness of the intrusion and the host denies it, has proved so durable that it remains in constant use today, making it almost redundant to establish its prevalence in the non-literary discourse of Shakespeare's day. While we have already seen how prevalent the "trouble" trope is in Elizabethan letter-writing in general, in the many existing letters negotiating Queen Elizabeth's progresses and her visits with her nobles we find it played out in the specific context of the verbal routines surrounding hospitality. For example, in 1577, the Earl of Leicester writes to the Earl of Sussex:

My good Lord, I have shewed your Letter to her Majesty, who did take your great care to have her welcome to your house in most kind and gracious part, thanking your Lordship many times. Albeit she saith very earnestly, that she wil by no means come this time to Newhal; saying, it were no reason, and less good manners, having so short warning this year to trouble you . . . and charged me so to let your Lordship know, that by no means she would have you prepare for her this time. Nevertheless, my Lord, for mine own opinion, I believe she wil hunt, and visit your house, coming so neer.[25]

The sociological stylistics of Mikhail Bakhtin can help to characterize this kind of verbal repetition in *Much Ado About Nothing*. Bakhtin conceives of all language use as dialogic, as in some sense answering or responding to previous speech events. One of many specific ways that concrete utterances respond to prior words or utterances is by repeating or "quoting" them.[26] But very often the repetition is not simply a matter of one individual's response to another's words. Utterances typically deploy speech genres, conventional patterns for performing actions in particular contexts.²⁷ The characters in *Much Ado About Nothing* do not merely deploy speech genres; they also make explicit observations about these routinized speech behaviors. For example, Benedick's friends identify in his talk a customary formula for concluding a letter. As he takes his leave of them, these words come out: "and so I commit you – ". Claudio picks up and continues the epistolary formula: "To the tuition of God: from my house if I had it – ." And Don Pedro concludes it with the date and signature: "The sixth of July: your loving friend Benedick" (1.1.209–11). To this mockery, Benedick rejoins that their talk also recycles used phrases: "Nay, mock not, mock not: the body of your discourse is sometime guarded with fragments . . . ere you flout old ends any further, examine your conscience . . ." (1.1.212–15).²⁸

The play also invites us to reflect on the link between the performance of social speech genres and the performance of repeatable artistic genres, like plays and songs. Actors in plays have scripted parts, which their characters appear to make up as they go along, for the benefit of an audience that overhears the conversation. In *Much Ado About Nothing*, this normal feature of dramatic performance is reproduced when Hero and Ursula prearrange a dialogue that Beatrice is to overhear (3.1). One consequence of this link is to suggest that everyday conversation is also made up of playlets at least minimally pre-scripted. The art genre is not being privileged above the speech genre here: a sense of the complex interest of social speech genres is stressed instead. Art and speech genres are also associated when Balthasar's singing performance is juxtaposed with a politeness ritual of self-deprecation and reassurance. When Don Pedro tells Balthasar that "we'll hear that song again" (2.3.35), he draws to our attention the nature of the song as a repeatable event. But an equally elaborate and repeatable social performance is enacted by Don Pedro and Balthasar in the process of eliciting and acknowledging Balthasar's musical performance. Balthasar responds to Don Pedro's bidding by deprecating his own skill ("Oh, good my lord, tax not so bad a voice, / To slander music any more than once" [2.3.36–37]), and Don Pedro counters with praise ("It is the witness still of excellency, / To put a strange face on his own perfection" [38–39]). The ritualized nature of Balthasar's part in the dialogue is readily confirmed if we look at the practice of self-deprecation common in the dedicatory letters of Renaissance literature. But as we have seen in chapter 4, there is no need to look to artistic genres: elaborate self-deprecatory strategies are standard routines used by speakers of lower relative status to negotiate self-assertive acts like performance, as in Henry Sidney's letter to Queen Elizabeth:

> In the lowliest Manner I can, I most humblye beseache youer most excellent Majestie, [he begins] to pardon me that I have so seldome written to your Highnes: So bad a Delyverie of my Minde I have by Pen, and so illeagible it is when I do it my selfe, as I rather thought it necessarye for me, to addresse that which I had to write to the Lordes of your Majesties Councell . . . then convenient to trouble your selfe with it.[29]

We might think that Balthasar overdoes it when Don Pedro's praise after the song ("By my troth a good song.") elicits his further insistence, "And an ill singer, my lord" (69–70), and a director may well be tempted to cut this short interchange altogether as irrelevant. But Balthasar's deference is less extreme than Sidney's, who returns at the end of his letter to further disclaimers of his "ill written" and "evell favored" lines. What Shakespeare turns our attention to here, then, is the interactive and recursive rhetoric by which social relations are produced and reproduced, to what Kenneth Burke calls "courtship," a term covering the wide range of social practices aimed at overcoming different kinds of estrangement.[30]

Indeed, replicated behavior is a constant motif of this play, and by no means restricted to verbal reproduction. The love plot centered on Beatrice and Benedick turns on how they are constrained finally to do "as other women [and men] do" (3.4.68) – that is to suffer tooth-aches, head-colds, and to marry. Benedick's friends take delight in seeing reproduced in his behavior the standard signs of heterosexual affection (here identified as shaving and melancholy), and their relationship moves towards their resistant voicing of the most inescapable of "old ends" – "I protest I love thee." Hero's restoration at the end of the play is not couched in a transcendent language of resurrection, but instead she is promised to Claudio as "Almost the copy of my child that's dead" (5.1.256) and she is delivered as Hero reproduced. In this way, replication or reproduction marks the large structures of the action in the play. In its finest detail too, this play – perhaps more than any other in the Shakespeare canon – stresses diurnal repetition, everyday routine: people are always being bid to dinner, Benedick "brushes his hat a-mornings" (3.3.32) and Hero, asked when she'll be married, anticipates being married "every day tomorrow" (3.1.101).

What are we to make of the insistence on verbal and social reproduction in this play? It was once common to dismiss as superficial the courtesies and the social formulas that are so prominent in *Much Ado About Nothing*, to see them as "appearances" to be displaced at the end of the play by "realities." Such a formulation entirely misses the point. If the play is, as Walter R. Davis and others have suggested, one of Shakespeare's most "realistic" of comedies, it is so because its world is built up, like everyday reality, of recurring social practices. Furthermore, contrary to Davis's claims, *Much Ado About Nothing* is not at all a play in which a superficial society is transformed;[31] it is, instead, very much a play in which existing social relations are reproduced. Characters like Beatrice and Benedick may initially give voice to some of the disincentives against marriage – for women, the pain of childbirth ("my mother cried," Beatrice tells us, when "I was born" [2.1.254–55]) and the grief of being "overmastered with a piece of valiant dust" (2.1.44); for men, the anxiety of being cuckolded. But in the end they go, in Beatrice's formulation, "to the world" (2.1.241): in Louis Althusser's formulation, they are "interpellated," or "hailed," as subjects into conventional roles.[32] Through its emphasis on reproduction, the play accents the social determination of human identity. The extent to which identity is caught up in social relations is particularly underlined when Benedick brings his formal challenge against Claudio: before Benedick can make his challenge, his former friends have drawn him into the routine patterns habitual to their usual conversation. Their banter reproduces their usual relations, and Benedick has extraordinary difficulty displacing these usual patterns, for, to change the conversation is to change who he is.

One further point before turning to the topic of verbal maintenance. One of the earliest instances of reproduction in the play is also the oddest, and it may suggest a more particular motivation for social reproduction. In the first scene, Don Pedro asks Leonato whether Hero is his daughter, and elicits this answer, "Her mother hath many times told me so" (1.1.78). This response, as recent feminist criticism has established, is by no means unusual in Shakespeare's works. It is particularly pertinent to this play, which dwells endlessly on the perils of cuckoldry and which personifies evil as the bastard son. Mary Beth Rose and others have drawn our attention to the obvious, but forgettable, fact that the physical part played by the male in biological reproduction is small and potentially anonymous. One cannot derive the important and continuing place of the father from the physical realities of biological reproduction.[33] Leonato's answer may be in jest, but it bespeaks the unassuageable anxiety that attends fatherhood in many cultures: the father has, ultimately, only a woman's word that his children are his own. This anxious moment in the play is quickly displaced by Don Pedro's courteous assertion of how physically like Leonato his daughter is: "Truly, the lady fathers herself: be happy, lady, for you are like an honourable father" (81–82). To secure and maintain the place and importance of the father in a patriarchal culture, what the play calls "fatherly and kindly power" (4.1.68), the continuous work of social reproduction – work that reproduces the privilege of the father within a hierarchical set of social relations – must supplement the practice of biological reproduction. One function that social and verbal reproduction fulfills in *Much Ado About Nothing* is to provide this supplement to biological reproduction. But I do not want to argue that this is the only function of verbal reproduction: it is only a part of the diffuse but powerful effect of repetition in making up the ordinary world.

I turn now to the foregrounding of verbal maintenance in *Much Ado About Nothing*. Many critics have observed that the play focuses attention on the perils of language. The New Cambridge editor observes that it "depends very much on the mistaking of words." For Sheldon Zitner it is an "encounter with the deficiencies of the verbal medium," and for Anthony Dawson, in an essay with a deconstructive edge, it is a "play of signification."[34] The accent in treatments of the language has been on how it fails to work, how signification and communication misfire. I want to shift that accent and to argue that the play deals not only with mistake-making and mis-taking in words, but also with their remedy and correction. Its concern is not with how language fails but with how language works. And this practical outlook on language is also the play's general outlook on life.

A view of language as productive of mistakes and misapprehensions is not the play's destination, but its starting point, what the characters take for granted. From the outset, the characters treat mistake-making as their normal expectation of language. They anticipate mistaken communications, and more important, they deploy a complex range of prevention and repair mechanisms to compensate.

"You must not, sir, mistake my niece" (1.1.45), says Leonato to the Messenger, anticipating and then working to correct the Messenger's potential misconstruction of Beatrice's loquacity as immodesty, or of her barbs against Benedick's reputation as hatred. "I pray you" (1.1.23) are Beatrice's first words as she joins in the conversation, anticipating and disarming the possible construction of her conversational contribution as interruptive or as unbeseeming a lady. "I was born to speak all mirth, and no matter" (2.1.251), says Beatrice to Don Pedro later in the play, repairing the possible offense to him given by her witty rejection of his marriage proposal. And when Claudio answers "No" to the Friar's ritual wedding question, "You come hither, my lord, to marry this lady?" Leonato, without any indication that he regards the mistaken response as out of place or disturbing, provides the reparative construction: "To be married to her: friar, you come to marry her" (4.1.3–5).

We have seen how discourse pragmatics offers a conception of remedial strategies not as exceptional measures undertaken to recover from communication breakdowns but instead as integral moves in the collaborative production of communication. This model envisions normal conversational exchange as involving a reciprocal process of mistake-making and correction. It has been a common practice in dramatic criticism to distinguish everyday conversation from dramatic dialogue partly by evincing the greater messiness of conversation – its false starts; its *hum*s, its *ha*s, and its *eh*s; its violations of grammar and its happenings into violations of decorum; and with these mistakes, the self- or other- correcting behavior that goes along. It is not my purpose here to contest the general applicability of this distinction between the composures of dialogue and the discomposures of everyday speech but to suggest that *Much Ado About Nothing* takes the normal mistake-making and repair procedures of conversation, even if these are more highly stylized in their representation in the play than in life, as a part of its theme.

Part of this stylized representation of mistake-making in communication consists in Dogberry's malapropisms, which not only confuse his individual speeches but also delay the communication of Borachio's and Don John's offenses to those who need this information. The eventual happy outcome of the play is, of course, brought about by the eventual success of Dogberry's muddled communications, so that the general effect of the Dogberry episodes is to underline not only mistake-makings in communication but also the correction mechanisms. Still, if a main part of speech competence is skill in deploying the repair structures of conversation, Dogberry is clearly being represented as an incompetent speaker. Nonetheless, in some of Dogberry's utterances, Shakespeare emphasizes that the maintenance work of language can operate apart from a speaker's control and competence. Redundancy, for example, is a very general feature of spoken language that compensates more usually for failures of speech reception than for errors of speech transmission, that is, for the varying degrees of inattention and distraction that attend listening. Even if Dogberry is not in full control of the messages he sends, nonetheless an audience does not find it difficult to understand roughly what he means by what he says. It is easy to illustrate that redundancy contributes to this effect, especially when Dogberry's malapropisms are wedded by coordinate conjunctions to their supposed synonyms to produce expressions like his announcement to "neighbour Seacoal" – "you are thought here to be the most *senseless and fit* man for the constable of the watch" (3.3.19–20; emphasis added) – or his instruction that the watch "make no noise in the streets: for, for the watch to babble and to talk, is *most tolerable and not to be endured*" (3.3.30–31; emphasis added).

Another kind of mis-taking in words that is placed on show in this play is that which generates the witty exchanges of Beatrice and Benedick. Earlier critics have, I think, been right in tracing the primarily literary rather than conversational affiliations of this sort of stylistic display, but one can nonetheless observe that the controlled punning of their exchanges construes conscious mistake-making in language as a productive resource of language rather than a deficiency in the medium.

We have already seen, in our examples of verbal reproduction, how the play accents politeness, or courtesy – Don Pedro's graceful exchanges with his host, Balthasar's modest derogation of his abilities, the deferential "father, as it please you" (2.1.39–40) that Beatrice attributes to Hero, only begin to illustrate the prevalence of polite forms. Brown and Levinson's understanding of politeness in terms of face-work can help illuminate the implications of politeness in *Much Ado About Nothing*, for the play is very much concerned with the characters' maintenance of "face." The polite words exchanged between Don Pedro and Leonato at the outset of their visit are easily understood as "face-work," and what is most seriously threatened in the crises of the play can be readily understood as loss of face, or – to use the play's word – "shame." Indeed, the play offers its own words and metaphors for a social logic of politeness involving threats to face and their remedies. Perhaps even more than other characters in the play, Claudio is a man apprehensive of potential mistakes that threaten his public self-image. This comes out when Benedick exposes to Don Pedro Claudio's desire for Hero. Claudio is extremely conscious of how this revelation might affect Don Pedro's image of him, and he regrets that Benedick's announcement forestalled his plans for managing any face risk. "But lest my liking might too sudden seem," he tells Don Pedro, "I would have salved it with a longer treatise" (1.1.240–41). Don Pedro's response offers a ready principle for judging the maintenance work needed to offset the potential damage of a speech action: "What need the bridge much broader than the flood?" (1.1.242).

We might also say that Dogberry offers insight into the psychology of politeness in his explanations of "the most peaceable way" (3.3.48) for the watch to live among its neighbors. The most characteristic action of a local constabulary, insofar as we can gather this from what Dogberry says, is the speech action of "bidding": the watch is to bid men to stand, to bid drunks to get them to bed, to bid nurses to quiet crying children, even to bid the "prince in the night," if "the prince be willing," to "stay." But Dogberry, like Brown and Levinson, is aware (even if his knowledge is tacit and not available to his conscious analysis) that in making a request a person risks threatening another's "negative face," or wish to be unimpeded. According to Dogberry, the watch or any man "may stay" the prince, but "marry, not without the prince be willing, for indeed the watch ought to offend no man, and it is an offence to stay a man against his will" (3.3.62–68). Hence Dogberry's "peaceable way" with policing works very much like politeness "to offend no man." As conversation analyst Gregory M. Matoesian puts it, "the organization of repair" is "conversation's central social control mechanism"[35] – an analogue at the level of discourse to law enforcement. The comic and seemingly absurd contradictions of this episode are Shakespeare's acute analysis of how politeness and policing – seeming opposites – intersect.

Mistake-making and repair form the pattern of the central comic action of the play just as they form the pattern of the play's language. In fact, we can say that the function served by comic form in the play and the function served by politeness forms and other verbal maintenance forms mirror one other. As the central action of the comedy, a mistake is made, but by the particular logic of this comedy, repair work offsets the mistake: the pieces are put back together. Indeed, the dreadful mistake takes the form of a speech action: words are spoken that should not have been spoken, and the chaste Hero is slandered. As in many Shakespearean comedies, the potential for tragedy is present, but it is muted: Hero, for example, is given no occasion to "tell the anger of [her] heart." The play instead treats Hero's slander as one more social mistake that can be repaired, like the misunderstanding attending Don Pedro's earlier courtship of Hero on behalf of Claudio. It is, I think, in this likeness between the maintenance work performed in the language and the social maintenance work performed in the comic action that we can locate the peculiar quality of the play's outlook. Interpreters have often taken issue with Claudio's casual representation of his behavior to Hero as merely mistake-making. His version of his behavior – "yet sinned I not, / But in mistaking" (5.1.240–41) – is often thought to be superficial and caddish. Nonetheless, once Hero is reproduced, this version of mistaking and correction is accepted by all the characters in the play, and it is the general outlook on life that the play itself tests out. This prosaic vision of social life as a matter not only of reproduction but also of maintenance is, finally, what gives this play its distinctive outlook. What my account has endeavored to establish is that this outlook is borrowed from everyday language use and is inscribed in the finest details of the conversations.

CHAPTER 7

"*Voice potential*": language and symbolic capital in Othello

Before Brabantio complains to the Venetian senators of Othello's marriage, Iago warns Othello that "the magnifico is much beloved, / And hath in his effect a voice potential / As double as the duke's." Brabantio's words will exert power – the power to "divorce you [Othello], / Or put upon you . . . restraint and grievance" (1.2.12–15).[1] Their power, however, will depend not upon Brabantio's rhetorical skill but instead upon his social position – that is, both on his aristocratic status ("magnifico") and on the accumulated credit he has with his auditors ("much beloved"). How his speech is received will depend less on what he says than on the social site from which it is uttered. Othello rebuts Iago's position, but he does not dispute Iago's presupposition that linguistic competence counts for less than rank or otherwise attributed status in this matter of "voice potential": "My services which I have done the signiory," he responds, "Shall out-tongue his complaints" (1.2.18–19). In the event, Othello's voice does outweigh Brabantio's, with an unanticipated element affecting the reception of their discourse and the outcome of the scene: that is, the exigency of the military threat to Cyprus.

In "The Economics of Linguistic Exchanges," Pierre Bourdieu develops a market analogy to explain how utterances receive their values in particular contexts and how, in turn, the conditions of reception affect discourse production. Giving discourse pragmatics a sociological turn, he asks questions critical to the Senate scene and to other situations in *Othello*: whose speech is it that gets recognized? Whose speech is listened to and obeyed? Who remains silent? and whose speech fails to gain attention or credit? In Bourdieu's account, language in any situation will be worth what those who speak it are deemed to be worth: its price will depend on the symbolic power relation between the speakers, on their respective levels of "symbolic capital."[2] The price a speaker receives for his or her discourse will not, however, be an invariable function of class position or relative status, even in a rigidly hierarchical society. Instead, as Othello's positive reception in the context of the Turkish threat suggests, the price will vary with varying market conditions.

Employing Bourdieu's model as a heuristic and focusing initially on a reading of the Senate scene (1.3), in this chapter I will sketch out the complex and variable linguistic market that shapes and refigures "voice potential" in *Othello*. Gender, class, race, necessity, linguistic ingenuity, and a number of other competing measures enter into the moment-by-moment relations of symbolic power that affect discourse value – that affect, for example, how Brabantio's charges against Othello or Desdemona's request to accompany Othello to Cyprus are heard. This chapter will explore not only discourse reception in *Othello*, but also the force within Shakespeare's play of Bourdieu's hypothesis that a person's discourse production is conditioned by anticipatory adjustments to discourse reception. Finally, I will focus on Iago as a rhetorician and argue for a new perspective on Iago's rhetorical performance in terms of his efforts to manipulate the linguistic market in *Othello*.

In enunciating a sociology of speech in opposition to formal linguistics, Bourdieu argues that "Language is not only an instrument of communication or even of knowledge, but also an instrument of power. A person speaks not only to be understood but also to be believed, obeyed, respected, distinguished."[3] One main event in Act 1 of *Othello* is the contest of voices between Brabantio and Othello. What is at issue between them is whose voice will be given credit, whose voice will have power to shape the ensuing course of events. This criterion for evaluating a particular discourse is foregrounded even before Brabantio and Othello enter the Senate chamber, as the Senators endeavor to digest the news of the Turkish fleets: the Duke observes that "There is no composition in these news / That gives them *credit*" (1.3.1–2; emphasis added); and the messenger from the governor of Cyprus urges:

>   Signior Montano,
> Your trusty and most valiant servitor,
> With his free duty recommends you thus,
> *And prays you to believe him.*   (1.3.39–42; emphasis added)

As the discursive contest between Brabantio and Othello proceeds, the verbal performance of each speaker receives a summary evaluation from the Duke. Whereas Brabantio's accusation draws the caution that "To vouch this is no proof" (106), the Duke responds with approval to Othello's colorful account of wooing Desdemona: "I think this tale would win my daughter too" (170). Although the Duke apparently evaluates intrinsic features of the linguistic performance of each speaker, it is situational context, as I have already suggested, more than verbal competence that accounts for Othello's profit and Brabantio's loss.

The carefully staged entrance of senator and general provides a vivid theatrical emblem for the dynamic variation in relative power. First, the significance of the entrance is prepared by the Duke's order that letters be sent "post-post-haste" to "Marcus Luccicos" (44–46), a character not otherwise identified except by his unavailability at this time of crisis. The verification of his absence heightens the importance of "the man," in Brabantio's words, "this Moor, whom now" the Duke's "special mandate for the state affairs / Hath hither brought" (71–73). A stage direction signals the arrival of a large group of characters, including "BRABANTIO, OTHELLO, CASSIO, IAGO, RODERIGO and OFFICERS." The First Senator announces the arrival selectively, singling out "Brabantio and the valiant Moor" (47) and relegating to lesser importance those left unnamed. The structure of the Duke's greeting encapsulates the power dynamic of the situation, articulating the priorities of the moment:

> Valiant Othello we must straight employ you
> Against the general enemy Ottoman.
> [*To Brabantio*] I did not see you: welcome, gentle signior;
> We lacked your counsel and your help tonight.   (1.3.48–51)

Othello is greeted first; the need for his military skills accounts for his precedence. Brabantio is greeted in second place, with the conversational repair work nonetheless signalling a recognition of his claim, based on rank, to first place.

This account of how Othello's voice gains ascendancy within the immediate situation in no way exhausts the complexity of the linguistic market depicted in the Senate scene. Another principal speaker whose voice power is at issue in the scene is Desdemona. Answering the Duke's summons, she speaks first to confirm Othello's account of their courtship and later to make a request of her own, to accompany Othello to the war zone. In both cases her speech wins credit, in the first instance solidifying the Duke's acceptance of the marriage and silencing Brabantio's complaint and in the second instance gaining her permission to go with Othello. An account of Desdemona's voice power in this situation must consider the subordinate relation it bears to Othello's discourse, although even this power relation is subtly modulated within the dialogue. In Desdemona's first speech, carefully weighing the duty owed to a father and to a husband, she seconds Othello's voice and adds in a straightforward way to his credibility. In making the request to accompany Othello, on the other hand, while Desdemona does show her devotion to Othello, she also asserts her separate and independent voice, her own claim to have her wish heard even after he has already publicly requested accommodation for her in Venice. In the chorus of dissent answering the Duke's suggestion that Desdemona reside with her father, her voice momentarily amplifies Othello's before she strikes off on her own, claiming the floor and elaborating an alternative plan:

> BRABANTIO   I'll not have it so.
> OTHELLO Nor I.
> DESDEMONA   Nor I; I would not there reside
>   To put my father in impatient thoughts
>   By being in his eye. Most gracious duke,
>   To my unfolding lend your prosperous ear
>   And let me find a charter in your voice
>   T'assist my simpleness.   (1.3.237–43)

The self-deprecating comment about her simplicity notwithstanding, Desdemona shows herself by Renaissance standards a bold and self-confident speaker in a setting whose formality and importance would silence most speakers, especially – one might expect – a woman. Nonetheless, any potential discomfort among her auditors at this mildly bold speech by a woman is in this instance quickly mitigated by Othello's appropriation of her voice to his own determinations. He takes ownership of her sentiments, asking that the Duke "Let her have your voice" (256) and internalizing any potential conflict as tension between his own affection for Desdemona and his military business.

Desdemona's verbal behavior in the scene and in the play as a whole is not consistent with any simple stereotype of feminine speech, especially not with the Renaissance commonplace concerning silence as woman's eloquence. In her initial appearances, Desdemona is an assured and self-confident speaker. That is not to say that stereotyped gender roles do not come into play here. Consider, for example, Othello's embedded narrative of the courtship as "mutual" recognition: "She loved me for the dangers I had passed, / And I loved her that she did pity them" (166–67). What could better exemplify the standard clichés about male and female roles in cross-sex conversation prevalent even today than Othello's account of how he talked and she responded?[4] When Othello told over "the story of my life" (128), Desdemona "gave me for my pains a world of sighs"[5] and "swore, in faith, 'twas strange, 'twas passing strange, / 'Twas pitiful, 'twas wondrous pitiful" (158–60). And yet, whatever we are to make of the accuracy of Othello's report, such self-effacing speech behavior is not Desdemona's predominant manner in the play.

Traditional readings of *Othello* have often focused, as I am doing now, on the complex speech patterns of the characters. In such readings, the *raison d'être* for an utterance is the speaker's character, or essential nature. Dramatic language is said to construct character: whereas in life language expresses character, in his plays Shakespeare shapes language to make it seem that language expresses pre-existing character.[6] In this view, the divergence from received stereotypes of female speech evident in Desdemona's self-assured and eloquent public speaking is to be explained as a particularizing and richly complicating mark of her essential character. But in a play so insistently dialogic as *Othello* – a play so intently focused on how one character's conversational contributions shape and direct the words, thoughts, and actions of another – it seems particularly pertinent to argue a different case, to take up Bourdieu's thesis that "[t]he *raison d'être* of a discourse . . . is to be found in the socially defined site from which it is uttered."[7] Bourdieu's account of the social production of discourse emphasizes anticipatory adjustment, and offers a fruitful way to account for the speech patterns of Desdemona and other characters in *Othello*.[8]

"[O]ne of the most important factors bearing on linguistic production," Bourdieu argues, is "the anticipation of profit which is durably inscribed in the language habitus, in the form of an anticipatory adjustment (without conscious anticipation) to the objective [i.e. ascribed] value of one's discourse."[9] What one says, how one says it, and whether one speaks at all in any given situation is strongly influenced, in this view, by the "practical expectation . . . of receiving a high or low price for one's discourse."[10] An utterance, then, inscribes an expectation of profit, an estimate of the likelihood that the speaker will be believed, recognized, obeyed. This expectation will not, in most instances, derive solely or even in the main part from an assessment of the immediate social situation; it cannot be entirely accounted for by the immediate relation of speaker to listener. The context of reception which shapes a speaker's linguistic production has a history, and it is that history Bourdieu tries to account for by positing the "language habitus" of the speaker. That language habitus is a practical memory, built up through the accumulated history of speech contexts in which a speaker has functioned and received recognition or censure. The language habitus is shaped by the history of a person's most sustained social connections, by a person's cumulative dialogue with others.

Bourdieu's practical application of this conception is to frame some generalizations about language and class position, generalizations about the speech entitlement of the dominant classes and the self-censorship of what he terms the petits bourgeois. Helpful as his preliminary ideas about language and class are, nonetheless these generalizations do not realize the full utility of his model. For, while the model can be of assistance in helping us to understand the speech positions of the dominant and subordinate classes, ultimately we are making only rough generalizations about any person's speech by positioning it as upper, middle, or lower class. We need a model for social discourse that can account for class and also for more particular linguistic trajectories, and Bourdieu's model can help us toward that particularity, toward an account of the social shaping even of highly individuated speech patterns.

But let us begin with Desdemona and class. Desdemona does not enter the play as the stereotypical silent and modest woman, but rather as an aristocratic speaker whose discourse is full of the assurance and self-confidence of her class habitus. This can be seen not only in the remarkable ease with which she speaks before the Duke and Senators, but also in the basic facts that she speaks at all and that she initiates speech topics. If we consider how it could be that speech patterns inscribe a speaker's expectation of profit, we need to look not only at the internal constitution of the speeches but also at turn-taking and access to the floor. "[T]he linguist," Bourdieu remarks, "regards the *conditions for the establishment of communication* as already secured, whereas, in real situations, that is the essential question."[11] To read the power relations of the scene one needs to observe the access to speech in this formal Senate setting of those who speak. Furthermore, one needs to consider what shapes the silence or non-participation of Roderigo, Cassio, the soldiers – and, most important for the developing action, the silence of Iago. Of course, in a play, considerations apart from those of real life will affect the access of speakers to the floor. The distinction, for example, between major and minor characters within any plot structure will help account for who speaks at length and whose speech is sparing. Nonetheless, one can still reasonably argue that the configuration of speakers Shakespeare represents in the Senate scene primarily reflects the power dynamics of the urgent situation as played out in a formal setting of the kind that regulates speaker access to a very high degree. Desdemona's confidence in her access to the floor, borne out by the Duke's solicitous question – "What would you, Desdemona?" (243) – suggests a history of access, the history of her class habitus.

This discourse history is also emphatically suggested by Desdemona's conversation with Cassio in 3.3 regarding her commitment to mediate on his behalf with Othello. "Be thou assured" is the opening phrase and repeated motif of her talk:

> *Be thou assured*, good Cassio, I will do
> All my abilities in thy behalf.   (3.3.1–2; emphasis added)

> ... *Do not doubt*, Cassio,
> But I will have my lord and you again
> As friendly as you were.   (3.3.5–7; emphasis added)

> ... and *be you well assured*
> He shall in strangeness stand no farther off
> Than in a politic distance.   (3.3.11–13; emphasis added)

> *Do not doubt* that. Before Emilia here,
> I give thee warrant of thy place. *Assure thee* ...
>   (3.3.19–20; emphasis added)

When she moves Cassio's suit to Othello, her whole manner bespeaks this assurance of a ready acquiescence to her request – her repetitive insistence that he set a time to see Cassio, her understated persuasion tactics, her assumption that she has a role to play in Othello's public affairs, her low assessment of the speech-act risk involved in making the request, and finally her minimizing of her suit:

> Why, this is not a boon;
> 'Tis as I should entreat you wear your gloves,
> Or feed on nourishing dishes, or keep you warm ...
> ... Nay, when I have a suit
> Wherein I mean to touch your love indeed,
> It shall be full of poise and difficult weight,
> And fearful to be granted.   (3.3.76–78; 80–83)

This is not simply the naïvety of a new wife about her power to sway a husband she scarcely knows. Desdemona's assurance inscribes the history of her prior speech reception, the ease that marks the dominant classes and exempts them from speech tension, linguistic insecurity, and self censoring. The crisis for Desdemona in this play comes as a surprising alteration in how her speech is received, specifically by Othello. The change in speech reception later in the play, it is possible to argue, also makes for a change in Desdemona.

If Desdemona's "voice potential" in the Senate scene and later bespeaks her class habitus, to what extent can we read a history of voice inscribed in Othello's speech? Othello's long speeches in Act 1 can be distinguished partly by their amplitude, by a high degree of elaboration and embellishment. Characteristic are the nominal and adjectival doublets, in some instances marked by syntactic strangenesses bearing some relation to hendiadys:[12] Othello speaks of "circumscription and confine" (1.2.27), "the flinty and steel couch of war" (1.3.227), "A natural and prompt alacrity" (229), "such accommodation and besort" (235), being "free and bounteous to her mind" (261), "serious and great business" (263), "speculative and officed instruments" (266), "all indign and base adversities" (269). In what George Wilson Knight called the "Othello music," there is, E. A. J. Honigmann has suggested, a complicating note of bombast.[13] It is an eloquence that displays its eloquent performance, not – like Desdemona's – an eloquence that bespeaks its adequacy. Apparently at odds with this high performance speech is Othello's disclaimer:

> Rude am I in my speech
> And little blessed with the soft phrase of peace,
> . . .
> And little of this great world can I speak
> More than pertains to feats of broil and battle;
> And therefore little shall I grace my cause
> In speaking for myself. Yet, by your gracious patience,
> I will a round unvarnished tale deliver
> Of my whole course of love . . .   (1.3.81–82; 86–91)

While I argued earlier that it is not primarily the distinction of Othello's verbal performance that accounts for his voice power in the scene, it is nonetheless untrue that he delivers "a round," or plain, "unvarnished tale" (90). Verbal virtuosity, and not plainness, marks his tale. Othello's discourse style, then, blends linguistic insecurity and linguistic effort. Not, as with Desdemona, ease and assurance, but instead some degree of tension characterizes Othello's discourse production. And, by the logic of Bourdieu's hypothesis that discourse production is shaped by anticipated discourse reception, it is not the aristocratic insider who will feel a performance compulsion, an impulse to linguistic overreaching, in the accustomed formality of the senate chamber. Hence we can see how Othello's distinctive speech patterns may have a social motive: a man of great talent without so consistent and homogeneous a history of speech-making and speech reception as the dominant speakers among the Venetians may well overreach in his speech, and a highly formalized, institutionalized setting will increase the likelihood of speech tension.[14] As Bourdieu argues in his efforts to characterize the speech of aspiring groups, "the greater the gap between recognition and mastery, the more imperative the need for the self-corrections aimed at ensuring the *revaluing of the linguistic product* by a particularly intensive mobilization of the linguistic resources, and the greater the tension and containment that they demand."[15] This helps to explain why Othello, a person of color and an exotic outsider, might – even without making conscious adjustments – tend to mobilize his verbal resources more fully than Venetian speakers of the dominant group. In language terms, what he does is to try harder.

As we have seen, trying harder to produce well-crafted discourse may not always pay off, since a discourse's value depends on the power relations obtaining in a particular market. Not all the characters in the play respond in the same way to a felt gap between the recognition they commonly receive and their verbal mastery. Consider Iago, who early on in the play registers his perception of a gap between recognition and mastery in the assertion: "I know my price, I am worth no worse a place" (1.1.11). Iago is keenly aware of a gap between his own considerable skills – including his verbal skills – and the limited advantages that readily come his way through their deployment. This shows in the extreme contempt he expresses for the linguistic accents of other characters – a contempt bound up in his recognition that the limited verbal repertoires of some others nonetheless garner them easy profits that his own greater rhetorical expertise cannot attain. At the start of the play, Iago derides the "bombast circumstance" (1.1.13) of Othello's talk, but the intensity of his resentment against the speech of others is most strongly illustrated in his reaction to Cassio's conversation with Desdemona upon their arrival in Cyprus. Shakespeare takes great care to draw his audience's attention to the courtierlike politeness of Cassio's speech here and elsewhere. Not only does Cassio himself associate his manner ostentatiously with a "courtesy" style, but he sets Iago's speech in antithetical (and insulting) relation to his own: "He speaks home, madam; you may relish him more in the soldier than in the scholar" (2.1.61–62). When Iago derogates Cassio's style, delivering sarcastic asides about his gestural and verbal courtesies, he is not, I think, voicing resentment that his lower class position excludes him from the verbal finesse of a gentlemanly discourse. Iago is a verbal chameleon; as we shall see, he knows how to speak like Cassio. What Iago resents is how easily Cassio's speech gains credit with his auditors, a credit Iago could not earn by employing the same speech patterns. Iago devalues the products of civil conversation not because he cannot replicate them but because he is not socially positioned to receive advantage from them. Cassio, Iago remarks to Roderigo, has "an eye can stamp and counterfeit advantages" (2.1.230–31). What Iago expresses is a keen awareness that different people can draw different profits from the same discourse – that Cassio's gentlemanly status and good looks make even the very motion of his eyes able to garner an advantage his own finest verbal performance could not attain in situations like the conversation with the aristocratic Desdemona. In *Othello*, Iago is – as many scholars have previously noted – a consummate rhetorician. But he is a rhetorician keenly aware that the prize for best speaker can't be won with excellent verbal skills.

The significant fact about Iago's discourse in the Senate scene is that he does not speak. His silence signals his slight chance of profit in that formal public setting. Whether with full consciousness or not, Iago as rhetorician assesses the conditions of the linguistic market in which he operates and chooses tools and timing that will work to gain him profit. Adapting Bourdieu's suggestions, we can generalize that rhetorical mastery consists not merely in the capacity for discourse production but also in "the capacity for appropriation and appreciation; it depends, in other words, on the capacity . . . to impose the criteria of appreciation most favorable to [one's] own products."[16] Iago as rhetorician works in the play to undo Cassio's and Desdemona's "credit with the Moor" and Othello's credit with the Venetian authorities; in so doing, he works to gain credit for his own discursive inventions. One striking feature of Iago's performance is his preference for private conversation as the scene of his verbal virtuosity. Indeed, the frequent conversations help to give this play its distinctive accent among Shakespeare's tragedies. As we have seen, Bourdieu distinguishes between the discourse constraints of formal situations and the less restricting discourse conditions of domestic settings, of talk among friends and family. Iago's choice of speech setting is, then, itself a key rhetorical strategy. Iago prefers conversational settings, for in the less restricted discourse conditions of talk between friends he can more readily capture the floor and win an appreciation for his speech products.

This is not to say that Iago's rhetorical expertise is never deployed on public occasions. It is, but his rhetorical strategies differ substantially from those he exhibits in conversation. One of his key strategies for public situations is voice mediation. Where his own voice has little chance of success, Iago appropriates other voices to his use. The play opens with Iago commenting on how he (like a typical Elizabethan suitor) negotiated through mediators for the place, lost to Cassio, as Othello's lieutenant: "three great ones of the city, / In personal suit to make me his lieutenant, / Off-capped to him; . . . / But he . . . / Nonsuits my mediators . . ." (1.1.8–16).

But Iago by no means restricts his tactics of voice mediation to this institutionalized form. Act 1, scene 1 also provides, in the role Iago constructs for Roderigo, a characteristic example of how Iago appropriates the credit of an intermediary voice. Iago, of course, deploys his own speaking voice in concert with Roderigo's in the effort to fire Brabantio up against Othello, and I will consider Iago's speech in the scene before exploring his appropriation of Roderigo's speech. To arouse Brabantio's emotions, Iago – keeping his personal identity obscure – takes on the voice of a "ruffian" (1.1.111), a voice from the gutter, whose lewd conceits prompt Brabantio to ask "What profane wretch art thou?" (114). Within the symbolic power relations and verbal economy of the polite Venetian society that Bourdieu's model has helped to describe, a ruffian's voice will have little power to secure appreciation and elicit belief. Nonetheless, the status-poor voice of the "ruffian" can certainly stir up trouble and do serious damage. Repeatedly in the play, Shakespeare associates a specific kind of destructive power with the untamed and uneuphemized speech of the status-less speaker. This association is most striking in the extended metaphor Montano and his interlocutors develop for the force beyond human control that defeats the Turks and endangers the Venetian fleets. The loud cursing speech of a "ruffian" is Shakespeare's metaphorical vehicle for the havoc played by the wind:

MONTANO Methinks the wind does *speak aloud* at land,
          A fuller blast ne'er shook our battlements.
          If it hath *ruffianed* so upon the sea,
          What ribs of oak, when mountains melt on them,
          Can hold the mortise? What shall we hear of this?
2 GENTLEMAN   A segregation of the Turkish fleet:
          For do but stand upon the banning shore,
          The *chidden* billow seems to pelt the clouds;
          . . .
          I never did like *molestation* view
          On the enchafèd flood.   (2.1.5–17; emphasis added)

The association between the low-status voice and a potential for doing damage operates at the level of tacit assumption, or ideological presupposition, among the characters in *Othello*. Emilia reflecting on Othello's slanders against Desdemona's chastity, for example, assumes that the damage has been done by the lies and insinuations of a low-status speaker: "The Moor's abused by some most villainous knave, / Some base notorious knave, some scurvy fellow" (4.2.138–39). Brabantio in 1.1 assumes from the clamorous voices and rude conceits that the men creating a disturbance outside are of low station, and, as I suggested earlier, Iago comments on the assumption – "you think we are ruffians" (1.1.110–11). While it may not be possible or even desirable to establish Iago's actual social station in this play with entire precision, it is clear that his background is of lower status than most of the other characters – he is a commoner, while other subordinate characters, the Clown excepted, are gentlemen (Cassio and Roderigo) or even noblemen (Lodovico and Gratiano). Nonetheless, it is not easy to determine whether Iago's "base" voice in 1.1 is that which is most "natural" to him, the dominant note of his linguistic habitus, or just one of many ventriloquized voices he is so adept at appropriating. Clearly, however, he has himself been often enough subjected to the negative judgments against low-status discourse that are a reflex among the Venetians to know precisely what kind of damaging power a clamorous voice can wield and what limits that power. What limits the voice power of the clamorous voice and makes it a rhetorical instrument Iago deploys only sparingly is that it cannot elicit the belief and recognition that gathers credit to the speaker. In seeking to secure profit on the linguistic markets of Venice and Cyprus, Iago aims for something more than the brute effect of making trouble.

To the end of shaping Brabantio's belief, Iago deploys the different accent of Roderigo's voice. Roderigo speaks as a gentleman, and calls upon Brabantio to "recognize" his voice ("Most reverend signior, do you know my voice?" [94]). He calls upon Brabantio not merely to recognize that it is Roderigo who speaks but to recognize that the speaker's social status guarantees his credit: "Do not believe / That from the sense of all civility / I thus would play and trifle with your reverence" (1.1.129–31). It is, indeed, this status-marked speech by Roderigo that finally draws Brabantio's acknowledgment that "Belief of it [Desdemona's elopement] oppresses me already" (142). Shrewdly calculating his slight chances of gaining such credit through his own voice in making this public disturbance, Iago appropriates to his own purposes the Cassio-like politeness and the matching status of Roderigo's voice. Of course, Iago's is a rough and improvisatory art here, for while he can direct Roderigo's general performance ("Rouse him, make after him, poison his delight" [69]), he cannot actually put the words into Roderigo's mouth. Nonetheless, Roderigo serves his turn. Iago tells the audience of how he makes "my fool my purse" (1.3.365), but we never actually see Iago spending Roderigo's money. What we see instead is how he spends the symbolic capital of Roderigo's voice.

Fundamental, then, to Iago's rhetorical mastery is his manipulation of what Bourdieu claims linguists long ignored: social context, understood as the conditions for speech profit. Iago is what he ironically calls Cassio – "a finder out of occasions" (2.1.29–30). Going beyond the usual dictates of decorum, he is not content merely to fit his speech to the occasion, since so many public occasions restrict his access to speech and opportunity for profit. Instead, he finds out or creates the occasions for speaking that afford him the greatest advantage. The riotous street scene is his public occasion of choice, the scene in which he most profitably draws speech credit away from others and toward himself. As I have suggested, Bourdieu distinguishes sharply between the communication conditions obtaining in situations of high formality and in situations of lesser formality. In situations of high formality the reproductive role of politeness is most pronounced, scripting in the language of participants a mutual recognition and acknowledgment of their relative social stations. In our analysis of the Senate scene, we have seen how the combination of formal scene and disruptive urgency made for a kind of re-ranking: the urgency of the moment meant that forms of symbolic capital apart from static social rank took on importance. But the adjustment in power relations was still relatively contained by the formal setting, keeping lesser ranking characters like Iago in their silent and inferior places. Lessen the formality and intensify the disruptive urgency of a scene, and Iago can make occasions in which even his speech can prevail over those of higher rank. Provide an outdoor setting, street fighting, darkness – as Iago does both when Cassio is discredited (2.3) and when Roderigo is murdered and Cassio badly hurt (5.1) – and restrictions on speech roles are relaxed or overturned.[17] As the murder scene in 5.1 draws towards its conclusion, Iago himself articulates this principle which has freed his speech, at least for a short space of time, from the perpetual obligation to "recognize" his subordinate relation to others: "Signior Gratiano!" he exclaims, pretending only then to make out who his interlocutor is and adjust his language to their prescribed social relation: "I cry your gentle pardon. / These bloody accidents must excuse my manners / That so neglected you" (5.1.93–95). Hence we see that Iago's instruction to Roderigo – "Do you find some occasion to anger Cassio" (2.1.250–51) – is as supreme a rhetorical act as any virtuoso speech of persuasion he makes in the play. It is through this construction of a favorable context that Iago can set up a contest of voices in which he is able to secure the floor ("Honest Iago, that looks dead with grieving, / Speak." [2.3.158–59]) and disable the voices of his superiors Cassio and Montano ("I pray you pardon me, I cannot speak" [170]; "Your officer Iago can inform you – / While I spare speech, which something now offends me –" [179–80]). Iago has full scope to elaborate his version of reality at extended length before important people. What he seeks and gains is not the hearers' simple belief in the facts as he represents them. What he is after is an enhancement of his "voice potential," or – in Bourdieu's terms – an accumulation of his symbolic capital, which is registered in the personal approbation of Othello's response: "I know, Iago, / Thy honesty and love doth mince this matter, / Making it light to Cassio" (2.3.227–29). Furthermore, Iago has engineered the loss of Cassio's lieutenancy with – perhaps more important – the loss of his annoying expectation that he can easily profit from the "show of courtesy" (2.1.99) characteristic of his discourse: "I will ask him for my place again; he shall tell me I am a drunkard. Had I as many mouths as Hydra, such an answer would stop them all" (2.3.276–78). A rhetorician able to understand the mechanisms by which the polite Venetian order, instantiated in its typical speech situations, stops talented voices and gives credit to the incompetent, Iago manages, if only for a short time, his own correction of the gap between linguistic capital and credit.

Let us turn briefly to a consideration of the arena of Iago's greatest rhetorical accomplishment – not the public occasion but the private space of conversation between "friends." Of course, the familiar and relaxed space of friendship is itself produced and sustained through discourse: utterance and context are co-constructive. It is made clear in *Othello* that Iago himself plays a large role in producing and reproducing the intimate register of the friendship discourses within which he finds his freedom to maneuver – the Iago–Roderigo dialogues, the Iago–Cassio dialogues, and the Iago–Othello dialogues:

[To Roderigo.] I have professed me thy friend, and I confess me knit to thy deserving with cables of perdurable toughness. (1.3.327–29)

[To Cassio.] And, good lieutenant, I think you think I love you. (2.3.282–83)

[To Othello.] My lord, you know I love you. (3.3.118)

Iago deploys the protestation of love or close affection as a rhetorical tactic, and the Brown and Levinson politeness model we have made use of in preceding chapters can help us to understand how it works to widen the scope of what speech is sayable and creditable for Iago. According to Brown and Levinson, the degree of polite reserve or deference expected of a low-ranking character like Iago speaking to social superiors like Roderigo, Cassio, and Othello is not dependent solely on their difference in social rank. In addition to relative power, the weight of the face-threatening act being negotiated and the social distance between the speakers will also serve to determine what politeness level is expected. As Brown and Levinson point out, a "fundamental ambiguity . . . derives from the compounding of the factors D [social distance], P [relative power], and R [culture-specific ranking of imposition] into a single index of risk." As we have seen with Sir Edward Warner's letter in chapter 4, a speaker may exploit this fundamental ambiguity for his or her own profit, by attempting "to re-rank the expectable weighting of one of the variables."[18] Iago does just this, using the assumption of greater intimacy or closeness than might otherwise obtain to permit franker and less formally polite utterance than his subordinate power relation would predict. In other words, he exploits the semblance of friendship to gain voice power. As a basic example, consider the relation between Iago's assurance to Cassio of friendship and the imperatives that surround it:

Come, be a man. Drown thyself? Drown cats and blind puppies! I have professed me thy friend, and I confess me knit to thy deserving with cables of perdurable toughness. I could never better stead thee than now. Put money in thy purse. Follow thou these wars; defeat thy favour with a usurped beard. I say, put money in thy purse. (1.3.326–32)

At work here is a "re-ranking" of the power relation obtaining between them, the commands unsuited to their relative social stations legitimized by the intimated closeness. As with Erasmus's self-consciously manipulated friendship language, Iago's is a style that accents presumption.

A more complex process of re-ranking occurs in the intense conversations in which Iago makes Othello believe Desdemona to be false. These conversations in 3.3 and 4.1 have been so often and so adequately analyzed in *Othello* criticism that I will restrict my consideration to a few points about Iago as a rhetorician of politeness and, more generally, of conversation. Iago's initial overtures are hedged in by ostentatiously polite forms, a deferential rhetoric which seems almost to ventriloquize Cassio's characteristic voice:

> I do beseech you,
> Though I perchance am vicious in my guess –
> As I confess it is my nature's plague
> To spy into abuses, . . .
> . . . that your wisdom then,
> From one that so imperfectly conceits,
> Would take no notice, nor build yourself a trouble
> Out of his scattering and unsure observance. (3.3.145–52)

> . . . – but I am much to blame,
> I humbly do beseech you of your pardon
> For too much loving you. (3.3.213–15)

> My lord, I would I might entreat your honour
> To scan this thing no farther . . .
> Yet, if you please to hold him off awhile,
> You shall by that perceive him and his means.
> (3.3.246–47; 250–51)

In these examples, Iago covers the whole range of negative-politeness behavior I have outlined in earlier chapters. The indirect and convoluted politeness forms are suited both to the large power difference between Iago and Othello and the serious face-threat involved in asserting Othello's wife's infidelity. Indeed, before the precise nature of the "abuses" hinted at reaches the level of direct statement, the uncharacteristically extreme (for Iago) politeness level invites Othello's inference-making about their extreme nature. Iago's concurrent insistence on his love for Othello, which would normally establish an expectation of more relaxed politeness forms, adds to the implied ranking of the face-threatening act being performed in unfolding Desdemona's wrongdoing as extreme. Hence, Iago employs a re-ranking technique first to elicit Othello's belief in Desdemona's and Cassio's crimes. Later we can measure in Iago's astonishingly altered politeness forms a re-ranking of the power relation between servant and master. Here is how Iago speaks to Othello in 4.1:

> Good sir, be a man:
> Think every bearded fellow that's but yoked
> May draw with you. (4.1.63–65)

> Stand you a while apart,
> Confine yourself but in a patient list.
> Whilst you were here, o'erwhelmèd with your grief –
> A passion most unsuiting such a man –
> Cassio came hither. (4.1.72–76)

This language, to the repetition of the phrase "be a man," is precisely the language Iago earlier addressed to Roderigo: Iago addresses Othello with what Brown and Levinson would call "bald on-record" commands, unmitigated by politeness repair. If Iago were challenged about this mode of address that undermines Othello's superior status, he would be able to claim as he did to Roderigo that "I have professed me thy friend" (1.3.327–28), with the implication that the close relation justifies the presumptuous language. In reality, Iago has maneuvered his master into a situation that affords the servant a "voice potential" above his master's. Iago, then, is a consummate rhetorician of politeness, but not – as should now be clear – because he employs polite eloquence. Iago's mastery of politeness consists in his ability to understand its full social logic and undermine its strong orientation to conservative reproduction of the entitlement of dominant speakers.

I have argued that Iago's rhetorical mastery is not a matter of his exceptional verbal skills but instead of his extraordinary command of how verbal process functions in context and of the conditions governing linguistic domination and speech profit. By offering an account of language performance that shifts the focus away from verbal eloquence, Bourdieu's model of how language operates as an instrument of power has helped to guide this reading of Iago as rhetorician. Bourdieu does not entirely discount the role of verbal skills: he simply treats verbal eloquence as only one among a number of competing forms of symbolic capital that enters into how discourse is valued. There can be no doubt that Iago is a skillful speaker as well as a skillful manipulator of context, but his eloquence is not that of the public orator. Iago is, above all, a rhetorician of conversation, and it is in his exploitation of some of its characteristic rhetorical forms and logic – including not only politeness forms but also the inference-generating strategies identified by H. Paul Grice as central to conversational logic – that his verbal skill or "linguistic capital" consists.[19]

Given Iago's unsurpassed ability to control the effects of speech, it is significant that his wife Emilia's speech is the instrument of his exposure. Shakespeare foregrounds the two exceptional circumstances that bring Iago's criminal actions to light: Emilia's persistence in speaking and people's belief in what she says. First, she has the boldness to interrupt her master and mistress in their bedchamber, after she has been explicitly dismissed: "O, good my lord, I would speak a word with you" (5.2.91), she insists, "I do beseech you / That I may speak with you. O, good my lord!" (102–03). Her access to speech in this situation can be explained in precisely the terms that Iago should understand: just as he has turned occasions of public disturbance into opportunities for his own exercise of language power, here the public disturbance surrounding Roderigo's and Cassio's injuries enables his wife to speak and be heard. Indeed, her cries of "What, ho!" (86, 90) directly echo the cries with which Iago and Roderigo awakened Brabantio (1.1.79–80). It may, nonetheless, be too reductive to argue that the rhetoric of social situation alone explains how Emilia sustains her resistance to Othello's and especially Iago's efforts to silence her ("What needs this iterance, woman?" [149]; "Go to, charm your tongue" [182]; "Be wise and get you home" [221]; "Filth, thou liest!" [229]) and her access to voice ("I will not charm my tongue; I am bound to speak" [183]; "let them all, / All, all cry shame against me, yet I'll speak" [219–20]). The surprise of Emilia's voice power is not simply a matter of everyday verbal economics: the play positions her speech as extraordinary and grants her a measure of heroic agency, as she asserts the priority of her moral responsibility over her social role ("'Tis proper I obey him, but not now" [195]). Indeed, social motives are inverted in Emilia's claim to speak not out of "power to do . . . harm" but out of power "to be hurt" (161–62).

How is it that Iago's rhetorical sophistication can fail to guard him against his wife's "voice potential," against her capacity to do him harm? His own brutal words in the scene of their arrival at Cyprus attest to his experience of Emilia's situated loquacity and should, one would think, forewarn him of what he so entirely fails to anticipate:

> IAGO   Sir, would she give you so much of her lips
> As of her tongue she oft bestows on me
> You would have enough.
> DESDEMONA   Alas, she has no speech.
> IAGO   In faith, too much:
> I find it still when I have list to sleep.
> Marry, before your ladyship, I grant

> She puts her tongue a little in her heart
> And chides with thinking.   (2.1.100–07)

Whether Iago's distinction between Emilia's talkativeness in the home and her self-censoring silence in her new mistress's presence is to be read as an accurate representation or an effect of his evident misogyny is ambiguous, but the pattern of variation he describes is consistent with Bourdieu's social logic of verbal fluency. Iago's carelessness about what he lets his wife know may be connected with his overly confident estimate that she will consistently put "her tongue a little in her heart" when she attends her superiors. He forgets that the exception he himself so cleverly manages to the general rule that an inferior's speech will receive little credit can be managed by someone else – even, in extraordinary circumstances, by the wife he so entirely discounts. The rough and improvisatory nature of Iago's rhetoric of situation makes his a particularly high-risk performance – and in the end he loses control of the play's speech outcomes. With his prospects in captivity affording him no further possibility of advantage through speech, he vows "never" to "speak word" (5.2.301).

In this chapter, I have used Bourdieu's economic model for linguistic exchange as a heuristic to explore speech reception and speech production in *Othello*. This enabled, first, an examination of how variable power relations affect discourse reception in a particular setting and, second, an account of how the history of a person's speech reception functions together with immediate context to shape speech production. As in chapter 1 but with another accent, this reading has allowed me to offer a different perspective on the interrelation Shakespeare represents between character and language than is usual in the stylistic criticism of Shakespeare's plays – a perspective that links linguistic performance not to the autonomous subject or to individual character but instead to character conceived as the locus of social and power relations. Here, as elsewhere in this study, it is clear that to discover the social shaping of Shakespeare's language is not to diminish the stature and accomplishment of his verbal art. Indeed, it is to enhance it by showing how much his art of dialogue goes beyond the formal manipulation of verbal patterns. Just as Bourdieu's model has helped to open up a new perspective for assessing Iago's rhetorical artistry as a mastery not only of speech forms but also of speech contexts, so the various models for social rhetoric considered in this book – from politeness theory, epistolary rhetoric, discourse and conversational analysis, and sociolinguistics – have helped to show Shakespeare's dialogic art as a mastery of social rhetoric going well beyond anything that was codified in the rhetorical texts of his day – or, except in broken glimpses, of ours.

Notes

INTRODUCTION

1 *The Dialogic Imagination: Four Essays by M. M. Bakhtin*, ed. Michael Holquist, trans. Caryl Emerson and Michael Holquist (Austin: University of Texas Press, 1981), p. 280.
2 Basic texts in the overlapping fields of discourse analysis and linguistic pragmatics include: Malcolm Coulthard, *An Introduction to Discourse Analysis*, 2nd edn. (London and New York: Longman, 1985); Stephen C. Levinson, *Pragmatics* (Cambridge University Press, 1983); Gillian Brown and George Yule, *Discourse Analysis* (Cambridge University Press, 1983).
3 See, for example, Norman Fairclough, *Language and Power* (London and New York: Longman, 1989) and *Discourse and Social Change* (Cambridge: Polity Press, 1992) and Jay L. Lemke, *Textual Politics: Discourse and Social Dynamics* (London: Taylor & Francis, 1995).
4 *Politeness: Some Universals in Language Usage* (1978; Cambridge University Press, 1987).
5 See Roger Brown and Albert Gilman, "The Pronouns of Power and Solidarity," in *Style in Language*, ed. Thomas A. Sebeok (Cambridge, Mass.: MIT Press, 1960), pp. 253–76; Clara Calvo, "Pronouns of Address and Social Negotiation in *As You Like It*," *Language and Literature*, 1 (1992), 5–27.
6 Trans. Charles Fantazzi, in *Collected Works of Erasmus*, vol. 25, ed. J. K. Sowards (Toronto, Buffalo, and London: University of Toronto Press, 1985), pp. 10–254.
7 William Fulwood, *The Enimie of Idlenesse* (1568; London, 1593); John Browne, *The Marchants Avizo* (London, 1590).
8 "On the Writing of Letters," p. 20.
9 Keir Elam's *Shakespeare's Universe of Discourse: Language-Games in the Comedies* (Cambridge University Press, 1984), pp. 177–234, and Andrew K. Kennedy's *Dramatic Dialogue: The Duologue of Personal Encounter* (Cambridge University Press, 1983), pp. 1–33 and 62–136, are two important exceptions. It is partly the long reign of a new critical discourse over discussions of Shakespeare's language that explains the neglect of dialogue. The features of dialogue do not fit anywhere in the traditional roll call of things to talk about when one considers verbal style in Shakespeare: diction, syntax,

prosody, imagery, tropes and figures. Dialogue was not prominent on the agenda of the New Critic who adapted his or her skills honed in reading short poems, imagined as self-sufficient utterances, to reading Shakespeare's plays. It was also not prominent on the agenda of the performance critic, who found in the languages of gesture and stage spectacle matters to displace the concerns of the verbal critic. And even actors, as far as I understand, tend to talk of searching out in *their* speeches the traces of *their* characters, of finding out the individuated psychology that can be construed as the well-spring for those particular words. We still need to develop a shared vocabulary, an inventory of categories and distinctions, for the detailed discussion of the interactive features of Shakespeare's language.

10 Andrew Kennedy argues for a "strong concept of dialogue" as "personal encounter" involving an "interchange of values" and "exchange of 'worlds'" (*Dramatic Dialogue*, pp. 5, 19). While this conception clearly puts an emphasis on the interactive nature of drama, it nonetheless focuses only on the immediate situation of two speakers engaging in interaction and not on the larger social shaping of discourse.

11 *Shakespearean Negotiations: The Circulation of Social Energy in Renaissance England* (Berkeley and Los Angeles: University of California Press, 1988), pp. 5, 4.

12 Dolores M. Burton (Austin and London: University of Texas Press, 1973); Madeleine Doran (Madison: University of Wisconsin Press, 1976); Philip Edwards, Inga-Stina Ewbank, and G. K. Hunter, eds. (Cambridge University Press, 1980); G. R. Hibbard (Toronto, Buffalo, and London: University of Toronto Press, 1981); Keir Elam; George T. Wright (Berkeley, Los Angeles, and London: University of California Press, 1988).

13 *Pragmatic Approaches to Shakespeare: Essays on "Othello," "Coriolanus," and "Timon of Athens"* (Lanham, New York, and London: University Press of America, 1993), pp. 1, 9.

14 Ed. Russ McDonald (Ithaca and London: Cornell University Press, 1994). Patricia Parker, in *Shakespeare From the Margins: Language, Culture, Context* (University of Chicago Press, 1996), also articulates the need to bring together language studies with sociohistorical criticism. Her approach is to contextualize and historicize important puns and key words.

15 In *The New Historicism*, ed. H. Aram Veeser (New York and London: Routledge, 1989), p. 15.

16 Greenblatt, *Shakespearean Negotiations*, p. 4.

17 In *The Dialogic Imagination*, pp. 259–422, especially p. 259.

18 "Discourse in the Novel," pp. 262–73. In a similar move, Pierre Bourdieu interrogates Noam Chomsky's opposition between *competence* and *utterance*, which also situates the speaker's utterance in relation to a unitary language system and entirely ignores the social situation of discourse production ("The Economics of Linguistic Exchanges," trans. Richard Nice, *Social Science Information*, 16 [1977], 646–47).

19 "Discourse in the Novel," pp. 273, 282, 276.

20 Ibid., p. 279.

21 Ibid., pp. 276–79, 293–94.
22 Ibid., p. 293.
23 Ibid., p. 280.
24 *Language and Symbolic Power*, ed. John B. Thompson, trans. Gino Raymond and Matthew Adamson (Cambridge, Mass.: Harvard University Press, 1991), pp. 76–77; see also "The Economics of Linguistic Exchanges," pp. 647, 653–56.
25 Brown and Levinson, *Politeness*, pp. 59–68.
26 "The Problem of Speech Genres," in *Speech Genres and Other Late Essays*, ed. Caryl Emerson and Michael Holquist, trans. Vern W. McGee (Austin: University of Texas Press, 1986), pp. 60–102. V. N. Vološinov, in *Marxism and the Philosophy of Language*, trans. Ladislav Matejka and I. R. Titunik (Cambridge, Mass. and London: Harvard University Press, 1986), speaks of "little behavioral genres" (p. 97).
27 Fairclough, *Discourse and Social Change*, p. 64.
28 Gary Saul Morson and Caryl Emerson, *Mikhail Bakhtin: Creation of a Prosaics* (Stanford University Press, 1990), pp. 33–35.
29 See, for example, Rosalie L. Colie's discussion of "unmetaphoring" as one of Shakespeare's main talents in her reading of *Romeo and Juliet* in *Shakespeare's Living Art* (Princeton University Press, 1974), p. 145.

1 POLITENESS AND DRAMATIC CHARACTER IN *HENRY VIII*

1 I quote throughout this chapter from *The Life of King Henry the Eighth*, ed. F. David Hoeniger, Pelican Shakespeare (Baltimore: Penguin Books, 1966). I assume that the play is written by Shakespeare, probably in collaboration with Fletcher, but I do not try in this chapter to distinguish between their respective shares. Nonetheless, a play that constitutes a collective invention in having shared authorship is a particularly apt starting place to make an argument for the importance of collective invention in the different sense I explore in this study. Quotations of other Shakespeare works, unless otherwise indicated, are taken from *The Complete Works of Shakespeare*, ed. David Bevington, 4th edn. (New York: HarperCollins, 1992).
2 This concept of fruitful redundancy is discussed by G. K. Hunter in "Hearing Shakespeare's Poetry," *The Elizabethan Theatre XII*, ed. A. L. Magnusson and C. E. McGee (Port Credit, Ontario: P. D. Meany, 1993), pp. 45–60, esp. pp. 47–48.
3 *Politeness: Some Universals in Language Usage* (1978; Cambridge University Press, 1987). Brown and Levinson's remains the leading model of politeness within the field of pragmatics. In their extensive introduction to the reissue in 1987 of their 1978 work on politeness, Brown and Levinson review applications and reassessments of their theory across many disciplines, with particular attention to work in anthropology, sociology, and psychology. More recent developments in the discussion of politeness are surveyed in Gabriele Kasper, "Linguistic Politeness: Current Research Issues," *Journal*

of *Pragmatics*, 14 (1990), 193–218. Other applications of the Brown and Levinson politeness model within Shakespeare studies include: Roger Brown and Albert Gilman's "Politeness Theory and Shakespeare's Four Major Tragedies," *Language in Society*, 18 (1989), 159–212, which tests its relevance to Early Modern English as represented by four Shakespearean tragedies; and chapter 6 of Juhani Rudanko's *Pragmatic Approaches to Shakespeare: Essays on "Othello," "Coriolanus," and "Timon of Athens"* (Lanham: University Press of America, 1993), which adapts the model to a reading of "nastiness" in *Timon of Athens*.

Writers such as Frank Whigham, in *Ambition and Privilege: The Social Tropes of Elizabethan Courtesy Theory* (Berkeley, Los Angeles, and London: University of California Press, 1984), have explored some of the rich resources of Renaissance courtesy theory for the illumination of a social rhetoric. By beginning with discourse pragmatics and conversational analysis, I come at some questions related to Whigham's from a different angle.

4 This concept of politeness as articulated within twentieth-century discourse pragmatics is consonant, in some significant ways, with Renaissance ideas about civility or courtesy. Wayne Rebhorn, for example, discusses how the social mechanisms of civility represented in Baldassare Castiglione's *The Book of the Courtier* are seen as operating "to minimize or eliminate the dangers posed by men's irrepressible aggression" (*Courtly Performances: Masking and Festivity in Castiglione's "Book of the Courtier"* [Detroit: Wayne State University Press, 1978], p. 133); in chapter 6, I explore interconnections between these conceptions further. Brown and Levinson's conception of politeness as anticipation and repair of speech threats should be distinguished from the eighteenth-century conception of a polite style marked by formality and restraint: as we shall see, their pragmatic model of politeness is inclusive of a very wide range of social discourse.

5 *Marxism and the Philosophy of Language*, trans. Ladislav Matejka and I. R. Titunik (Cambridge, Mass. and London: Harvard University Press, 1986), p. 86.

6 For some of the classic texts of speech-act theory see J. L. Austin, *How to Do Things with Words* (1962), ed. J. O. Urmson and Marina Sbisà, 2nd edn. (Cambridge, Mass.: Harvard University Press, 1975); John R. Searle, "What is a Speech Act?" in *Philosophy in America*, ed. Max Black (Ithaca, N.Y.: Cornell University Press, 1965), pp. 220–39, and "Indirect Speech Acts" in *Speech Acts*, ed. Peter Cole and Jerry L. Morgan, vol. 3 of *Syntax and Semantics* (New York: Academic Press, 1975), pp. 59–81. For two applications to Shakespeare, see Stanley E. Fish, "How To Do Things with Austin and Searle: Speech-Act Theory and Literary Criticism," *Modern Language Notes*, 91 (1976), 983–1025; and Keir Elam, *Shakespeare's Universe of Discourse: Language-Games in the Comedies* (Cambridge University Press, 1984), pp. 199–234.

7 Brown and Levinson, *Politeness*, p. 94.

8 Erving Goffman, "On Face-Work," in *Interaction Ritual: Essays on Face-to-Face Behavior* (Garden City, N.Y.: Doubleday, 1967), pp. 5–45.

9 Brown and Levinson, *Politeness*, pp. 61, 58, 60.
10 *The Elements of Drama* (Cambridge University Press, 1963), pp. 11–26, esp. p. 11.
11 In Cole and Morgan, eds., *Speech Acts*, pp. 41–58.
12 Brown and Levinson, *Politeness*, p. 79.
13 Ibid., pp. 68–74.
14 One of few relatively recent essays concerning style in *Henry VIII* is Pierre Sahel's "The Strangeness of a Dramatic Style: Rumour in *Henry VIII*," *Shakespeare Survey*, 38 (1985), 145–51. The essay is less concerned with details of verbal texture than is my essay, and it touches on none of the same instances; but it does look at a social practice motivating a style. Since I completed this chapter, W. F. Bolton has made use of linguistic pragmatics (but not the politeness model) as a point of entry into the language of the play in *Shakespeare's English: Language in the History Plays* (Cambridge, Mass. and Oxford: Basil Blackwell, 1992), pp. 186–220. Most recent criticism of *Henry VIII* has been more concerned with its visual language than with the verbal language. See, for example, Linda McJ. Micheli, "'Sit By Us': Visual Imagery and the Two Queens in *Henry VIII*," *Shakespeare Quarterly*, 38 (1987), 452–66, and F. Schreiber-McGee, "'The View of Earthly Glory': Visual Strategies and the Issue of Royal Prerogative in *Henry VIII*," *Shakespeare Studies*, 20 (1988), 191–200. G. Wilson Knight's brilliant but eccentric essay – "*Henry VIII* and the Poetry of Conversion," in *The Crown of Life* ([London: Methuen, 1948] pp. 256–336) – remains the most detailed critical account of the play's styles. In Wilson Knight's account, the languages of the play reveal the innermost souls of Shakespeare's characters and of Shakespeare himself. Hence we get explanations like this: "It is, very roughly, the speech of lonely souls, of persons rejected, thrown back on themselves, concentrating on their own, or someone else's, individual selves" (p. 267). Most other stylistic studies concern the authorship question. These have been summarized by John Margeson in the 1990 New Cambridge edition (pp. 4–14).
15 This formulation can help us to link Brown and Levinson's model to the contemporary rhetorical tradition. For Kenneth Burke, "identification" is the main principle of persuasion. In *A Rhetoric of Motives* (Berkeley: University of California Press, 1969), he emphasizes the "ingredient of rhetoric in all *socialization*" (pp. 19–27 and 39).
16 See, for example, the effusive talk between Lovell and Gardiner at 5.1.5–55.
17 What I have marked at *b* is Norfolk's vocative use of the titles "your grace" and "my lord." Brown and Levinson's theory may contribute to a new understanding of the use in general of such titles of address in Shakespeare's works. Carol Replogle (in "Shakespeare's Salutations: A Study of Stylistic Etiquette," *Studies in Philology*, 70 [1973], 172–86) offers an excellent introductory account of "appellative etiquette" in Elizabethan usage and in Shakespeare's plays. She stresses the precise deployment of forms of address in greetings and farewells; she also draws attention to the frequent repetition of such forms throughout conversations and letters, especially where the

speaker or writer addresses a person of superior social station. Replogle offers no rationale for the distribution within a discourse of these deferential forms of address but speaks of them instead as "scattered" throughout (p. 175). If Brown and Levinson's theory has predictive force for Elizabethan usage, then we should expect to find increased frequencies of vocative titles in the contexts of "face-threatening acts." A brief survey shows that this is true at least of *Henry VIII*, 1.1. This scene contains twelve such vocatives, including three repetitions of "your grace" ("a title," according to Replogle, "proper only for royalty, for dukes and duchesses, and archbishops and their wives" [pp. 183–84]), four of "my lord" and one of "my Lord Aberga'ny," and four of "sir." One of these instances of "sir" is followed up by the high formality of "My lord the Duke of Buckingham, and Earl / Of Hereford, Stafford, and Northampton (198–200). The occasion of this address by the Sergeant-at-Arms is the gravest and most ceremonial face-threatening act of the scene, the ritual of Buckingham's arrest for high treason. The first and the final two occurrences of deferential forms of address accompany the salutations and farewells. Of the others, Buckingham's "I pray you who, my lord?" (49) repairs his interruption of Norfolk's talk to repeat a question that Norfolk had been slow to answer; Norfolk's "Surely, sir" (57) prefaces an opinion contradicting Buckingham's; the First Secretary's highly deferential "Ay, please your grace" (117) redresses a social inferior's presumption in entering the conversation (even where his part is required by his superior's question); in Buckingham's "Sir, / I am thankful to you" (149–50), the *sir* accompanies his thanks for Norfolk's advice; and in Buckingham's "Pray give me favor, sir" (168), the *sir* redresses his request to continue his account of Wolsey's treacheries undisturbed by Norfolk's placating interruptions. Only in Buckingham's exclamation when he is arrested – "Lo you, my lord, / The net has fall'n upon me!" (202–03) – does minimization of a face-threatening act provide an inadequate motive for the use of an address form. At least in this scene, then, Brown and Levinson's theory of politeness as redress of face-threatening acts seems to help account for the distribution of address forms.
18 "Discourse in Life and Discourse in Art" (1926), trans. I. R. Titunik, in *Contemporary Literary Criticism: Literary and Cultural Studies*, ed. Robert Con Davis and Ronald Schleifer, 2nd edn. (New York and London: Longman, 1989), pp. 392–410, esp. p. 408; "Discourse in the Novel," p. 280.
19 Brown and Levinson, *Politeness*, p. 129.
20 Both Kim H. Noling, "Grubbing Up the Stock: Dramatizing Queens in *Henry VIII*" (*Shakespeare Quarterly*, 39 [1988], 291–306, esp. pp. 293–94), and Micheli ("Visual Imagery," pp. 454–56) emphasize how Katherine's strong presence is represented in the visual scene.
21 Brown and Levinson, *Politeness*, p. 204.
22 Vološinov, *Marxism*, pp. 93 and 90.
23 Brown and Levinson touch very tentatively on such possibilities in *Politeness*, p. 232.

24 In 2.4, a scene regularly allotted not to Fletcher but to Shakespeare, Katherine says to Wolsey, "I am a simple woman" (104).
25 Raphael Holinshed, *Holinshed's Chronicles of England, Scotland, and Ireland* (1587), 6 vols. (London, 1808; rpt. New York: AMS Press, 1965), vol. 3, p. 740.
26 "The Economics of Linguistic Exchanges," trans. Richard Nice, *Social Science Information*, 16 (1977), 645–68, esp. p. 657.
27 Noling discusses the use Shakespeare makes of Anne's silence and her visual presence ("Dramatizing Queens," p. 299) to reinforce her overall point that the "dramaturgy of queens .. endorses Henry's patriarchal will" (p. 291).
28 Consider, for example, the rebuke Anne is said to have written to Cardinal Wolsey in 1529 (quoted here from *Letters of Royal and Illustrious Ladies of Great Britain*, ed. Mary Anne Everett Wood, 2 vols. [London: Henry Colburn, 1846], vol. 2, pp. 48–49):

... Though you are a man of great understanding, you cannot avoid being censured by every body for having drawn on yourself the hatred of a king who had raised you to the highest degree to which the greatest ambition of a man seeking his fortune can aspire. I cannot comprehend, and the king still less, how your reverend lordship, after having allured us by so many fine promises about divorce, can have repented of your purpose, and how you could have done what you have, in order to hinder the consummation of it. What, then, is your mode of proceeding? ...

... The wrong you have done me has caused me much sorrow; but I feel infinitely more in seeing myself betrayed by a man who pretended to enter into my interests only to discover the secrets of my heart. I acknowledge that, believing you sincere, I have been too precipitate in my confidence; it is this which has induced, and still induces me, to keep more moderation in avenging myself, not being able to forget that I *have* been
     Your servant,
      Anne Boleyn

29 Margaret Patterson Hannay's introduction to *Silent But for the Word* ([Kent, Ohio: Kent State University Press, 1985], pp. 1–14) dwells on how Tudor women were almost exclusively restricted in their writing to religious subjects. Her emphasis, however, is on how this situation prevented them from "speak[ing] or writ[ing] their own ideas" (p. 7).
30 Recent research on early modern women writers has explored how "[r]eligious fervor opened up spaces for women's speech and writing" (Mary Ellen Lamb, *Gender and Authorship in the Sidney Circle* [Madison: Wisconsin University Press, 1990], p. 14) and how "[t]he utilization of permitted areas, especially of religion, became an indirect way of self-assertion in literary expression" (Tina Krontiris, *Oppositional Voices: Women as Writers and Translators of Literature in the English Renaissance* [London and New York: Routledge, 1992], p. 21).
31 Here again I quote from Wood, ed., *Letters*, vol. 2, pp. 198–99. Since, as Wood indicates, the letter is a translation of the lost original, the word choice here will not be Katherine's.
32 Holinshed, *Chronicles*, vol. 3, p. 738.

33 See 3.1.50–53 and 3.2.166–79. A particularly interesting and complicated example occurs at 2.4.91–103.
34 "Greenes Groats-worth of Wit," in *The Life and Works of Robert Greene*, ed. Alexander B. Grosart, 15 vols. (New York: Russell & Russell, 1964), vol. 12, p. 144.
35 Wilson Knight finds a "spiritual" class resemblance not between Shakespeare and Wolsey but between Shakespeare and Buckingham: "The lines [of Buckingham's farewell] are spoken from that deeper, spiritual, aristocracy that underlies all Shakespeare's noblest thought. Buckingham shows here a sweetness and serenity distilled from the finest essence of nobility, courtesy, suffering and religious faith . . ." (*Crown of Life*, p. 275).

2 "POWER TO HURT": LANGUAGE AND SERVICE IN SIDNEY HOUSEHOLD LETTERS AND SHAKESPEARE'S SONNETS

1 I quote here from Arthur Collins, ed., *Letters and Memorials of State*, 2 vols. (London, 1746; rpt. New York: AMS Press, 1973), vol. 1, pp. 293–94; emphasis added. The long "s" has been modernized in all quotations.
2 *Christian Oeconomy*, in *The Work of William Perkins*, ed. Ian Breward (Appleford: Sutton Courteny Press, 1970), p. 434.
3 Analyzing Elizabethan suitors' letters, Frank Whigham led the way in emphasizing their rhetorical interest in "The Rhetoric of Elizabethan Suitors' Letters," *PMLA*, 96 (1981), 864–82. Jonathan Goldberg's discussion of epistolary handbooks in *Writing Matter: From the Hands of the English Renaissance* (Stanford University Press, 1990) makes interesting suggestions about how to read "the space of writing as the index of social relations" (p. 253).
4 In "Editing Out: The Discourse of Patronage and Shakespeare's Twenty-Ninth Sonnet," John Barrell argues that the historically specific discourse of patronage shaped sonnet 29, and his argument is consistent with my emphasis on social invention (in *Poetry, Language and Politics* [Manchester University Press, 1988], pp. 18–43). Arthur F. Marotti also argues that the young-man sonnets enact a patronage relationship (see "'Love is Not Love': Elizabethan Sonnet Sequences and the Social Order," *ELH*, 49 [1982], 396–428, especially pp. 410–13; and "Shakespeare's Sonnets as Literary Property," in *Soliciting Interpretation: Literary Theory and Seventeenth-Century English Poetry*, ed. Elizabeth D. Harvey and Katharine Eisaman Maus [Chicago and London: University of Chicago Press, 1990], pp. 143–73, esp. pp. 145–50). My argument also connects the Poet's discourse to a specific relation with a social superior, but the politeness model helps us to see that modes of address even within a specific social relation vary significantly with speech-act risk.
5 *The Subject of Tragedy: Identity and Difference in Renaissance Drama* (London and New York: Methuen, 1985), p. 5.
6 "Discourse in Life and Discourse in Art" (1926), trans. I. R. Titunik, in

Contemporary Literary Criticism: Literary and Cultural Studies, ed. Robert Con Davis and Ronald Schleifer, 2nd edn. (New York and London: Longman, 1989), p. 408.
7 *Language and Symbolic Power*, ed. John B. Thompson, trans. Gino Raymond and Matthew Adamson (Cambridge, Mass.: Harvard University Press, 1991), p. 67.
8 See, for example, Peter Laslett, *The World We Have Lost: Further Explored*, 3rd edn. (London: Methuen, 1983), p. 38; Carol Replogle, "Shakespeare's Salutations: A Study in Stylistic Etiquette," *Studies in Philology*, 70 (1973), 172–86; Roger Brown and Albert Gilman, "The Pronouns of Power and Solidarity," in *Style in Language*, ed. Thomas A. Sebeok (Cambridge, Mass.: MIT Press, 1960), pp. 253–76.
9 *Language and Symbolic Power*, p. 72.
10 "The Economics of Linguistic Exchanges," trans. Richard Nice, *Social Science Information*, 16 (1977), 662.
11 *Politeness: Some Universals in Language Usage* (1978; Cambridge University Press, 1987), p. 68.
12 *Marxism and the Philosophy of Language*, trans. Ladislav Matejka and I. R. Titunik (Cambridge, Mass. and London: Harvard University Press, 1973), pp. 83–98.
13 For a lucid and suggestive account of how the disparity in social status enacted in the sonnets affects the psychology of the speaker, see Sheldon P. Zitner, "In the Sonnet Workshop," in *All's Well That Ends Well* (New York and London: Harvester Wheatsheaf, 1989), pp. 23–39. He argues that "the emotions are mediated by status" (p. 34), but does not investigate the relation between social speech repertoires and the speaker's language. Anne Ferry, in *The "Inward Language": Sonnets of Wyatt, Sidney, Shakespeare, Donne* (Chicago and London: University of Chicago Press, 1983), and Joel Fineman, in *Shakespeare's Perjured Eye: The Invention of Poetic Subjectivity in the Sonnets* (Berkeley and Los Angeles: University of California Press, 1986), explore inwardness and poetic subjectivity in the sonnets, but without emphasizing the social inflections of the speaker's psychology.
14 *Shakespeare's Perjured Eye*, p. 297.
15 Collins, *Letters*, vol. 1, p. 88.
16 Ibid., pp. 145–46.
17 Ibid., p. 187.
18 See Ann Kussmaul, *Servants in Husbandry in Early Modern England* (Cambridge University Press, 1981), pp. 3–5; see also David Cressy, "Describing the Social Order of Elizabethan and Stuart England," *Literature and History*, 3 (1976), 29–44, esp. p. 41.
19 See Alice T. Friedman, *House and Household in Elizabethan England: Wollaton Hall and the Willoughby Family* (Chicago and London: University of Chicago Press, 1989), pp. 41–46 and Kussmaul, *Servants in Husbandry*, p. 4.
20 I. M., *A Health to the Gentlemanly Profession of Serving-Men* (London, 1598), B2v–B3.

21 Ibid., B3.
22 Ibid., B3v.
23 Ibid., c3–c3v.
24 Ibid., c2v.
25 *House and Household*, p. 44.
26 Collins, *Letters*, vol. 1, p. 145.
27 *The Enimie of Idlenesse* (London, 1593), B3.
28 *The Dictionary of National Biography from the Earliest Times to 1900*, ed. Sir Leslie Stephen and Sir Sidney Lee, 22 vols. (London: Oxford University Press, 1937–38), vol. 13, pp. 580–81.
29 Replogle, "Shakespeare's Salutations," pp. 180–81.
30 Lawrence Stone, *The Crisis of the Aristocracy, 1558–1641* (Oxford: Clarendon Press, 1965), p. 747.
31 Collins, *Letters*, vol. 1, p. 9.
32 Quoted from Margaret P. Hannay, *Philip's Phoenix: Mary Sidney, Countess of Pembroke* (New York and Oxford: Oxford University Press, 1990), p. 56.
33 On Mary (Dudley) Sidney, see Katherine Duncan-Jones, *Sir Philip Sidney, Courtier Poet* (New Haven and London: Yale University Press, 1991), esp. pp. 3–7; see also Hannay, *Philip's Phoenix*, esp. pp. 17–21.
34 On the context of the quarrel, see Duncan-Jones, *Sir Philip Sidney*, p. 197 and Ronald A. Rebholz, *The Life of Fulke Greville, First Lord Brooke* (Oxford: Clarendon Press, 1971), pp. 22–23. This was not the first disagreement between them. In 1578, Philip Sidney wrote a threatening letter accusing Molyneux of showing letters Philip wrote his father to others, and Molyneux answered back, asserting his honesty and innocence (see Collins, *Letters*, vol. 1, p. 256). Duncan-Jones reads the episode as an example of Philip Sidney's tendency towards "vehement outbursts of rage" (*Sir Philip Sidney*, pp. 22–23). I would add that the level of passion may also reflect the servant–master's child tensions that Friedman suggests could eventuate from a servingman's constant proximity and access to the master and his resultant capacity to exert influence (*House and Household*, p. 44).
35 Collins, *Letters*, vol. 1, p. 293.
36 Ibid., p. 296.
37 Ibid.
38 Angel Day, *The English Secretary, or Methods of Writing Epistles and Letters* (1599 edn.), intro. Robert O. Evans (Gainesville, Fla.: Scholars' Facsimiles & Reprints, 1967), p. 105.
39 Collins, *Letters*, vol. 1, p. 271.
40 Ibid., p. 272.
41 *Politeness*, pp. 74–84.
42 *Holinshed's Chronicles of England, Scotland, and Ireland*, 6 vols. (London, 1808; rpt. New York: AMS Press, 1965), vol. 4, p. 879. See Lamb, *Gender and Authorship in the Sidney Circle* (Madison: University of Wisconsin Press, 1990), pp. 122–23; and Hannay, *Philip's Phoenix*, pp. 55–56.

43 Weil, "'Household Stuff': Maestrie and Service in *The Taming of the Shrew*," in *The Elizabethan Theatre XIV*, ed. A. Lynne Magnusson and C. E. McGee (Toronto: P. D. Meany, 1996), pp. 71–82, esp. p. 75; see also Belsey, *The Subject of Tragedy*, pp. 154–60; Friedman, *House and Household*, p. 46.
44 *The Subject of Tragedy*, pp. 150, 6.
45 Thomas Wright, ed., *Queen Elizabeth and Her Times, A Series of Original Letters*, 2 vols. (London: Henry Colburn, 1838), vol. 1, p. 24.
46 "Inward Language," pp. 7–13.
47 P. 90; emphasis added.
48 The sexual overtones of the word are highlighted by Kerrigan in the New Penguin edition (245).
49 "Poet, Friend, and Poetry: The Idealized Image of Love in Shakespeare's Sonnets," *The American Journal of Psychoanalysis*, 45 (1985), 176–90, esp. 176–77.
50 Lewis, "Poet, Friend and Poetry," p. 184.
51 Bruce R. Smith, *Homosexual Desire in Shakespeare's England: A Cultural Poetics* (Chicago and London: University of Chicago Press, 1991), p. 229.
52 *Homosexuality in Renaissance England* (Boston: Gay Men's Press, 1982), pp. 44–53.
53 *Shakespeare the Actor and the Purposes of Playing* (Chicago and London: Chicago University Press, 1993), pp. 42, 85.
54 "The Motive for Interiority: Shakespeare's *Sonnets* and *Hamlet*," *Style*, 23 (1989), pp. 430–44, esp. 431–42.
55 Ibid., 431.
56 *Marxism and the Philosophy of Language*, pp. 88, 91, 93.
57 Steven Guazzo, *The Civile Conversation of M. Steeven Guazzo*, trans. George Pettie and Barth. Young, intro. Sir Edward Sullivan, 2 vols. (London: Constable, 1925), vol. 2, p. 110; emphasis added.

3 SCRIPTING SOCIAL RELATIONS IN ERASMUS AND DAY

1 For a full list and brief history of the English manuals, see Jean Robertson, *The Art of Letter Writing: An Essay on the Handbooks Published in England During the Sixteenth and Seventeenth Centuries* (Liverpool and London: University Press of Liverpool and Hodder & Stoughton Ltd., 1942). For another detailed survey, see Katherine Gee Hornbeak, "The Complete Letter-Writer in English, 1568–1800," *Smith College Studies in Modern Languages*, 15 (1934), 1–150.
2 For a detailed account of the medieval *ars dictaminis*, see James J. Murphy, "*Ars dictaminis*: The Art of Letter-Writing," in *Rhetoric in the Middle Ages: A History of Rhetorical Theory from Saint Augustine to the Renaissance* (Berkeley, Los Angeles and London: University of California Press, 1974), pp. 194–268. For insights into its institutional contexts and its "phatic rhetoric," see Les Perelman, "The Medieval Art of Letter Writing: Rhetoric as Institutional Expression," in *Textual Dynamics of the Professions*, ed. Charles Bazerman

and James Paradis (Madison: University of Wisconsin Press, 1991), pp. 97–119. Judith Rice Henderson offers useful accounts of how humanist epistolographers influenced Erasmus and Vives in "Erasmus on the Art of Letter-Writing," in *Renaissance Eloquence: Studies in the Theory and Practice of Renaissance Rhetoric*, ed. James J. Murphy (Berkeley, Los Angeles, London: University of California Press, 1983), pp. 331–55 and in "Defining the Genre of the Letter: Juan Luis Vives' *De conscribendis epistolis*," *Renaissance and Reformation*, n.s. 7 (1983), 89–105. Erika Rummel also reviews humanist epistolography in relation to Erasmus in "Erasmus' Manual of Letter-Writing: Tradition and Innovation," *Renaissance and Reformation*, n.s. 13 (1989), 299–312.

3 For a brief account of the revision and publication history, see J. K. Sowards, "Introduction," vol. 25 of *Collected Works of Erasmus* (Toronto, Buffalo, and London: University of Toronto Press, 1985), pp. li–lii.

4 Sowards, "Introduction," p. lii.

5 Angel Day, *The English Secretary, or Methods of Writing Epistles and Letters* (1599), introduced by Robert O. Evans (Gainesville, Fla.: Scholars' Facsimiles & Reprints, 1967), sig. A3. This revised edition includes "A declaration of such Tropes, Figures, and Schemes . . ." and "the parts and office of a Secretarie." Further references in this chapter, given parenthetically in the text, are to this edition.

6 For Erasmus's handbook, the text cited is "On the Writing of Letters" (*De conscribendis epistolis*), trans. Charles Fantazzi, in *Collected Works of Erasmus*, vol. 25, ed. J. K. Sowards (Toronto, Buffalo, and London: University of Toronto Press, 1985), pp. 10–254. See pp. 12 and 15. Further references in this chapter are given parenthetically in the text.

7 See especially p. 350. The vibrant evocation of the interlocutor's presence is in keeping with Erasmus's advice on letter-writing. This quality of "addressivity" is, for Michael Mendelson in "A Dialogical Model for Business Correspondence" (*Journal of Business and Technical Communication*, 7 [1993], 283–311), at the very centre of Erasmus's teaching in the epistolary handbook and closely related to Bakhtin's philosophy of discourse.

8 I rely here on Henderson's account, especially pp. 340–42 and p. 333.

9 Henderson, "Erasmus on the Art of Letter-Writing," pp. 341–42.

10 In Henderson's view, by introducing this transformed classification, Erasmus widens the range of potential uses of the letter well beyond the affairs of friends. She regards "On the Writing of Letters" as a synthesis of the medieval and humanist traditions in that Erasmus extends the letter genre to permit both public and private subject matters. Describing the formal elements Erasmus rejects and maintains from each tradition, Henderson characterizes Erasmus's innovation in terms of the formal changes he makes to traditional models. But Erasmus's reconceptualization of rhetorical form may suggest that his innovation is even more thoroughgoing than Henderson argues.

11 *Shaping Written Knowledge: The Genre and Activity of the Experimental Article in*

Science (Madison: University of Wisconsin Press, 1988), p. 319.
12 Bazerman, *Shaping Written Knowledge*, p. 320.
13 See "The Problem of Speech Genres," in *Speech Genres and Other Late Essays*, ed. Caryl Emerson and Michael Holquist, trans. Vern W. McGee (Austin: University of Texas Press, 1986), pp. 60–102.
14 *The Philosophy of Literary Form: Studies in Symbolic Action* (Berkeley and Los Angeles: University of California Press, 1973), p. 303.
15 *Renaissance Self-Fashioning: From More to Shakespeare* (Chicago and London: University of Chicago Press, 1980).
16 "Discourse in the Novel," in *The Dialogic Imagination: Four Essays by M. M. Bakhtin*, ed. Michael Holquist and trans. Caryl Emerson and Michael Holquist (Austin: University of Texas Press, 1981), p. 331.
17 Jacques Revel points out that Erasmus's highly influential contribution to the literature of civility, his *Manners for Children* (*De civilitate morum puerilium*), is innovative in that "it was addressed to all children, without distinction" and "it aimed to teach a code of manners valid for everyone": "Erasmus sought to use a common code of manners as a basis for establishing social transparency, which he considered a necessary precondition for broader social intercourse" ("The Uses of Civility," in *Passions of the Renaissance*, vol. 3 of *A History of Private Life*, ed. Roger Chartier, trans. Arthur Goldhammer [Cambridge, Mass. and London: Harvard University Press, 1989], pp. 170–71). "On the Writing of Letters" works toward the same ideal.
18 Since I completed this chapter, Lisa Jardine's fascinating work on the "technology of affect" in relation to Erasmus's letters and to the reception of letters in *King Lear* has appeared in *Reading Shakespeare Historically* (London and New York: Routledge, 1996), pp. 78–97. Her discussion complements the treatment of friendship as a discursive construct in this chapter.
19 "Greetings and Salutations in Erasmus," *Renaissance and Reformation*, n.s. 13 (1989), 257.
20 Friar Laurence employs something like this speech genre with Romeo in his consolation inquiring "Art thou a man?" in *Romeo and Juliet*, 3.3.108–58.
21 "The Economics of Linguistic Exchanges," *Social Science Information*, 16 (1977), 645–68, esp. p. 652. In chapter 7, I develop a reading of *Othello* that takes this conception as its starting point.
22 Pierre Bourdieu develops the idea of double profit, also referred to as "strategies of condescension" and "profit of distinction," in *Language and Symbolic Power*, ed. John B. Thompson, trans. Gino Raymond and Matthew Adamson (Cambridge, Mass.: Harvard University Press, 1991), esp. pp. 68–69 and 55–56. Norman Fairclough sees many modern institutional orders of discourse as exercising social control through "simulated egalitarianism, and the removal of surface markers of authority and power" (*Language and Power* [London and New York: Longman, 1989], p. 37).
23 See *Ambition and Privilege: The Social Tropes of Elizabethan Courtesy Theory* (Berkeley, Los Angeles, and London: University of California Press, 1984), esp. chapter 1, pp. 1–31.

24 Whigham, *Ambition and Privilege*, p. 5.
25 Jonathan Goldberg offers a wonderfully suggestive account of Day's appended section on the office of secretary in *Writing Matter: From the Hands of the English Renaissance* (Stanford University Press, 1990), pp. 265–72. My point here modifies his claim that the manual "provides instructions for a secretary whose literate skills . . . equip him to rise into aristocratic employment" (p. 255).
26 In classifying English works on logic and rhetoric, Sister Miriam Joseph places Angel Day among the "figurists" (*Rhetoric in Shakespeare's Time: Literary Theory of Renaissance Europe* [New York: Harcourt, Brace & World, Inc., 1962], p. 14). This is misleading: the "Declaration" of figures of speech did not even appear in the first edition of 1586 and, in later editions, it has the status of an appendix. Figures of speech are incidental to the book's discussion of letter-writing. Wilbur Samuel Howell's classification of *The English Secretary* as "a formulary and a stylistic rhetoric" (*Logic and Rhetoric in England, 1500–1700* [New York: Russell & Russell, Inc., 1961], p. 330) is less misleading, although the interest in fitting this and other works into one of "three patterns" still contributes to a cursory treatment of Day's project.
27 *Writing Matter*, pp. 254–55. Frank Whigham's brief account of *The English Secretary* in his ground-breaking article, "The Rhetoric of Elizabethan Suitors' Letters," *PMLA*, 96 (1981), 865– 66, emphasizes literary elements, perhaps more to legitimize the rhetorical study of letter-writing within literary criticism before cultural criticism had become prominent than to discount Day's practical orientation.
28 Perelman, "Medieval Art of Letter Writing, p. 106.
29 Ibid., p. 107.
30 Ibid., pp. 113–14.
31 Goldberg, *Writing Matter*, p. 253. Goldberg concentrates on how such material forms as the placement of the signature and the choice of script serve as indices to social relation and does not treat the stylistics of the letter.
32 In his treatment of petition and commendation, Day does not offer any specific treatment of Brown and Levinson's third variable, social distance. Roger Brown and Albert Gilman have, indeed, argued on the limited evidence of their study of politeness in four Shakespeare tragedies against the relevance of social distance as Brown and Levinson define it to Early Modern English ("Politeness Theory and Shakespeare's Four Major Tragedies," *Language in Society*, 18 [1989], 159–212, especially pp. 166–68 and 195–96). While I will argue in later chapters that social distance does enter into the stylistic figuration of relations, relative power is certainly given more weight.
33 *English Society, 1580–1680* (New Brunswick, N.J.: Rutgers University Press, 1982), p. 51.
34 Wrightson, *English Society*, p. 51.
35 Ibid., p. 53.
36 Ibid., p. 55.

37 Ibid., p. 55.
38 "The Rhetoric of Elizabethan Suitors' Letters," *PMLA*, 96 (1981), 864–82.
39 Wallace Chafe and Johanna Nichols, eds., *Evidentiality: The Linguistic Coding of Epistemology* (Norwood, N.J.: Ablex Publishing Corporation, 1986).
40 *Evidentiality*, p. xi.
41 "The Rhetoric of Elizabethan Suitors' Letters," p. 870.
42 *The Complete Works*, The Oxford Shakespeare, gen. ed. Stanley Wells and Gary Taylor (Oxford: Clarendon Press, 1986), pp. 254 and 270; emphasis added.
43 Charlotte Carmichael Stopes, *The Life of Henry, Third Earl of Southampton, Shakespeare's Patron* (1922; New York: AMS Press, 1969), p. 49.

4 READING COURTLY AND ADMINISTRATIVE LETTERS

1 Frank Whigham, "The Rhetoric of Elizabethan Suitors' Letters," *PMLA*, 96 (1981), 864–82, esp. 866–67. Most of the other valuable work on the Elizabethan vernacular letter has aimed at a general overview rather than at practices of close reading. See, for example, Gary R. Grund, "From Formulary to Fiction: The Epistle and the English Anti-Ciceronian Movement," *Texas Studies in Language and Literature*, 17 (1975), 379–95; and Claudio Guillén, "Notes toward the Study of the Renaissance Letter," in *Renaissance Genres: Essays on Theory, History, and Interpretation*, ed. Barbara Kiefer Lewalski (Cambridge and London: Harvard University Press, 1986), pp. 70–101. Those working on early modern women writers have recently focused some attention on letter-writing. See, for example, Sara Jayne Steen's edition of *The Letters of Lady Arbella Stuart* (New York and Oxford: Oxford University Press, 1994); here close attention has been paid to textual questions and to textual annotation, but the emphasis is more on recovering the life and "gaining access to the mind of an unapologetically bright and learned aristocratic woman" (p. 105) than on stylistic or rhetorical analysis of the letters. Focusing on humanist letters, which I do not consider in this chapter, Judith Rice Henderson cautions against unproblematized "use of . . . letters as historical and biographical sources" and stresses the need to read for rhetorical persuasion in "On Reading the Rhetoric of the Renaissance Letter," in *Renaissance-Rhetorik/Renaissance Rhetoric*, ed. Heinrich F. Plett (Berlin and New York: Walter de Gruyter, 1993), pp. 143–62.
2 Whigham, "Rhetoric of Suitors' Letters," p. 864.
3 Ibid., pp. 869, 870.
4 Pierre Bourdieu, "The Economics of Linguistic Exchanges," trans. Richard Nice, *Social Science Information*, 16 (1977), 662.
5 See, for example, David Cressy, "Describing the Social Order of Elizabethan and Stuart England," *Literature and History*, 3 (1976), 29–44; Keith Wrightson, "Estates, Degrees and Sorts in Tudor and Stuart England," *History Today*, 37 (1987), 17–22, and chapter 1, "Degrees of People," in *English Society, 1580–1680* (New Brunswick, N.J.: Rutgers University Press, 1982),

pp. 17–38.
6 For this account of the difficulties in Scotland at this time, I have depended on Conyers Read's chapter on "Scotland, 1558–60" in *Mr. Secretary Cecil and Queen Elizabeth* (London: Jonathan Cape, 1955), pp. 135–72.
7 Quoted in Read, *Mr. Secretary Cecil and Queen Elizabeth*, p. 153, from the instructions written by Cecil for Sadler, which are printed in Ralph Sadler, *The State Papers and Letters*, ed. Arthur Clifford, 2 vols. (London, 1809), vol. 1, pp. 388ff. Hereafter cited as *Sadler Papers*.
8 Quoted from Thomas Wright, ed., *Queen Elizabeth and Her Times, A Series of Original Letters*, 2 vols. (London: Henry Colburn, 1838), vol. 1, pp. 18–19. The letter is followed by a postscript concerning an enclosed letter by John Knox.
9 Barrett L. Beer and Sybil M. Jack, eds., *The Letters of William, Lord Paget of Beaudesert, 1547–63*, in *Camden Miscellany Vol. XXV* (London: Royal Historical Society, 1974), pp. 1–141. For the advice I quote, see pp. 77–78 (emphasis added). Paget, who functioned as a close confidential advisor to Somerset, was certainly capable of giving him very direct advice, with little politeness mitigation, as in a letter of May 1549: "Howsoever it cometh to pass I cannot tell, but of late Your Grace is grown in great choleric fashions, whensoever you are contraried in that which you have conceived in your head. A king which shall give men an occasion of discourage to say their opinions frankly, receiveth thereby great hurt and peril in his reign. But a subject in great authority, as your Grace is, using such fashion, is like to fall into great danger and peril of his own person, besides that of the common weal; which, for the very love I bear to your Grace, I beseech you and for God's sake consider and weigh well" (quoted in Read, *Mr. Secretary Cecil and Queen Elizabeth*, p. 55).
10 *DNB*, vol. 17, pp. 599–601 and vol. 5, pp. 110–12.
11 *Sadler Papers*, vol. 1, pp. 392–94. The style in which the councillors issue their directives in the letter may nonetheless retain a note of consdescension signaling their authority over the men.
12 Read, *Mr. Secretary Cecil and Queen Elizabeth*, p. 152. As an example of meanings not made explicit between them, Cecil writes in his letter of 24 August 1559, "If Mr Lee be not *come*, tell hym that he shall have his lettre of lycnes at my house, by Stamford. I trust you, Mr Sadler, knowe his meaning." (*Sadler Papers*, vol. 1, p. 405). It is true, of course, that there are signs in the letters of Cecil's authority over Sadler: Cecil is, in a sense, Sadler's controller in this secret mission to further the cause of the Scottish Protestants, Sadler his (and the queen's) agent. And, as is Cecil's characteristic habit whenever those who are the state's ears and eyes in distant parts seem to him to fall short of precision or of requisite details in their epistolary reports on the nation's business, the secretary is as ready to remonstrate with his friend Sadler as with any other, as in a letter written during the northern insurrection in 1569: "We are never well satisfyed with generall advertisements. You must let us know what is become of Norton, Marcan-

feld, Tempest, sir John Novell, and such lyke" (*Sadler Papers*, vol. 2, p. 78).
13 Letter from Ralph Sadler to William Cecil of 29 August 1559, *Sadler Papers*, vol. 1, pp. 409–10; letter of William Cecil to Ralph Sadler and James Croft of 31 August 1559, vol. 1, pp. 417–18.
14 *Sadler Papers*, vol. 1, p. 526; emphasis added; quoted in part in Read, *Mr. Secretary Cecil and Queen Elizabeth*, pp. 155–56.
15 See *Sadler Papers*, vol. 1, pp. 375–732.
16 I draw on Jonathan Goldberg's account of the letter as administrative instrument and quote from his sources in this paragraph. See *Writing Matter: From the Hands of the English Renaissance* (Stanford University Press, 1990), pp. 255–59.
17 Hilary Jenkinson, "The Teaching and Practice of Handwriting in England," *History*, 11 (1926), 215, as quoted in Goldberg, *Writing Matter*, p. 258; G. R. Elton, *The Tudor Revolution in Government* (Cambridge University Press, 1959), p. 299, as quoted in Goldberg, *Writing Matter*, p. 258.
18 Sig. A3; quoted from Goldberg, *Writing Matter*, p. 257.
19 Arthur Collins, *Letters and Memorials of State*, 2 vols. (London, 1746; rpt. New York: AMS Press, 1973), vol. 1, pp. 180–85.
20 Collins, *Letters*, vol. 1, pp. 185–89.
21 Collins, *Letters*, vol. 1, p. 184. Much is at stake in this letter, and it also accomplishes much: within a week, Waterhouse writes that the soldiers, ships, arms, and treasure are being made ready (vol. 1, p. 191), and Sidney learns from Sir Francis Walsingham of his opponents' submission and brief imprisonment in the Fleet (vol. 1, p. 202). Nonetheless, Sidney's correspondence is not entirely successful in sustaining his working relations with the court in good repair: he hears from Waterhouse how "Hir Majestie angry at the first, when Money was demaundid, said, that *Henry Sidney* did allwaies seek to put her to Charge" (vol. 1, p. 191), and Walsingham writes to him of "suche lewde Brutes of a generall Discontentment in that Realme" as "makethe her [the Queen] to write somewhat offensively" to him (vol. 1, p. 199). As Edmund Molyneux, his biographer in Holinshed's *Chronicles*, explains the problem,
In one thing his fortune was most hard, and he more than twise unhappie, that his service (for the most part) was subject to the eare, and not object to the eie, by meanes whereof his noble vertues and deserts were manie times suppressed, and seldome or never seene, but his faults often told and willinglie heard; and so consequentlie his service obedient to great misreport, slander, and calumniation. (vol. 4, p. 877)
Clearly, the letter was not the ideal vehicle for Sidney's hard service in Ireland, a service which seems to have relied more on force than on civility.
22 Collins, *Letters*, vol. 1, pp. 180, 184–85.
23 "The Rhetoric of Elizabethan Suitors' Letters," p. 867.
24 Sir Harris Nicolas, ed., *Memoirs of the Life and Times of Sir Christopher Hatton, K.G., Vice-Chamberlain and Lord Chancellor to Queen Elizabeth* (London: Richard Bentley, 1847), p. 265; emphasis added. This volume prints Hatton's "Letter Book" and is the volume from which Frank Whigham draws letters by

Doctor Toby Mathew that he analyzes in "The Rhetoric of Elizabethan Suitors' Letters."

25 I have not commented on the issue of gender in relation to this letter, mainly because the letter does not strike me as different from male-authored letters emphasizing relational maintenance. Without an awareness of the typical "trouble" tropes I am analyzing here, a reader might judge the writer's self-consciousness about troubling her addressee to be characteristically feminine, but this would be a mistake: it is part of the general currency of the courtly letters. It is interesting to note that at least one poem has been attributed to the Countess of Arundel, a woman whose Catholic commitment was to bring difficulties for her and her husband, Philip Howard. The poem – a verse prayer – is printed and analyzed in Louise Schleiner's *Tudor and Stuart Women Writers* (Bloomington and Indianapolis: Indiana University Press, 1994), pp. 93–95.

Letters by women (Queen Elizabeth and Mary Queen of Scots excepted) are infrequent among the sixteenth-century collections relating to Elizabethan government from which I draw in this chapter. Where women's letters occur, they are usually suitors' letters, petitioning to powerful men for assistance when a husband has been imprisoned, executed, or subject to other disgrace.

26 Wright, *Queen Elizabeth and Her Times*, vol. 2, pp. 21–24, especially pp. 22 and 24; ibid., vol. 1, pp. 60–61; Henry Ellis, ed., *Original Letters, Illustrative of English History*, First Series, 3 vols. (London, 1824; New York: AMS Press, 1970), vol. 2, pp. 271–72; Ellis, *Original Letters* vol. 2, p. 148; Nicolas, ed., *Memoirs of Sir Christopher Hatton*, pp. 265–66.

27 Nicolas, ed., *Memoirs of Sir Christopher Hatton*, p. 338; Wright, *Queen Elizabeth and Her Times*, vol. 2, pp. 161–62.

28 Wright, *Queen Elizabeth and Her Times*, vol. 1, p. 80; ibid., vol. 1, p. 103; ibid., vol. 1, p. 116.

29 Ibid., vol. 1, p. 72.

30 *Holinshed's Chronicles*, vol. 4, p. 872.

31 Wright, *Queen Elizabeth and Her Times*, vol. 2, p. 34; ibid., vol. 1, p. 506.

32 Ibid., vol. 1, pp. 139–40.

33 Ibid., vol. 2, p. 48; emphasis added.

34 Ibid., vol. 1, pp. 140–41.

35 Ibid., vol. 1, p. 141.

36 *The Complete Works of Shakespeare*, ed. David Bevington, 4th edn. (New York: HarperCollins, 1992).

5 LINGUISTIC STRATIFICATION, MERCHANT DISCOURSE, AND SOCIAL CHANGE

1 Another early English book on letter writing, Abraham Fleming's *A Panoplie of Epistles* (1576), is a collection of letters, mainly in translation, by famous and learned men; it is addressed to "the learned and the unlearned reader."

2 Quotations from *The Enimie of Idlenesse* (1568; London, 1593) and from *The Marchants Avizo* (London, 1590) are cited parenthetically in the text throughout this chapter.
3 "Describing the Social Order of Elizabethan and Stuart England," *Literature and History*, 3 (1976), 37. Ian W. Archer's *The Pursuit of Stability: Social Relations in Elizabethan London* (Cambridge University Press, 1991), analyzes social relations among the citizens of London.
4 Katherine Gee Hornbeak, "The Complete Letter-Writer in English, 1568–1800," *Smith College Studies in Modern Languages*, 15 (1934), 3.
5 Jean Robertson identifies this source in *The Art of Letter Writing* (Liverpool and London: University Press of Liverpool and Hodder & Stoughton Ltd., 1942), p. 15.
6 Peter Quince's prologue to "Pyramus and Thisbe" raises the possibility that the players may offend at the same time as it disclaims the intention to offend (5.1.108–10); in the earlier rehearsal, Starveling, worried about giving offense, argues that "we must leave the killing out" (3.1.13); for all their care, the craftsmen are judged by the less generous in their aristocratic audience to be "asses" (5.1.153). Similarly, in *Love's Labour's Lost*, the players take some care to anticipate and "to make an offence gracious" (5.1.127) and the verbal and other mishaps in their performance receive scathing comments from the elite audience. Theodore B. Leinwand discusses the teetering of Quince's prologue between deference and offensiveness in "'I believe we must leave the killing out': Deference and Accommodation in *A Midsummer Night's Dream*," *Renaissance Papers* (1986), 11–30, esp. p. 22. This article takes a helpful look at the social negotiation between the craftsmen and the aristocracy.
7 The "great feast of language" in *Love's Labour's Lost* has been very fully and adequately anatomized by William C. Carroll, in *The Great Feast of Language in "Love's Labor's Lost"* (Princeton University Press, 1976), and by Keir Elam, in *Shakespeare's Universe of Discourse: Language-Games in the Comedies* (Cambridge University Press, 1984), esp. pp. 235–308. In this chapter, I take their detailed analysis as given and try to accent the social basis of some of the linguistic productions. The play is more usually read as literary satire, parodying such styles as "euphuism ... Arcadianism, Petrarchism, sonneteering, inkhornism, Nashe's idiosyncratic pamphlets, and whatever species of style Gabriel Harvey may be said to have produced" (Carroll, *Great Feast of Language*, p. 25). My argument in what follows is not meant to contest but to supplement these readings. For a social perspective on Shakespeare's malapropisms, see Margaret Schlauch, "The Social Background of Shakespeare's Malapropisms," *Poland's Homage to Shakespeare* (1965), 203–31; rpt. in *A Reader in the Language of Shakespearean Drama*, ed. Vivian Salmon and Edwina Burness (Amsterdam and Philadelphia: John Benjamins, 1987), pp. 71–99.
8 Keir Elam discusses a possible borrowing from Angel Day's *The English Secretary* (*Shakespeare's Universe of Discourse*, pp. 268–69).

9 Quotations from *Love's Labour's Lost* are from G. R. Hibbard's Oxford edition (Oxford and New York: Oxford University Press, 1990).
10 In the Oxford Shakespeare, G. R. Hibbard glosses the phrase as a "legal tag that found its way into common parlance" (1.1.202n). Fulwood's use is far more specific to the context of utterance.
11 For "remuneration," see *LLL*, 3.1.127, 132, 134–35, 141–42, 165–67 and *Enimie*, p. 5, sig. E1v; for "abhominable" and "abhomination," see *LLL*, 5.1.23–24 and *Enimie*, p. 42, sig. D1v; for "condign," see *LLL*, 1.2.25 and *Enimie*, p. 48, sig. D4v).
12 Keith Wrightson comments on this "dichotomous use of the language of sorts" in "Estates, Degrees, and Sorts in Tudor and Stuart England," *History Today*, 37 (1987), 21–22.
13 Penelope Brown and Stephen C. Levinson, *Politeness: Some Universals in Language Usage* (1978; Cambridge University Press, 1987), p. 186.
14 *Language and Symbolic Power*, ed. John B. Thompson, trans. Gino Raymond and Matthew Adamson (Cambridge, Mass.: Harvard University Press, 1991), p. 62. Bourdieu's analysis builds on and theorizes the empirical observations developed by William Labov in *Sociolinguistic Patterns* (Oxford: Basil Blackwell, 1972).
15 *Shakespeare's Comic Commonwealths* (Toronto, Buffalo, and London: University of Toronto Press, 1993), p. 82. She interprets the stylistic similarity as among "the unifying effects of educational expansion" (p. 85). Despite a general similarity among the styles, I think that William Carroll is nonetheless correct to comment that "The play continually forces us to make distinctions" (*Great Feast of Language*, p. 57). I am linking this tension between stylistic likeness and distinction-making to the dynamic of assimilation and dissimilation Bourdieu sees occurring in the social negotiation of linguistic change.
16 *Language and Symbolic Power*, p. 63.
17 Quoted from the title-page.
18 David Harris Sacks interprets the collection as the record of one actual venture, probably occurring sometime between February 1582 and 1584, involving the five vessels named in the letters – the *Joseph*, the *Gabriel*, the *Minion*, the *Unicorne*, and the *Pleasure* – but it is not clear to me how one draws the line between what is Browne's invention and what is historical record in relation to this manual (see *The Widening Gate: Bristol and the Atlantic Economy, 1450–1700* [Berkeley, Los Angeles, and Oxford: University of California Press, 1991], pp. 66–68).
19 *Worlds Apart: The Market and the Theater in Anglo-American Thought, 1550–1750* (Cambridge University Press, 1986), p. 59.
20 Ibid., p. 43; Agnew is quoting Marx.
21 Ibid., p. 68.
22 For Bakhtin's thinking about linguistic change, I draw partly on the interpretation in Gary Saul Morson and Caryl Emerson, *Mikhail Bakhtin: Creation of a Prosaics* (Stanford University Press, 1990), esp. pp. 27–40 and 142–45.
23 David Cressy, *Literacy and the Social Order: Reading and Writing in Tudor and*

Stuart England (Cambridge University Press, 1980), pp. 130, 140, 134–35.
24 Sacks, *The Widening Gate*, pp. 19–53, 331–43.
25 Sacks, *The Widening Gate*, pp. 196–209, 336; see also Patrick McGrath, *The Merchant Venturers of Bristol* (Bristol: The Society of Merchant Venturers of the City of Bristol, 1975), pp. 10–21.
26 Sacks, *The Widening Gate*, pp. 103–24.
27 *Textual Politics: Discourse and Social Dynamics* (London: Taylor & Francis, 1995), p. 20.
28 *Creation of a Prosaics*, pp. 134 and 143.
29 *The English Secretary, or Methods of Writing Epistles and Letters* (1599), introduced by Robert O. Evans (Gainesville, Fla.: Scholars' Facsimiles & Reprints, 1967), Book 1, pp. 97–98.
30 *Shakespearean Pragmatism: Market of His Time* (Chicago and London: University of Chicago Press, 1993), p. 83.
31 Engle, *Shakespearean Pragmatism*, p. 82; Marianne Novy is quoted from Engle, p. 240.
32 "The Ideology of *The Merchant of Venice*," *English Literary Renaissance*, 20 (1990), 436.
33 Ferber, "The Ideology of *The Merchant of Venice*," 448.
34 Shakespeare makes this stylistic dispute more explicit and open later in the play. This occurs, first, in the miscommunications of the trial scene, where the demand for an "answer" is repeatedly foregrounded to accent the incommensurable styles, and the "pleasures" style is further called into dispute by Shylock's literalizing answers. Beyond this, Shylock explicitly rejects the reciprocal contract the "pleasuring" form of exchange takes for granted: "I am not bound to please thee with my answers" (4.1.65). And the dispute takes its final and most obvious form in Portia's "ring" lesson, where she embarrasses her husband for the overly liberal exchange he has made to "pleasure" his new friend and sets the marital relation in competition with the friendship exchanges.
35 "'Magic of Bounty': *Timon of Athens*, Jacobean Patronage, and Maternal Power," *Shakespeare Quarterly*, 38 (1987), 34–57, esp. p. 48.

6 THE PRAGMATICS OF REPAIR IN *KING LEAR* AND *MUCH ADO ABOUT NOTHING*

1 I am adapting these terms for the various functional levels of discourse from M. A. K. Halliday, *An Introduction to Functional Grammar* (London: Edward Arnold, 1985).
2 On the turn-taking model for conversation, see H. Sacks, E. Schegloff, and G. Jefferson, "A Simplest Systematics for the Organization of Turn-Taking for Conversation," *Studies in the Organization of Conversational Interaction*, ed. J. Schenkein (New York: Academic Press, 1978), pp. 7–55.
3 On conversational implicature, see H. Paul Grice, "Logic and Conversation," in *Speech Acts*, ed. Peter Cole and Jerry L. Morgan, vol. 3 of *Syntax and*

Semantics (New York: Academic Press, 1975), pp. 41–58.
4 For linguistic approaches to background knowledge, see Stephen C. Levinson on presupposition in *Pragmatics* (Cambridge University Press, 1983), pp. 167–225 and Gillian Brown and George Yule on given and new information in *Discourse Analysis* (Cambridge University Press, 1983), pp. 153–89.
5 "The Avoidance of Love: A Reading of *King Lear*," *Disowning Knowledge in Six Plays of Shakespeare* (Cambridge University Press, 1987), pp. 39–123.
6 *The Bonds of Love: Psychoanalysis, Feminism, and the Problem of Domination* (New York: Pantheon Books, 1988), esp. pp. 11–36.
7 In *Structures of Social Action: Studies in Conversational Analysis*, ed. J. Maxwell Atkinson and John Heritage (Cambridge University Press, 1984), p. 17.
8 Stephen Levinson provides a good brief summary in *Pragmatics*, pp. 339–45.
9 Margaret L. McLaughlin summarizes the work on preventatives and repairs in chapter 6 of *Conversation: How Talk is Organized* (Beverly Hills, London, and New Delhi: Sage Publications, 1984), pp. 201–33. I quote her definition from p. 208. Emanuel Schegloff, Gail Jefferson, and Harvey Sacks contributed what remains the most influential article on repair structures in conversation – "The Preference for Self-Correction in the Organization of Repair in Conversation," *Language*, 53 (1977), 361–82.
10 McLaughlin, *Conversation*, p. 202.
11 *Politeness: Some Universals in Language Usage* (1978; Cambridge University Press, 1987), p. 58.
12 *The New Rhetoric: A Treatise on Argumentation*, trans. John Wilkinson and Purcell Weaver (Notre Dame and London: University of Notre Dame Press, 1969), esp. pp. 293–305 and 310–16.
13 *The Dialogic Imagination: Four Essays by M. M. Bakhtin*, ed. Michael Holquist, trans. Caryl Emerson and Michael Holquist (Austin: University of Texas Press, 1981), p. 280.
14 *Outline of a Theory of Practice*, trans. Richard Nice (Cambridge University Press, 1977), pp. 81–82.
15 Roger Brown and Albert Gilman also note that the power difference between the Doctor and Cordelia is evident in the politeness usage in "Politeness Theory and Shakespeare's Four Major Tragedies," *Language in Society*, 18 (1989), 187. In an excellent essay that considers language and the social construction of identity in the play, David Aers and Gunther Kress comment briefly on the change in Cordelia's language in 4.7 ("The Language of Social Order: Individual, Society and Historical Process in *King Lear*," *Literature, Language and Society in England 1580–1680* [Dublin: Gill and Macmillan, 1981], pp. 75–99, esp. pp. 93–94).
16 *Outline of a Theory of Practice*, p. 82.
17 Cordelia is weeping, and her tears may inhibit long speech turns, but they are not a sufficient explanation for the formality of her address.
18 *Outline of a Theory of Practice*, p. 78.
19 Ibid., pp. 79, 81.
20 Rosalie L. Colie, "Reason and Need: *King Lear* and the 'Crisis' of the

Aristocracy," *Some Facets of King Lear*, ed. Colie and F. T. Flahiff (Toronto and Buffalo: University of Toronto Press, 1974), pp. 185–219; Paul Delany, "*King Lear* and the Decline of Feudalism," *PMLA*, 92 (1977), 429–40.

21 For an excellent account of Kent's plain language here as an alternative to superficial decorum, see Sheldon P. Zitner, "*King Lear* and Its Language," in *Some Facets of King Lear: Essays in Prismatic Criticism*, ed. Rosalie L. Colie and F. T. Flahiff (Toronto and Buffalo: University of Toronto Press, 1974), pp. 3–22, esp. pp. 9–11.

22 *How Conversation Works* (Oxford and New York: Basil Blackwell, 1985), p. 55.

23 *Outline of a Theory of Practice*, p. 79.

24 Citations of *Much Ado About Nothing* are from the New Cambridge edition, ed. F. H. Mares (Cambridge University Press, 1988).

25 Henry Ellis, ed. *Original Letters, Illustrative of English History*, 3 vols. (London, 1824; rpt. New York: AMS Press, 1970), vol. 2, pp. 272–73.

26 M. M. Bakhtin, *The Dialogic Imagination*, p. 339.

27 M. M. Bakhtin, "The Problem of Speech Genres," in *Speech Genres and Other Late Essays*, trans. Vern W. McGee, ed. Caryl Emerson and Michael Holquist (Austin: University of Texas Press, 1986), pp. 60–102, *passim*.

28 Camille Wells Slights opens her chapter on *Much Ado About Nothing* with a useful reading of this exchange. While she recognizes Benedick's glimpse here at how language provides "the material of the social self," her emphasis is on Benedick's wariness about "the capacity of language to obscure truth" (*Shakespeare's Comic Commonwealths* [Toronto, Buffalo, and London: University of Toronto Press, 1993], p. 171).

29 Arthur Collins, ed., *Letters and Memorials of State*, vol. 1, p. 180.

30 *A Rhetoric of Motives* (Berkeley: University of California Press, 1969), p. 208.

31 "Introduction," *Twentieth-Century Interpretations of "Much Ado About Nothing"* (Englewood Cliffs, N.J.: Prentice-Hall, 1969), pp. 2, 12–13.

32 Louis Althusser, "Ideology and Ideological State Apparatuses," in *Lenin and Philosophy and Other Essays*, trans. Ben Brewster (London: New Left Books, 1971), pp. 127–86.

33 Mary Beth Rose, "Where are the Mothers in Shakespeare? Options for Gender Representation in the English Renaissance," *Shakespeare Quarterly*, 42 (1991), 291–314. In "Fatherly Authority: The Politics of Stuart Family Images," *Rewriting the Renaissance: The Discourses of Sexual Difference in Early Modern Europe*, ed. Margaret W. Ferguson, Maureen Quilligan, and Nancy J. Vickers (Chicago and London: University of Chicago Press, 1986), pp. 3–32, Jonathan Goldberg discusses the ideological function of the family and of family portraiture in negotiating the tension between the mother's reproductive creativity and the father's power.

34 F. H. Mares, ed., "Introduction," *Much Ado About Nothing*, p. 37; Zitner, "*King Lear* and Its Languages," p. 6; Anthony B. Dawson, "Much Ado About Signifying," *Studies in English Literature*, 22 (1982), 221.

35 *Reproducing Rape: Domination through Talk in the Courtroom* (University of Chicago Press, 1993), p. 90.

7 "VOICE POTENTIAL": LANGUAGE AND SYMBOLIC CAPITAL IN *OTHELLO*

1 Citations of *Othello* are from the New Cambridge edition, ed. Norman Sanders (Cambridge University Press, 1984).
2 "The Economics of Linguistic Exchanges," *Social Science Information*, 16 (1977), 645–68, esp. p. 648. Much of the material in this essay is recirculated as "Price Formation and the Anticipation of Profit" in *Language and Symbolic Power*, ed. John B. Thompson (Cambridge, Mass.: Harvard University Press, 1991), pp. 66–89.
3 "The Economics of Linguistic Exchanges," p. 648.
4 For overviews of research on cross-sex conversations, see Deborah James and Sandra Clarke, "Women, Men, and Interruptions: A Critical Review" and Deborah James and Janice Drakich, "Understanding Gender Differences in Amount of Talk: A Critical Review of Research," in *Gender and Conversational Interaction*, ed. Deborah Tannen (New York and Oxford: Oxford University Press, 1993), pp. 231–80 and 281–312.
5 Where Q1 reads "a world of sighs," F offers "a world of kisses." While still a non-verbal response, the Folio's version gives a significantly different turn to Desdemona's portrayal here. If Desdemona is so forward here with her kisses, it is hard to reconcile with Othello's remark later in the speech that he spoke of his love upon a "hint" (165) from her. I am grateful to Paul Werstine for drawing my attention to this variant.
6 Virginia Mason Vaughan notes critics' fascination with language in *Othello* and the general tendency to relate language patterns to essential character in the introduction to *"Othello": New Perspectives* (London and Toronto: Associated University Presses, 1991), pp. 14–15.
7 "The Economics of Linguistic Exchanges," p. 657.
8 Both Bakhtin and Bourdieu offer an account of the social production of discourse which emphasizes anticipatory adjustment. To the best of my knowledge, no one has pointed out this shared orientation or demonstrated how the one can reinforce the other. In Bakhtin's account of discourse as social and language as dialogic, he makes this somewhat elusive claim: "The word in living conversation," he asserts, "is directly, blatantly, oriented toward a future answer-word: it provokes an answer, anticipates it and structures itself in the answer's direction" ("Discourse in the Novel," in *The Dialogue Imagination: Four Essays by M. M. Bakhtin*, ed. Michael Holquist, trans. Caryl Emerson and Michael Holquist [Austin: University of Texas Press, 1981], p. 280). In this formulation, a dialogic utterance is not structured to answer a preceding utterance, in the way we might normally think of conversational sequence. It is structured to answer its own answer. Intriguing as this idea sounds, it is perhaps not immediately obvious how it might apply to practical speech situations. In what way might the structure of an utterance be shaped by "a future answer-word"? Elsewhere I have suggested that politeness theory is consistent with Bakhtin's anticipatory hypothesis: speakers deploy politeness strategies to mitigate potentially

threatening effects of their speech acts, repairing the damage – so to speak – before it occurs. But Bourdieu's economic model for linguistic exchange offers a fuller account of how anticipated reception may shape discourse production.
9. "The Economics of Linguistic Exchanges," p. 653.
10. Ibid., p. 655.
11. Ibid., p. 648.
12. On hendiadys in Shakespeare, see George T. Wright, "Hendiadys and *Hamlet*," *PMLA*, 96 (1981), 168–93.
13. G. Wilson Knight, "The *Othello* Music," in *The Wheel of Fire: Interpretations of Shakespearian Tragedy* (Oxford University Press, 1930), pp. 97–119; E. A. J. Honigmann, "Shakespeare's 'Bombast,'" in *Shakespeare's Styles: Essays in Honour of Kenneth Muir*, ed. Philip Edwards, Inga-Stina Ewbank, and G. K. Hunter (Cambridge University Press, 1980), pp. 151–62, esp. pp. 158–59.
14. Clearly, with Othello, this linguistic overreaching, with its exotic touches, has become a habit that has itself received a positive reception in various settings (e.g., in Brabantio's household), thus adding a motive beyond linguistic insecurity for Othello to reproduce the style. Hence, this encoded discourse history may even be consistent with a proud and apparently self-assured delivery in 1.3, but it nonetheless anticipates Othello's susceptibility to Iago's persuasions.
15. "The Economics of Linguistic Exchanges," p. 658.
16. *Language and Symbolic Power*, p. 67.
17. Brown and Levinson, *Politeness: Some Universals in Language Usage* (1978: Cambridge University Press, 1987), pp. 95–96 and p. 282, make the point that in situations of urgency and desperation, when maximum efficiency of communication is required, the face-redress work of politeness is unnecessary.
18. *Politeness*, p. 228.
19. Roger Brown and Albert Gilman, in "Politeness Theory and Shakespeare's Four Major Tragedies," *Language in Society*, 18 (1989), 169, and Juhani Rudanko, in *Pragmatic Approaches to Shakespeare: Essays on "Othello," "Coriolanus," and "Timon of Athens"* (Lanham, New York, and London: University Press of America, 1993), pp. 24–26, have already offered brief but illuminating suggestions about how Grice's model can account for Iago's tactics for triggering Othello's inference-making in the famous "seduction" scene (3.3), and I will not repeat their analyses here.

Bibliography

PRIMARY SOURCES

Beer, Barrett L., and Sybil M. Jack, eds. *The Letters of William, Lord Paget of Beaudesert, 1547–63*. In *Camden Miscellany Vol. XXV*. London: Royal Historical Society, 1974, pp. 1–141.

Browne, John. *The Marchants Avizo*. London, 1590.

Collins, Arthur. *Letters and Memorials of State*. 2 vols. London, 1746; rpt. New York: AMS Press, 1973.

Day, Angel. *The English Secretary, or Methods of Writing Epistles and Letters* (1599). Introduced by Robert O. Evans. Gainesville, Fla.: Scholars' Facsimiles & Reprints, 1967.

Ellis, Henry, ed. *Original Letters, Illustrative of English History . . . from Autographs in the British Museum, and One or two other collections*. First Series. 3 vols. London, 1824; New York: AMS Press, 1970. Vol. 2.

Erasmus, Desiderius. "On the Writing of Letters" (*De conscribendis epistolis*). Trans. Charles Fantazzi. *Collected Works of Erasmus*. Vol. 25. Ed. J. K. Sowards. Toronto, Buffalo, and London: University of Toronto Press, 1985, pp. 10–254.

Fleming, Abraham. *A Panoplie of Epistles*. London, 1576.

Fulwood, William. *The Enimie of Idlenesse*. 1568; London, 1593.

Gainsford, Thomas. *The Secretaries Studie*. London, 1616. Rpt. as No. 658 of The English Experience series. Amsterdam and Norwood, N.J.: Theatrum Orbis Terrarum, Ltd. and Walter J. Johnson, Inc., 1974.

Greene, Robert. *The Life and Works of Robert Greene*. Ed. Alexander B. Grosart. 15 vols. New York: Russell & Russell, 1964.

Guazzo, Steven. *The Civile Conversation of M. Steeven Guazzo*. Trans. George Pettie and Barth. Young. Intro. Sir Edward Sullivan. 2 vols. London: Constable, 1925.

Holinshed, Raphael. *Holinshed's Chronicles of England, Scotland, and Ireland* (1587). 6 vols. London, 1808; rpt. New York: AMS Press, 1965.

M., I. *A Health to the Gentlemanly Profession of Serving-Men*. London, 1598.

Nicolas, Sir Harris, ed. *Memoirs of the Life and Times of Sir Christopher Hatton, K.G., Vice-Chamberlain and Lord Chancellor to Queen Elizabeth*. London: Richard Bentley, 1847.

Perkins, William. *Christian Oeconomy. The Work of William Perkins*. Ed. Ian Breward. Appleford: Sutton Courteny, 1970, pp. 411–39.
Sadler, Ralph. *The State Papers and Letters*. Ed. Arthur Clifford. 2 vols. London, 1809.
Shakespeare, William. *The Complete Works of Shakespeare*. Ed. David Bevington. 4th edn. New York: HarperCollins, 1992.
 The Complete Works. The Oxford Shakespeare. Gen. ed. Stanley Wells and Gary Taylor. Oxford: Clarendon Press, 1986.
 The Life of King Henry the Eighth. Ed. F. David Hoeniger. Pelican Shakespeare. Baltimore: Penguin Books, 1966.
 Love's Labour's Lost. Ed. G. R. Hibbard. Oxford and New York: Oxford University Press, 1990.
 Much Ado About Nothing. Ed. F. H. Mares. New Cambridge edn. Cambridge University Press, 1988.
 Othello. Ed. Norman Sanders. New Cambridge edn. Cambridge University Press, 1984.
 The Sonnets and *A Lover's Complaint*. Ed. John Kerrigan. Harmondsworth: Penguin, 1986.
Wood, Mary Anne Everett, ed. *Letters of Royal and Illustrious Ladies of Great Britain*. 2 vols. London: Henry Colburn, 1846.
Wright, Thomas, ed. *Queen Elizabeth and Her Times, A Series of Original Letters*. 2 vols. London: Henry Colburn, 1838.

SECONDARY SOURCES

Aers, David, and Gunther Kress. "The Language of Social Order: Individual, Society and Historical Process in *King Lear*." In David Aers, Bob Hodge, and Gunther Kress, *Literature, Language and Society in England 1580–1680*. Dublin: Gill and Macmillan, 1981, pp. 75–99.
Agnew, Jean-Christophe. *Worlds Apart: The Market and the Theater in Anglo-American Thought, 1550–1750*. Cambridge University Press, 1986.
Althusser, Louis. "Ideology and Ideological State Apparatuses." In *Lenin and Philosophy and Other Essays*. Trans. Ben Brewster. London: New Left Books, 1971, pp. 127–86.
Archer, Ian W. *The Pursuit of Stability: Social Relations in Elizabethan London*. Cambridge University Press, 1991.
Atkinson, J. Maxwell, and John Heritage, eds. *Structures of Social Action: Studies in Conversational Analysis*. Cambridge University Press, 1984.
Austin, J. L. *How to Do Things with Words*. 1962. Ed. J. O. Urmson and Marina Sbisà. 2nd edn. Cambridge, Mass.: Harvard University Press, 1975.
Bakhtin, M. M. "Discourse in Life and Discourse in Art." 1926. Trans. I. R. Titunik. *Contemporary Literary Criticism: Literary and Cultural Studies*. Ed. Robert Con Davis and Ronald Schleifer. 2nd edn. New York and London: Longman, 1989, pp. 392–410.
 "Discourse in the Novel." *The Dialogic Imagination: Four Essays by M. M.*

Bakhtin. Ed. Michael Holquist, trans. Caryl Emerson and Michael Holquist. Austin: University of Texas Press, 1981, pp. 259–422.

"The Problem of Speech Genres." *Speech Genres and Other Late Essays*. Ed. Caryl Emerson and Michael Holquist, trans. Vern W. McGee. Austin: University of Texas Press, 1986, pp. 60–102.

Barrell, John. "Editing Out: The Discourse of Patronage and Shakespeare's Twenty-Ninth Sonnet." *Poetry, Language, and Politics*. Manchester University Press, 1988, pp. 18–43.

Bazerman, Charles. *Shaping Written Knowledge: The Genre and Activity of the Experimental Article in Science*. Madison: University of Wisconsin Press, 1988.

Belsey, Catherine. *The Subject of Tragedy: Identity and Difference in Renaissance Drama*. London and New York: Methuen, 1985.

Benjamin, Jessica. *The Bonds of Love: Psychoanalysis, Feminism, and the Problem of Domination*. New York: Pantheon Books, 1988.

Bolton, W. F. *Shakespeare's English: Language in the History Plays*. Cambridge, Mass. and Oxford: Basil Blackwell, 1992.

Bourdieu, Pierre. "The Economics of Linguistic Exchanges." Trans. Richard Nice. *Social Science Information*, 16 (1977), 645–68.

Language and Symbolic Power. Ed. John B. Thompson, trans. Gino Raymond and Matthew Adamson. Cambridge, Mass.: Harvard University Press, 1991.

Outline of a Theory of Practice. Trans. Richard Nice. Cambridge University Press, 1977.

Bray, Alan. *Homosexuality in Renaissance England*. Boston: Gay Men's Press, 1982.

Brown, Gillian and George Yule. *Discourse Analysis*. Cambridge University Press, 1983.

Brown, Penelope, and Stephen C. Levinson. *Politeness: Some Universals in Language Usage*. 1978; Cambridge University Press, 1987.

Brown, Roger, and Albert Gilman. "Politeness Theory and Shakespeare's Four Major Tragedies." *Language in Society*, 18 (1989), 159–212.

"The Pronouns of Power and Solidarity." *Style in Language*. Ed. Thomas A. Sebeok. Cambridge, Mass.: MIT Press, 1960, pp. 253–76.

Burke, Kenneth. *The Philosophy of Literary Form: Studies in Symbolic Action*. Chicago and London: University of Chicago Press, 1980.

A Rhetoric of Motives. Berkeley: University of California Press, 1969.

Burton, Dolores M. *Shakespeare's Grammatical Style: A Computer-Assisted Analysis of "Richard II" and "Antony and Cleopatra."* Austin and London: University of Texas Press, 1973.

Calvo, Clara. "Pronouns of Address and Social Negotiation in *As You Like It*." *Language and Literature*, 1 (1992), 5–27.

Carroll, William C. *The Great Feast of Language in "Love's Labor's Lost."* Princeton University Press, 1976.

Cavell, Stanley. "The Avoidance of Love: A Reading of *King Lear*." *Disowning Knowledge in Six Plays of Shakespeare*. Cambridge University Press, 1987, pp. 39–123.

Chafe, Wallace, and Johanna Nichols, eds. *Evidentiality: The Linguistic Coding of Epistemology*. Vol. 20 of *Advances in Discourse Processes*. Norwood, N.J.: Ablex Publishing Corporation, 1986.
Chartier, Roger, ed. *Passions of the Renaissance*. Vol. 3 of *A History of Private Life*. Trans. Arthur Goldhammer. Cambridge, Mass. and London: Harvard University Press, 1989.
Cherry, Roger D. "Politeness in Written Persuasion." *Journal of Pragmatics*, 12 (1988), 63–81.
Colie, Rosalie L. "Reason and Need: *King Lear* and the 'Crisis' of the Aristocracy." *Some Facets of King Lear*. Ed. Colie and F. T. Flahiff. Toronto and Buffalo: University of Toronto Press, 1974, pp. 185–219.
 Shakespeare's Living Art. Princeton University Press, 1974.
Coulthard, Malcolm. *An Introduction to Discourse Analysis*. 2nd edn. London and New York: Longman, 1985.
Cressy, David. "Describing the Social Order of Elizabethan and Stuart England." *Literature and History*, 3 (1976), 29–44.
 Literacy and the Social Order: Reading and Writing in Tudor and Stuart England. Cambridge University Press, 1980.
Dalzell, Alexander. "Greetings and Salutations in Erasmus." *Renaissance and Reformation*, n.s. 13 (1989), 251–61.
Davis, Walter R., ed. *Twentieth-Century Interpretations of "Much Ado About Nothing."* Englewood Cliffs, N.J.: Prentice-Hall, 1969.
Dawson, Anthony B. "Much Ado About Signifying." *Studies in English Literature*, 22 (1982), 211–21.
De Grazia, Margreta. "The Motive for Interiority: Shakespeare's *Sonnets* and *Hamlet*." *Style*, 23 (1989), 430–44.
Delany, Paul. "*King Lear* and the Decline of Feudalism." *PMLA*, 92 (1977), 429–40.
Doran, Madeleine. *Shakespeare's Dramatic Language*. Madison: University of Wisconsin Press, 1976.
Duncan-Jones, Katherine. *Sir Philip Sidney, Courtier Poet*. New Haven and London: Yale University Press, 1991.
Edwards, Philip, Inga-Stina Ewbank, and G. K. Hunter, eds. *Shakespeare's Styles: Essays in Honour of Kenneth Muir*. Cambridge University Press, 1980.
Elam, Keir. *Shakespeare's Universe of Discourse: Language-Games in the Comedies*. Cambridge University Press, 1984.
Elton, G. R. *The Tudor Revolution in Government*. Cambridge University Press, 1959.
Engle, Lars. *Shakespearean Pragmatism: Market of His Time*. Chicago and London: University of Chicago Press, 1993.
Fairclough, Norman. *Discourse and Social Change*. Cambridge: Polity Press, 1992.
 Language and Power. London and New York: Longman, 1989.
Ferber, Michael. "The Ideology of *The Merchant of Venice*." *English Literary Renaissance*, 20 (1990), 431–64.
Ferry, Anne. *The "Inward Language": Sonnets of Wyatt, Sidney, Shakespeare, Donne*.

Chicago and London: University of Chicago Press, 1983.
Fineman, Joel. *Shakespeare's Perjured Eye: The Invention of Poetic Subjectivity in the Sonnets*. Berkeley and Los Angeles: University of California Press, 1986.
Fish, Stanley E. "How To Do Things with Austin and Searle: Speech-Act Theory and Literary Criticism." *Modern Language Notes*, 91 (1976), 983–1025.
Friedman, Alice T. *House and Household in Elizabethan England: Wollaton Hall and the Willoughby Family*. Chicago and London: University of Chicago Press, 1989.
Goffman, Erving. *Interaction Ritual: Essays on Face-to-Face Behavior*. Garden City, N.Y.: Doubleday, 1967.
Goldberg, Jonathan. "Fatherly Authority: The Politics of Stuart Family Images." *Rewriting the Renaissance: The Discourses of Sexual Difference in Early Modern Europe*. Ed. Margaret W. Ferguson, Maureen Quilligan, and Nancy J. Vickers. Chicago and London: University of Chicago Press, 1986, pp. 3–32.
― *Writing Matter: From the Hands of the English Renaissance*. Stanford University Press, 1990.
Greenblatt, Stephen. *Renaissance Self-Fashioning: From More to Shakespeare*. Chicago and London: University of Chicago Press, 1980.
― *Shakespearean Negotiations: The Circulation of Social Energy in Renaissance England*. Berkeley and Los Angeles: University of California Press, 1988.
Grice, H. Paul. "Logic and Conversation." *Speech Acts*. Ed. Peter Cole and Jerry L. Morgan. Vol. 3 of *Syntax and Semantics*. New York: Academic Press, 1975, pp. 41–58.
Grund, Gary R. "From Formulary to Fiction: The Epistle and the English Anti-Ciceronian Movement." *Texas Studies in Language and Literature*, 17 (1975), 379–95.
Guillén, Claudio. "Notes toward the Study of the Renaissance Letter." *Renaissance Genres: Essays on Theory, History, and Interpretation*. Ed. Barbara Kiefer Lewalski. Cambridge and London: Harvard University Press, 1986, pp. 70–101.
Hagge, John, and Charles Kostelnick. "Linguistic Politeness in Professional Prose: A Discourse Analysis of Auditors' Suggestion Letters." *Written Communication*, 6 (1989), 312–39.
Halliday, M. A. K. *An Introduction to Functional Grammar*. London: Edward Arnold, 1985.
Hannay, Margaret P. *Philip's Phoenix: Mary Sidney, Countess of Pembroke*. New York and Oxford: Oxford University Press, 1990.
― *Silent But for the Word*. Kent, Ohio: Kent State University Press, 1985.
Henderson, Judith Rice. "Defining the Genre of the Letter: Juan Luis Vives' *De conscribendis epistolis*." *Renaissance and Reformation*, n.s. 7 (1983), 89–105.
― "Erasmus on the Art of Letter-Writing." *Renaissance Eloquence: Studies in the Theory and Practice of Renaissance Rhetoric*. Ed. James J. Murphy. Berkeley, Los Angeles, and London: University of California Press, 1983, pp. 331–55.

"On Reading the Rhetoric of the Renaissance Letter." *Renaissance-Rhetorik/Renaissance Rhetoric*. Ed. Heinrich F. Plett. Berlin and New York: Walter de Gruyter, 1993, pp. 143–62.

Hibbard, G. R. *Shakespeare's Dramatic Poetry*. Toronto, Buffalo, and London: University of Toronto Press, 1981.

Hornbeak, Katherine Gee. "The Complete Letter-Writer in English, 1568–1800." *Smith College Studies in Modern Languages*, 15 (1934), 1–150.

Howell, Wilbur Samuel. *Logic and Rhetoric in England, 1500–1700*. New York: Russell & Russell, Inc., 1961.

Hunter, G. K. "Hearing Shakespeare's Poetry." *The Elizabethan Theatre XII*. Ed. A. L. Magnusson and C. E. McGee. Port Credit, Ontario: P. D. Meany, 1993, pp. 45–60.

Jardine, Lisa. *Reading Shakespeare Historically*. London and New York: Routledge, 1996.

Jenkinson, Hilary. "The Teaching and Practice of Handwriting in England." *History*, 11 (1926), 130–38, 211–18.

Joseph, Sister Miriam. *Rhetoric in Shakespeare's Time: Literary Theory of Renaissance Europe*. New York: Harcourt, Brace & World, Inc., 1962.

Kahn, Coppelia. "'Magic of Bounty': *Timon of Athens*, Jacobean Patronage, and Maternal Power." *Shakespeare Quarterly*, 38 (1987), 34–57.

Kasper, Gabriele. "Linguistic Politeness: Current Research Issues." *Journal of Pragmatics*, 14 (1990), 193–218.

Kennedy, Andrew K. *Dramatic Dialogue: The Duologue of Personal Encounter*. Cambridge University Press, 1983.

Knight, G. Wilson. *The Crown of Life*. London: Methuen, 1948.

The Wheel of Fire: Interpretations of Shakespearian Tragedy. Oxford University Press, 1930.

Krontiris, Tina. *Oppositional Voices: Women as Writers and Translators of Literature in the English Renaissance*. London and New York: Routledge, 1992.

Kussmaul, Ann. *Servants in Husbandry in Early Modern England*. Cambridge University Press, 1981.

Labov, William. *Sociolinguistic Patterns*. Oxford: Basil Blackwell, 1972.

Lamb, Mary Ellen. *Gender and Authorship in the Sidney Circle*. Madison: University of Wisconsin Press, 1990.

Laslett, Peter. *The World We Have Lost: Further Explored*. 3rd edn. London: Methuen, 1983.

Leinwand, Theodore B. "'I believe we must leave the killing out': Deference and Accommodation in *A Midsummer Night's Dream*." *Renaissance Papers* (1986), 11–30.

Lemke, Jay L. *Textual Politics: Discourse and Social Dynamics*. London: Taylor & Francis, 1995.

Levinson, Stephen C. *Pragmatics*. Cambridge University Press, 1983.

Lewis, Catherine R. "Poet, Friend, and Poetry: The Idealized Image of Love in Shakespeare's Sonnets." *The American Journal of Psychoanalysis*, 45 (1985), 176–90.

Margeson, John. "Introduction." *King Henry VIII*. Cambridge University Press, 1990.
Marotti, Arthur F. "'Love is Not Love': Elizabethan Sonnet Sequences and the Social Order." *ELH*, 49 (1982), 396–428.
  "Shakespeare's Sonnets as Literary Property." *Soliciting Interpretation: Literary Theory and Seventeenth-Century English Poetry*. Ed. Elizabeth D. Harvey and Katharine Eisaman Maus. Chicago and London: University of Chicago Press, 1990, pp. 143–73.
Matoesian, Gregory M. *Reproducing Rape: Domination through Talk in the Courtroom*. University of Chicago Press, 1993.
McDonald, Russ, ed. *Shakespeare Reread: The Texts in New Contexts*. Ithaca and London: Cornell University Press, 1994.
McGrath, Patrick. *The Merchant Venturers of Bristol*. Bristol: The Society of Merchant Venturers of the City of Bristol, 1975.
McLaughlin, Margaret L. *Conversation: How Talk is Organized*. Beverly Hills, London, and New Delhi: Sage Publications, 1984.
Mendelson, Michael. "A Dialogical Model for Business Correspondence." *Journal of Business and Technical Communication*, 7 (1993), 283–311.
Micheli, Linda McJ. "'Sit By Us': Visual Imagery and the Two Queens in *Henry VIII*." *Shakespeare Quarterly*, 38 (1987), 452–66.
Montrose, Louis A. "Professing the Renaissance: The Poetics and Politics of Culture." *The New Historicism*. Ed. H. Aram Veeser. New York and London: Routledge, 1989, pp. 15–36.
Morson, Gary Saul, and Caryl Emerson. *Mikhail Bakhtin: Creation of a Prosaics*. Stanford University Press, 1990.
Murphy, James J. "*Ars dictaminis*: The Art of Letter-Writing." *Rhetoric in the Middle Ages: A History of Rhetorical Theory from Saint Augustine to the Renaissance*. Berkeley, Los Angeles, and London: University of California Press, 1974, pp. 194–268.
Noling, Kim H. "Grubbing Up the Stock: Dramatizing Queens in *Henry VIII*." *Shakespeare Quarterly*, 39 (1988), 291–306.
Parker, Patricia. *Shakespeare from the Margins: Language, Culture, Context*. University of Chicago Press, 1996.
Perelman, Chaim, and L. Olbrechts-Tyteca. *The New Rhetoric: A Treatise on Argumentation*. Trans. John Wilkinson and Purcell Weaver. Notre Dame and London: University of Notre Dame Press, 1969.
Perelman, Les. "The Medieval Art of Letter Writing: Rhetoric As Institutional Expression." *Textual Dynamics of the Professions: Historical and Contemporary Studies of Writing in Professional Communities*. Ed. Charles Bazerman and James Paradis. Madison: University of Wisconsin Press, 1991, pp. 97–119.
Read, Conyers. *Mr. Secretary Cecil and Queen Elizabeth*. London: Jonathan Cape, 1955.
Rebholz, Ronald A. *The Life of Fulke Greville, First Lord Brooke*. Oxford: Clarendon Press, 1971.

Rebhorn, Wayne A. *Courtly Performances: Masking and Festivity in Castiglione's "Book of the Courtier."* Detroit: Wayne State University Press, 1978.

Replogle, Carol. "Shakespeare's Salutations: A Study of Stylistic Etiquette." *Studies in Philology*, 70 (1973), 172–86.

Robertson, Jean. *The Art of Letter Writing: An Essay on the Handbooks Published in England During the Sixteenth and Seventeenth Centuries.* Liverpool and London: University Press of Liverpool and Hodder & Stoughton Ltd., 1942.

Rose, Mary Beth. "Where are the Mothers in Shakespeare? Options for Gender Representation in the English Renaissance." *Shakespeare Quarterly*, 42 (1991), 291–314.

Rudanko, Juhani. *Pragmatic Approaches to Shakespeare: Essays on "Othello," "Coriolanus," and "Timon of Athens."* Lanham, New York, and London: University Press of America, 1993.

Rummel, Erika. "Erasmus' Manual of Letter-Writing: Tradition and Innovation." *Renaissance and Reformation*, n.s. 13 (1989), 299–312.

Sacks, David Harris. *The Widening Gate: Bristol and the Atlantic Economy, 1450–1700.* Berkeley, Los Angeles, and Oxford: University of California Press, 1991.

Sacks, H., E. Schegloff, and G. Jefferson. "A Simplest Systematics for the Organization of Turn-Taking for Conversation." *Studies in the Organization of Conversational Interaction.* Ed. J. Schenkein. New York: Academic Press, 1978, pp. 7–55.

Sahel, Pierre. "The Strangeness of a Dramatic Style: Rumour in *Henry VIII.*" *Shakespeare Survey*, 38 (1985), 145–51.

Schegloff, E., G. Jefferson, and H. Sacks. "The Preference for Self-Correction in the Organization of Repair in Conversation." *Language*, 53 (1977), 361–82.

Schlauch, Margaret. "The Social Background of Shakespeare's Malapropisms." *Poland's Homage to Shakespeare* (1965), 203–31; rpt. in Vivian Salmon and Edwina Burness, eds., *A Reader in the Language of Shakespearean Drama.* Amsterdam and Philadelphia: John Benjamins, 1987, pp. 71–99.

Schleiner, Louise. *Tudor and Stuart Women Writers.* Bloomington and Indianapolis: Indiana University Press, 1994.

Schreiber-McGee, F. "'The View of Earthly Glory': Visual Strategies and the Issue of Royal Prerogative in *Henry VIII.*" *Shakespeare Studies*, 20 (1988), 191–200.

Searle, John R. "Indirect Speech Acts." *Speech Acts.* Ed. Peter Cole and Jerry L. Morgan. Vol. 3 of *Syntax and Semantics.* New York: Academic Press, 1975, pp. 59–81.

"What is a Speech Act?" *Philosophy in America.* Ed. Max Black. Ithaca, N.Y.: Cornell University Press, 1965, pp. 220–39.

Skura, Meredith Anne. *Shakespeare the Actor and the Purposes of Playing.* Chicago and London: University of Chicago Press, 1993.

Slights, Camille Wells. *Shakespeare's Comic Commonwealths.* Toronto, Buffalo, and London: University of Toronto Press, 1993.

Smith, Bruce R. *Homosexual Desire in Shakespeare's England: A Cultural Poetics.*

Chicago and London: University of Chicago Press, 1991.

Steen, Sara Jayne. *The Letters of Lady Arbella Stuart*. New York and Oxford: Oxford University Press, 1994.

Stephen, Sir Leslie, and Sir Sidney Lee. *The Dictionary of National Biography from the Earliest Times to 1900*. 22 vols. London: Oxford University Press, 1937–38.

Stone, Lawrence. *The Crisis of the Aristocracy, 1558–1641*. Oxford: Clarendon Press, 1965.

Stopes, Charlotte Carmichael. *The Life of Henry, Third Earl of Southampton, Shakespeare's Patron*. 1922; New York: AMS Press, 1969.

Styan, J. L. *The Elements of Drama*. Cambridge University Press, 1963.

Tannen, Deborah, ed. *Gender and Conversational Interaction*. New York and Oxford: Oxford University Press, 1993.

Vaughan, Virginia Mason, ed. *"Othello": New Perspectives*. London and Toronto: Associated University Presses, 1991.

Vološinov, V. N. *Marxism and the Philosophy of Language*. Trans. Ladislav Matejka and I. R. Titunik. Cambridge, Mass. and London: Harvard University Press, 1986.

Wardhaugh, Ronald. *How Conversation Works*. Oxford and New York: Basil Blackwell, 1985.

Weil, Judith. "'Household Stuff': Maestrie and Service in *The Taming of the Shrew*." *The Elizabethan Theatre XIV*. Ed. A. Lynne Magnusson and C. E. McGee. Toronto: P. D. Meany, 1996, pp. 71–82.

Whigham, Frank. *Ambition and Privilege: The Social Tropes of Elizabethan Courtesy Theory*. Berkeley, Los Angeles, and London: University of California Press, 1984.

"The Rhetoric of Elizabethan Suitors' Letters." *PMLA*, 96 (1981), 864–82.

Wright, George T. "Hendiadys and *Hamlet*," *PMLA*, 96 (1981), 168–93.

Shakespeare's Metrical Art. Berkeley, Los Angeles, and London: University of California Press, 1988.

Wrightson, Keith. *English Society, 1580–1680*. New Brunswick, N.J.: Rutgers University Press, 1982.

"Estates, Degrees and Sorts in Tudor and Stuart England." *History Today*, 37 (1987), 17–22.

Zitner, Sheldon P. *All's Well That Ends Well*. New York and London: Harvester Wheatsheaf, 1989.

"*King Lear* and Its Languages." *Some Facets of King Lear: Essays in Prismatic Criticism*. Ed. Rosalie L. Colie and F. T. Flahiff. Toronto and Buffalo: University of Toronto Press, 1974, pp. 3–22.

Index

acknowledgment 13, 142–43, 146, 150, 153
administrative letter 92, 93–108, 198 n.12
advice 17–18, 21–24, 95–99, 198 n.9
Agnew, Jean-Christophe 124, 128, 130
Aldworth, Robert 123
Aldworth, Thomas 114, 123, 125
Althusser, Louis 10, 157
Aristotle 92
Arundel, Anne Dacre Howard, Countess of 102–03, 200 n. 25
Austin, J. L. 141

Bacon, Francis 74
Bakhtin, M. M. 2, 7, 8–11, 19, 36, 65, 66, 124, 131, 135
   "alien words" 9, 11
   "future answer-word" 1, 4, 24, 146
   "quotation" 9, 10, 154
   see also dialogue, heteroglossia, language and social change, reaccentuation, speech genres, stylistic "dispute"
Bazerman, Charles 65, 74
Bebel, Heinrich 63
Belsey, Catherine 36, 48–49
Benjamin, Jessica 143, 144
Boleyn, Anne, Queen of England 29, 189 n.28
Booth, Stephen 6
Bourdieu, Pierre 2, 7, 13, 29, 38, 49, 73, 93, 121, 122, 149, 195 n.22
   market analogy for linguistic exchange 9, 163–64, 167–68, 170–71, 172, 181
   interpersonal relations and social structure 36–37, 147
   see also discourse, habitus, hypercorrection, legitimate language, linguistic domination, politeness, symbolic capital
Bray, Alan 54
Brown, Penelope 2, 7, 11, 17–27, 38, 69, 79, 93, 120, 144, 146, 160, 177, 185 n.3
Browne, John

The Marchants Avizo 3, 13, 62, 114, 115, 122–30, 131–32, 134
Buckhurst, Thomas Sackville, Baron 104
Burghley, Sir William Cecil, Baron 41, 51, 93–95, 98, 99, 103, 104, 105–06, 109–12
Burke, Kenneth 66, 156
Burton, Dolores M. 5, 184 n.12

Carroll, William C. 201 n.7, 202 n.15
Cavell, Stanley 142
Cecil, Sir William *see* Burghley
Chafe, Wallace 86
character construction 5, 11, 14, 27, 29, 34, 54, 167, 181
Chomsky, Noam 2, 184 n.18
Cicero 10, 62, 63, 73
civility, early modern 11, 37, 38, 44, 91, 102, 103, 108, 130, 186 n.4, 195 n.17
   see also politeness
class 93, 190 n.35
   cross-class encounters 120
   and language 1, 3, 18, 168–70
   resentment 22, 171–72
   and social mobility 12, 74–75, 111, 112
   status and voice power 173–75
   trajectory 31–34
   see also habitus
client–patron relation 71, 84, 88–90
Colie, Rosalie 151, 152
competence
   interpretive 112–13
   legitimate standard of 120
   linguistic 119–20, 159, 163
   in situated discourse 66, 90
conversation 1, 2, 10, 13, 20
   as achievement 141
   Iago as rhetorician of 164, 178–79
   and ideology 153
   and prosaic vision 162
   rhetoric of 2, 14, 142, 153
conversational analysis 13, 143–44, 182

217

cooperation 152
creativity in social language 10–11
Cressy, David 114, 125
Croft, Sir James 93, 94–97, 98–100
cultural poetics 5, 6–7, 10, 19, 91

Dalzell, Alexander 68–69, 70
Davis, Walter R. 157
Dawson, Anthony B. 158
Day, Angel
  The English Secretary 3, 12, 13, 37, 44, 48, 61, 62, 74–88, 96, 114, 123, 124, 128, 131, 133
Day, Thomas 75
De Grazia, Margreta 55
deconstruction 2, 7, 8, 91, 158
decorum 64, 65, 78, 115, 116–17, 118, 122, 150, 175
dedicatory epistles 88–90, 155
defamiliarization 126
deference 25–26, 37, 41–42, 51–52, 55, 66–67, 83, 85, 89–90, 92, 101–02, 107–08, 119–20, 127, 156
Delany, Paul 151, 152
dialogue
  Bakhtinian 8–9, 131, 135
  and conversation 159
  and discourse analysis 2
  dramatic 4, 20, 183–84 n.9, 184 n.10
  external and internal 9
  and social rhetoric 1, 181–82
discourse 5, 7
  as anticipatory 9, 167, 206 n.8
  as a social phenomenon 2, 4–5, 7, 8–11
  conditions of production and reception 9, 14, 112, 163, 167
discourse analysis 1–2, 8, 182
Duxwell, Thomas 75

Edward VI, King of England 97, 104
Edwards, Philip 5, 184 n.12
Elam, Keir 5, 183 n.9, 184 n.12
Elizabeth I, Queen of England 39, 41, 42, 44, 51, 56, 74, 93, 94, 95, 96, 98, 100–02, 104–08, 109–11
Elton, G. R. 99
Engle, Lars 133
epistemology, linguistic coding of 86, 89–90
epistolary rhetoric 3, 12, 61–88, 92, 181–82, 193 n.1 and 2
  ars dictaminis, medieval 61, 63, 64, 75, 77–78
  and classical oratory 61, 63, 77, 92
  classification of letters 63–64, 65, 69, 76, 77, 79–80, 115–16
  humanist epistolography 63, 64
  and mercantile adaptation 122–30

and social stratification 114–15
Erasmus, Desiderius
  "On the Writing of Letters" (*De conscribendis epistolis*) 2, 12, 61–74, 77, 79, 88, 90, 115, 177
ethos (in rhetoric) 68
evidentiality 86–87
Ewbank, Inga-Stina 5, 184 n.12

face-threatening acts 17–18, 20, 24, 46
female speech 122, 200 n.25
  and politeness strategies 28–31, 47–49
  and religious discourse 29–31, 189 n.30
  situated loquacity 180
  stereotypes 166–67
Ferber, Michael 134
Ferry, Anne 51
figures of speech 76
Fineman, Joel 38–39
Fletcher, John 28, 185 n.1
Fletewood, William 104
formality, situations of 121, 168, 171, 172, 175
Foucault, Michel 8
Freud, Anna 133
Friedman, Alice T. 41, 48–49
friendship, discourse of 12, 13, 61, 68, 69, 72, 80–84, 94, 108–12, 113, 116, 128–37, 176–77
Fulwood, Willliam
  The Enimie of Idlenesse 3, 13, 41, 62, 114, 115–19, 123

gender and language 18, 122, 200 n.25
Goffman, Erving 20
Goldberg, Jonathan 76, 78, 99, 100, 196 n.25 and 31
Greenblatt, Stephen 5–6, 7, 66, 144
Greene, Robert 33
Grey, Lady Jane 42
Greville, Fulke 39, 43, 51
Grey, Lady Katherine 109, 111
Grice, H. Paul 20, 179
Guazzo, Steven 56
guest–host relation 154

habitus 37, 151, 152–53, 167–68
  and class 169, 170, 174
handwriting 100, 107
  writing in one's own hand 107–08
Hannay, Margaret P. 47
Harrison, William 93
Hatton, Sir Christopher 84, 102–03, 104
Henderson, Judith Rice 63, 194 n.10
heteroglossia 8, 131
Hewitt, J. P. 144

Hibbard, G. R. 5, 184 n.12
Hicks, Michael 89
Holinshed's *Chronicles* 29, 33, 47
Honigmann, E. A. J. 170
Hunsdon, Henry Carey, Baron 103
Hunter, G. K. 5, 184 n.12, 185 n.5
hypercorrection 120–21

identity and discourse 10, 13, 66, 142
   act–person liaison 145
   in communication breakdown 147
   in conversation 144
   intersubjective theory of 143
   social determination 157
ideology 5, 7, 10, 88, 100, 153
inner and outer speech 38, 55–56
interaction scripts, or styles 1, 61, 76, 80–88, 94, 97, 114, 115, 123, 130, 133, 137
interiority 12, 27, 38, 49, 51, 55, 57
interpellation 157
intersubjectivity 11, 13, 143–44
intertextuality 9
inwardness *see* interiority

Jefferson, Gail 143
Jenkinson, Sir Hilary 99

Kahn, Coppelia 137
Katherine of Aragon, Queen of England 29
Kennedy, Andrew 183 n.9, 184 n.10
Knight, George Wilson 170, 190 n.35
knowledge claims 86–90, 100
Knox, John 94

Labov, William 121
Lamb, Mary Ellen 47
language
   and social change 11, 13, 88, 115, 121, 130, 131, 137, 151–53
   and mistake-making 158–62
   and social invention 1, 10–11, 12, 38–39, 123, 124–25, 130
langue and *parole* 8
legitimate language 120–22
Leicester, Robert Dudley, Earl of 41, 42, 154
Lemke, Jay L. 130
letters
   reading of 112–13
Levinson, Stephen C. 2, 7, 11, 17–27, 38, 69, 79, 93, 120, 144, 146, 160, 177, 185 n.3
Lewis, Catherine R. 53–54, 55
linguistic domination 9, 115, 120–22

M., I.
   A Health to the Gentlemanly Profession of Serving-Men 40–41
maintenance work
   practical outlook on language 158–62
   reciprocal self-maintenance 143–45, 147, 150, 152
   in social language 10, 11, 13, 18, 38, 81, 92–93, 99, 153
Malone, Edmond 55
Markham, Gervase 99
Mary, Queen of Scots 94
Mary I, Queen of England 94
Mathew, Toby 87, 91
Matoesian, Gregory M. 161
McDonald, Russ 6
mediation
   rhetorical strategy of Iago 173
merchant discourse 13, 122–35, 137
Merchant Venturers, Society of 114, 125, 130
Mildmay, Sir Walter 108
Molyneux, Edmund 12, 35–55, 107
Montrose, Louis A. 6–7

negative face 20, 144, 161
negative politeness 21, 24, 69, 95–96
   and character 29
   and Elizabethan hierarchy 74, 93
   Iago 178
   and inner speech 55
   Katherine in *Henry VIII* 25–27, 29, 30
   non-symmetrical response 73, 93
   and subordination 46–47, 50–53, 101–02
   Wolsey in *Henry VIII* 32–33
neighborliness 83–84
new criticism 5, 6
new historicism 5, 7, 8
Nichols, Johanna 86
Northumberland, Henry Percy, Earl of 110
Northumberland, John Dudley, Duke of 42
Novy, Marianne 133, 203 n.32

Olbrechts-Tyteca, L. 145
Oxford, Edward de Vere, Earl of 41, 62, 75

Paget, William, Baron 97
pathos (in rhetoric) 68
pedagogy, language of 70, 73, 74
Pembroke, William Herbert, Earl of 41
Percy, Henry *see* Northumberland
Perelman, Chaim 145
Perelman, Les 77–78
Perkins, William 36, 46
personality 27–28, 34
Pettie, George 56
pleasuring friends 13, 80–84, 124, 128–37

politeness 2, 17–27, 46–47, 79, 106, 109, 160, 185 n.3
   as anticipation 9
   and Elizabethan civility 11, 81, 102, 186 n.4
   and epistolary theory 92
   forms of address 187–88 n.17
   and ideology 99–100
   politics of 96, 120
   recognition of hierarchy 38, 93
   rhetorical method of Iago 177–79
   and self-construction 144
   and social speech position 36
   see also negative and positive politeness
positive face 20, 144
positive politeness 21–24, 25, 46, 47, 67
   flattery 69
   presumptuous style in Erasmus 70–73
practical criticism 2, 7, 11, 91
pragmatics, linguistic 1, 6, 13, 61, 65, 143, 146, 159
prestige language 120, 121
preventatives 144
pronouns of address 2, 149, 150
prosaic creativity 11, 125, 126, 130
psychology
   and social rhetoric 1, 27, 53–57, 134, 137, 161

Radcliffe, Anthony 114
Randolph, Thomas 106
reaccentuation 124, 131, 132, 137
Read, Conyers 98
recognition
   self and other 143
   theatre staple 142
   see also acknowledgment, intersubjectivity
recontextualization 11, 13, 124, 130, 132
redundancy in language 17, 160
repair, verbal 13, 17, 18, 37, 38, 56, 70, 88, 92–93, 99, 103
   in ordinary conversation 142
   and self-construction 147
   self-repair and other-repair 143–44
social control mechanism 161
repetition 10, 131, 158
   and artistic genres 155
   daily routines 156
   of everyday speech forms 153–55
   and realistic play world 157
requests 71, 79–88, 94, 133
re-ranking 112, 175, 177–79
rhetoric
   of division, or dissociation 21, 46, 109
   of identification, or association 21, 23, 46, 49, 81, 109
   of social context 175–76, 179–81

rhetorical genre 65
Rudanko, Juhani 6

Sacks, David Harris 125, 126, 129–30
Sacks, Harvey 143
Sackville, Thomas *see* Buckhurst
Sadler, Sir Ralph 93, 94–97, 98–100
Sandys, Edwyn, Archbishop of York 104
Schlegloff, E. 143
secretary, office of 75–76, 99, 100, 105–06, 107
self-fashioning 143, 144
semiotics 2
servants and service 1, 12, 35–57, 90
servingmen, gentlemen 40–42, 53–57
Shakespeare, William
   social position 33–34
   letters 88–90
   All's Well That Ends Well 49
   Hamlet 29
   Henry IV Part 1 90, 112–13
      Prince Hal 90, 112
      Hotspur 112–13
   Henry VIII 11, 17–34
      Anne Bullen 29
      Katherine 11, 18, 25, 26–31, 32
      Norfolk 17–18, 21–24
      Wolsey 11, 19, 22, 25, 26, 27, 28, 31–34
   King Lear 13, 18, 26, 29, 142–53
      Cordelia 148–51
      Kent 145–46, 148–49, 151–53
   Love's Labour's Lost 13, 90, 115, 116, 117, 118–19, 120, 121–12
   The Merchant of Venice 13, 115, 124, 131, 132–35
   A Midsummer Night's Dream 13, 115, 116, 118, 119, 120, 121
   Much Ado About Nothing 13, 117, 119, 142, 153–62
   Othello 13–14, 163–82
      Desdemona 14, 165–70
      Emilia 180–81
      Iago 14, 171–81
      Othello 13, 170–71
   The Rape of Lucrece (dedicatory epistle) 88–90
   sonnets 35–36, 50, 54–55
      sonnet 57 36, 52, 55
      sonnet 58 12, 36, 37, 38, 52–57
      sonnet 85 36
      sonnet 88 36, 52
      sonnet 89 36, 52
      sonnet 94 35–36, 49–50
      sonnet 149 52
   The Taming of the Shrew 142
   Timon of Athens 13, 115, 124, 131, 135–37, 153
   Troilus and Cressida 143

Index

Venus and Adonis (dedicatory epistle) 88–90
The Winter's Tale 18
Sidney, Sir Henry 39, 41–42, 44–45, 47–48, 93, 100–02, 105, 106–08, 156
Sidney, Lady Mary (Dudley) 39, 42, 44–45, 46, 47–50
Sidney, Sir Philip 12, 35–36, 39, 42, 43, 44, 45–46, 50–52, 56
Sidney, Sir Robert 39, 41, 44, 45–46
Skura, Meredith Anne 54
Slights, Camille Wells 122, 202 n.15, 205 n.28
Smith, Sir Thomas 93, 105, 106
social reproduction 10, 11, 12, 39, 67, 74, 88, 93, 121, 150
   supplement to biological 157–58
   see also repetition, maintenance
solidarity rhetoric 116, 130
Somerset, Edward Seymour, Duke of 97
sorts
   meaner and better 119, 120, 122
   middling 115, 120
Southampton, Henry Wriothesley, Earl of 89–90
Spanish Company 125
speech acts 32, 141
   business of letters 99, 109
   and categories in epistolary rhetoric 65, 69, 79
   and power relations 39, 42
   risk and mitigation 9, 17–18, 19–20, 46, 72, 85, 88, 93, 109, 146
speech-act theory 2, 19, 186 n.6
speech genres 1, 10, 65, 66, 72, 154–55
speech position 11, 27, 29–31, 33–34, 36
speech vs. exchange 4
spoken and written language 3, 18
Stanley, Sir George 103
Stokes, R. 144
stratification

social and linguistic 3, 8, 13, 37, 114–22
Styan, J. L. 20
style
   in Shakespeare criticism 5, 6
stylistic collision 134–35
stylistic "dispute" 124, 130, 131, 134, 135, 203 n.34
stylistics
   affective 2
   formalist 2, 5, 6, 91
   sociological 11, 154
subject position 36, 39, 49
subjectivity 9, 12, 27, 36, 38–39, 49, 57
superior, speech of 149
Sussex, Thomas Radcliffe, Earl of 44, 45, 48, 103, 104, 105, 154
symbolic capital 38, 42, 54, 90, 163, 175, 179
symbolic domination 3, 11

Tremaine, Edmund 107
trouble-making trope 100, 102–06, 154
trouble-taking trope 100–03, 106–08

Vendler, Helen 6
voice power 14, 163, 164, 165, 170, 177, 180
Vološinov, V. N. 19, 27, 38, 55

Walsingham, Sir Francis 39
Wardhaugh, Ronald 152
Warner, Sir Edward 94, 109–12
Warwick, Ambrose Dudley, Earl of 42
Waterhouse, Edward 100, 107
Weil, Judith 48–49
Whigham, Frank 74, 84, 87, 91–93, 99, 102
White, Sir Nicholas 108
Willoughby, Sir Francis 41
Wright, George T. 5, 184 n.12
Wrightson, Keith 83–84, 93

Zitner, Sheldon P. 158, 191 n.13